Sean _____

Best Wishes.

Jett Hébert

Mortgaged and Armed

A Key to Understanding Mortgage Industry Tactics

Peter Hébert

FREEDOM HOUSE PRESS
United States of America

Published in the United States of America by Freedom House Press
Cover Design by David Dees of DeesIllustration.com
Printed by CreateSpace, An Amazon.com Company.

www.MortgagedAndArmed.com

This publication is designed to provide accurate and authoritative information in regard to the subject matter covered. It is sold with the understanding that neither the author nor the publisher is engaged in rendering legal, accounting, or other professional service. If legal advice or other expert assistance is required, the services of a competent professional person should be sought.
—*From a declaration of principles jointly adopted by a Committee of the American Bar Association and a committee of publishers.*

I am a mortgage lending and real estate industry insider by virtue of my past employment and consulting engagements over the span of over 20 years. I worked as a mortgage loan officer and was on the front lines of the refinance and housing boom while researching and writing this book. This book is an outgrowth of academic research that took place at Mount St. Mary's University in Emmitsburg, Maryland between 2005 and 2008, where I earned a Master of Business Administration degree.

The information secured for this book rests on professional experience, academic training, and extensive research. I reviewed annual reports, newspaper and magazine articles, and industry studies. I read government agency reports and Congressional testimony. I visited the public library, Googled the Internet, viewed numerous You Tube video clips, looked at social networking websites like Facebook to better understand the public's pulse beat, and queried Lexis/Nexis®. I also interviewed and consulted numerous industry experts to secure their insights. Although some of the information came from the public domain, or through the fair use doctrine, some was obtained through phone calls to several

I

government agencies and through numerous Freedom of Information Act requests. Other material was used with express permission. For your benefit, the research has been documented.

There is no stated or implied affiliation between me as an author or any real estate firm, financial institution, trade association, regulatory or enforcement agency, or consumer advocacy group referenced in this book. All opinions expressed in this book belong to those quoted or to me and do not represent the opinions of any institution, any industry, any banking or housing-related trade association, any of my past employers, or any government agency.

Library of Congress Cataloging-in-Publication Data

Hébert, Peter
Mortgaged and armed: a key to understanding mortgage industry tactics
/ Peter Hébert – 1st ed.

Includes end notes, references, glossary, and index.

ISBN: 1439260664
EAN-13: 9781439260661
LCCN: 2009910327

First Edition

To the American people, who deserve to better understand the tactics the mortgage finance industry uses in its war on the household and investor.

Contents

About the Author

Peter Hébert has a Masters of Business Administration degree in finance and marketing from Mount St. Mary's University in Emmitsburg, Maryland. He was the keynote speaker for his MBA graduating class at Mount St. Mary's University on its 200th anniversary. He has a Bachelor of Arts degree in journalism and history from the University of Maryland in College Park, Maryland. Hébert has over 20 years experience in residential mortgage lending; residential property management and leasing; commercial and residential real estate marketing and sales; and secondary market experience in due diligence, commercial loan servicing, multi-family loan registrations, and residential loss mitigation. Hébert is a communicator and educator at heart with a passion in taking complex concepts and distilling them so that they are easily understandable for those with an interest in better understanding. He has experience teaching corporate finance as an adjunct business professor. He has designed and taught several state approved continuing education courses to licensed real estate agents and loan officers. His professional experience includes working with attorneys, plaintiffs, and defendants as a litigation consultant and as an expert witness.

Acknowledgments

I need to first acknowledge the most important people in my life, which are the members of my immediate family. They provided me with the needed safe harbor essential for deep inquiry. Because of them, I had the opportunity to withdraw, reflect, research, and write.

To my late father Raymond Joseph Hébert (1928 - 1990), you were right to warn that another Great Depression could happen. I never fully understood what you experienced and how it shaped your views towards Wall Street, the federal government, and towards money. Today, I have a better understanding. Thank you for sharing the many stories with us over the years about an era that resembles the early 21st century. You taught me by example to turn off the television, and to instead read and really think. I have done my best to live up to your counsel. We miss you.

To my mother Meryem Hébert, thank you for always making known your doubts concerning the claims of advertisers in banking, propagandists in government that use the media as its floodgate, and the prevailing wisdom that promotes perpetual financial servitude. You were always right, "The best mortgage is the one that is paid off." You taught me by example to stand up for what is right, even when it meant going up against the establishment. I have done my best to live up to your example. I thank you also for your words of support to stay focused and help everyday Americans so that they can be empowered to fight back.

I could not have researched or written *Mortgaged and Armed* without the patience, understanding, and support of my wife, Mabel Ramírez. She lived through the process with me and understands, like any other author's spouse, what is required of an author to research, write, edit, complete a book, and then go through the publishing process. Thank you for your patience and understanding.

To my brother Jonathan Hébert, your support and words of continued encouragement as I worked on my manuscript, published *Mortgaged and Armed*, and completed the sequel *Predator Nation*, have been invaluable. I cannot thank you enough.

I thank David Dees of DeesIllustration.com. David produced the creative art for the book's front and back cover as well as the cartoon work. Political art is meant to be controversial and irritate those who are under criticism. Dees' work has a substantial following on the Internet, and he has indeed irritated organizations that prefer to maintain a lopsided narrative on issues of importance to all.

I would like to recognize Dr. Jo McLaughlin and Brian O'Brien for persuading me to transform my three part 800-plus page manuscript into three different books. I especially thank Dr. McLaughlin for reviewing several of the last chapters, then the larger three part manuscript in its entirety, and for providing constructive feedback that included publishing stand alone articles and consumer oriented resources. Your patience in our several meetings and words of support were greatly appreciated!

To the extent possible, this book serves to describe mortgage lending and its relationship with investment banking, the political process, regulation, and the economy. This book is the end result of working with a variety of people and sources that together served to provide me with the information contained here. I consulted the work of many industry analysts. Their careful analyses permitted for a better understanding of a complex industry. I spoke with many business reporters and carefully followed the work of others. I also looked with interest at the positions of different consumer advocates. In addition, I examined the positions of the different trade associations that represent their dues paying members. More importantly, I researched the difficult task regulators and policy makers face when investigating, understanding, and determining an appropriate course of action.

I engaged validators and readers who helped me determine this book's final form. I would like to thank the following people, who freely gave of themselves in order to help me to research, write, edit, and complete this book: Dr. Michael Berenhaus, Dr. Richard Brocato, Guy Cecala, Matthew Chorley, Tracey A. Cullen, Esq., Dr. Kirk Davidson, Jeff Fraley, Mike Frank, Kim R. Gerald, Budd Hallberg, my cousin John Hébert, my brother Jonathan Hébert, Cynthia Maubert, Dr. Jo McLaughlin, Dr. David Olson, Scott Paintner, Mabel Ramírez, Rob Snow, Ray Speciale, Esq., and Dr. Dileep Wagle. Because of their constructive remarks, guidance, and encouragement, I was able to produce this book for you, the reader, whom I always had in mind. This book does not represent the views or opinions of those who served as validators, readers, or reviewers since their comments were provided while this book was still taking shape. Any shortcomings in the final product are mine alone.

I thank my nephew José Julian Ramírez for his research assistance. The research exposed him to the world of finance, real estate, insurance, regulation, and economics as well as to the critical role of the media in controlling the narrative and shaping public perception.

I thank Kelli Christiansen of Bibliobibuli.com for providing professional editing services for the book's preliminary manuscript. Her critique forced me as a communicator of complex ideas to stay on task with my primary mission: to produce a readable book to arm readers with actionable information and solutions.

I thank Nina Brauer of BookSurge™ (now CreateSpace™), who coached me with this simple axiom: "The slower you go, the faster you get there." As a result of these guiding words, I worked more patiently to research thousands of details that were taken and transformed into readable analysis with clear explanations suitable for homeowners, real estate investors, mortgage borrowers, policy makers, regulators, licensed real estate brokers and loan officers, students, and readers abroad.

And, I thank Zach J. Coddington of CreateSpace™ doing business as On-Demand Publishing LLC for his patience as I completed this book. I also thank Angela Johnson at CreateSpace™ for facilitating the book's interior design, printing, and publishing process on behalf of Freedom House Press.

Finally, I thank Claudia Kpotor, Steve Price, and Kristen Vesper at FedEx Office for printing and binding chapter drafts as well as the entire manuscript on short notice during the development process on behalf of the book's readers and reviewers.

Disclaimer

This book was written to describe the mortgage lending industry, mortgages, the subprime crisis, the collapse of home prices, the wave of foreclosures, the credit crunch, the global financial crisis, and the political crisis. The information contained here has been well researched; is deemed reliable, but not necessarily guaranteed given the fluid nature of the markets and the industry. This book contains legal information, but should not be construed as legal advice. This is not a get-rich-quick book, nor should it be viewed in that manner. There should be no impact on homeowners with mortgages when any lender or institution may experience hardship. Moreover, this book should not be viewed as an advertisement for any person or company mentioned herein.

Consumers entering into a serious commitment such as a real estate purchase or a mortgage finance transaction should seek appropriate counsel. Consumers should consult with their tax office, the land planning office, a qualified attorney who is a practicing specialist in the area of concern, a certified financial planner, a tax accountant, an experienced and licensed real estate agent, and an experienced and licensed loan officer when entering into any complex transaction. This book, although informative, should not be regarded as a substitute for specific and competent counsel.

I strongly encourage consumers to engage in serious due diligence when shopping for mortgages and even credit cards and not just rely on advertisements or what the neighbors are doing. The Better Business Bureau, U.S. Department of Housing and Urban Development, and the Federal Trade Commission archive Consumer Alerts and information about rogue lenders. Moreover, review the blogs and examine what others have said. Past business behavior can be an indicator of future conduct.

I want to make this clear: There are high caliber, ethical, and hard working people in the lending industry. Some are unsung heroes who work extra hours on short notice in processing and underwriting to make sure a purchase loan closes on time to meet the expectations of real estate agents and their clients; or that it is denied to due to blatant fraud. Some are wholesale account executives who are diligent when it comes to dotting the "i's" and crossing the "t's" as they provide updates that allow the professionals in the industry to genuinely serve the public. Some are retail loan officers and their managers who together do what they can to meet the challenging needs of borrowers looking to lenders in their times of need. They enjoy the work, and count it an honor to serve customers.

After many years in this industry working as a direct lender, as a correspondent lender, and as a mortgage broker carefully observing the caliber of people hiring managers bring into companies and the types of issues that the human resource departments have to deal with, I firmly believe that the high caliber and ethical loan officer is the exception, not the rule. Loan officers come and go, and during the boom, the average length of experience was just two or three years. Moreover, a high performing rogue loan officer is a cash cow. Management in many companies provide them the shield of cover needed since the revenues they pull in more than offset any potential liability that may arise from a lawsuit that is difficult to assemble, litigate, and then win. The federal government knows this, which is why there will be a national database of all mortgage originators, which is only one step in the right direction. This book addresses several other steps for consumers, tax payers and voters, and property owners to immediately address without having to wait on the world's greatest deliberative body.

Although this book's intention is to equip readers, it should not be seen as a means for readers to believe they know more than many lenders. Financial corporations have an asymmetrical relationship with consumers. After a few years of experience, the most inexperienced loan officer will have the upper hand. There is an adage that holds true here: a little knowledge can be a dangerous thing. Although there is a lot of information contained in these pages, this should not be seen as a substitute for allowing a lender of choice to provide good service. This book is simply intended to outline a framework of understanding so that the reader is no longer overwhelmed by terms and protocols and options, nor likely to be taken advantage of by the big banker or the predator where loopholes in laws and regulations may permit less than ethical business conduct. Finally, this book should not be regarded as the last word, but rather as the beginning of an inquiry on every issue that is covered.

This is a book that needed to be written ... and needs to be read. Peter Hébert in this undertaking, *Mortgaged and Armed: A key to understanding mortgage industry tactics,* has done us all a service. It is a detailed exploration of the mortgage lending industry—the "good, the bad, and the ugly"—from an insider who is not afraid to name names, expose the dirt where it exists, and make bold predictions, some of which, unfortunately, are already coming true. And throughout the book there runs a strong moral current so badly needed as we scramble to put the pieces of our tattered economy back together.

Mr. Hébert tells us that the book is designed to "deconstruct mortgage marketing," to bring to light the "problems tied to how mortgage loans were engineered and marketed." It is meant, as the title suggests, to educate and forewarn home buyers and would-be buyers about the complexities and the pitfalls of the mortgage market. But in fact it is much more than that. *Mortgaged and Armed* skillfully connects the dots between consumers, financial institutions, government regulators, Capitol Hill, and the central bank. It is a carefully constructed description of why and how the housing bubble burst leading to skyrocketing foreclosure rates, the freezing of mortgage lending and subsequently all forms of credit, and stark predictions of a steep recession still to come.

There is little that escapes Mr. Hébert's attention. He explains in layman's language the wide variety of mortgage products from the straightforward, traditional 30-year fixed loan to the bewildering Option ARM. He tells us—sometimes in chilling detail—how these products are marketed, advertised, and sold to us. And he lays out the "unintended consequences" that are the certain results of this often excessive promotion.

Along the way we are given a close look at two of the giant corporate mortgage lenders which played such major roles in inflating the housing bubble: the now-defunct Ameriquest and its founder Roland Arnall who "institutionalized predatory lending," and Countrywide Financial, now a part of Bank of America, which Mr. Hébert describes as a "bellwether for the financial crisis" where aggressive lending practices put in jeopardy both borrowers and ultimately investors as well.

Over and over again Mr. Hébert returns to the subject of greed, that all-too-common moral failure: greed on the part of lenders who so easily and readily took advantage of unsophisticated borrowers; greed on the part of Wall Street financiers who packaged and leveraged and promoted these risky investments; and, yes, greed on the part of some home buyers who believed that they could afford to own a home far in excess of what their incomes and their assets would allow.

In *Mortgaged and Armed*, Peter Hébert has given us a book that details with rock-solid analysis the problems that got us into the mess we are in, provides sound recommendations for corporate and public policies to help us get out of that mess, and offers some dire predictions for what lies ahead. We can thank him for his painstaking efforts on the first two counts while hoping against hope for a somewhat less harsh future.

Dedication

This book is dedicated to my parents, who showed me from a young age through example the importance of commitment to each other, planning ahead, budgeting and saving, and homeownership as a vehicle to building enduring wealth. Because of their combined efforts, they were able to leverage their savings and incomes into a first home, and later, a move-up home. I owe my mother thanks for instilling within me a passion for social justice and gratitude towards my father for showing me through example the patience and dedication that is required to research and write.

As a child of the Great Depression, my late father (1928 – 1990) often warned that an economic depression could happen again in our life times. Just prior to his death, he told me that the end of the world as we know it will be the result of war between the Islamic world and the West. When I was a child of seven years of age, I remember asking my father what made the world go round. His blunt answer was money. Looking back, I know that I was looking for an answer that recognized God or addressed astronomy and physics. Consequently, his approach to money was pragmatic and quite conservative. He never owned or drove a car, and did not need one since public transportation provided him access to and from work. In today's dollars, that saved him close to $750 per month in the overall cost of car ownership. But, when it came to enjoying life, he was the first to take the family to an opening of a new restaurant with a celebrated chef or to see a film by an acclaimed director. His views towards politics were rooted in the observation of history that power had an inherent tendency towards control and corruption. As a result, he was pragmatic and believed that the best government was one that was stalled by opposing political interests, which meant politicians could do little harm to the nation by passing new laws with unforeseen consequences. He despised the filibuster since it suggested that inferior minds were at work. And, he feared any party in control of both the White House and Congress since that meant too much political power. He understood human nature and the wisdom of our nation's founding fathers.

My late father was a numismatist and worked for the majority of his career at the Smithsonian Institution in Washington, D.C. While our periodic conversations about coins and history did not directly revolve around economics, they did from time to time focus on a crude form of inflation history's despots used to bank roll a war campaign—clipping coins or debasing the currency. By debasing the value of a currency, a percentage from each gold or silver coin could be appropriated for expenses without resorting to an unpopular move to raise existing taxes or to impose new ones. As a result, it became clear to me early on that the warrior kings of the past and war time presidents of the present shared something in common. They tended to be thieves and liars.

Our first home was a post-Korean War rambler in the suburbs that my parents purchased in 1966 on the resale market for $20,000. They used my late father's Veterans Administration eligibility to finance the purchase, and the payments were about $158 per month. During the Korean War, my dad worked in an intelligence unit with aerial photos taken from reconnaissance missions. His job was to identify targets that needed to be "softened," and then he conducted the bomb damage assessment afterward. When his service was over, he was entitled to veteran's benefits.

That first home provided us with a three bedrooms and one full bath. The lower level was partially finished and, because it sat on a walk-out grade, there was an outside entrance to a fenced back yard. The great thing about the house from their perspective was that it was walking distance to schools and on the bus line.

Several years later, my mother served as the driving force in the family to trade up, and my father reluctantly went along with the idea of a new home, given that older homes required maintenance. That little brick rambler had everything going against it. It was functionally obsolete and in constant need of costly upkeep—and it was just too small. So, my parents targeted larger homes in new home communities, shopped using the process of elimination, and settled on one community that was close to schools, shopping, parks, and transportation. The home of their dreams was the classic two-storey brick colonial with a two-car garage sitting on about one fourth of an acre. The back yard had an easement at the back of the property to protect mature tress and to provide a landscape buffer between the neighbors.

But, they faced obstacles every step of the way. Richard Nixon was president, Paul Volcker ran the Federal Reserve, and a Middle East oil embargo in the wake of the 1973 Yom Kippur War pushed the United States economy into an energy crisis. The inflationary environment that followed was of historic proportions. To make matters worse, no new building permits were being issued in the county at that time due to a sewer moratorium. The timing to move up could not have been worse.

My parents, however, were determined. They made a financial plan with targets and a timeline. They then cut back, saved, and worked overtime. I remember eating every variation of the potato imaginable, because my parents had cut the food budget back as far as they could in order to save more. My parents even got on a first-name basis with the car mechanic since they chose to service and repair their one old car rather than buy a new one. The nights out to foreign films and elegant restaurants were cut back. But, I do not remember those sacrifices as being unbearable.

The $62,000 model home they desired started inching up in price and then started skyrocketing. Eventually the builder exhausted its inventory, no new homes remained, and the community sat unfinished until the county regained control of the infrastructure and its ability to meet the demands of growth. So, my parents bought the first resale in the community for $100,500—close to double what they originally were looking to spend. They suffered under a crushing $650-per-month house payment. The original owner sold due to a job transfer abroad. When the seller returned two years later, he was completely priced out of the community. His income did not come close to keeping pace with inflation or the laws of supply and demand. More importantly, he was priced out of the market, because the United State went off the gold standard and embraced a fiat currency as a result of the costs of the Vietnam War.

The "elasticity" that fiat currency enables, as advocates of the Federal Reserve like to say, was essential in no longer constraining the nation's fiscal limits. The result over time was a rapid devaluation of the dollar as a result of a rapid rise in growing government debt.

For both their first-time and move-up purchases, my parents worked with the same real estate broker. Not only did this agent handle the real estate transactions, but she also assisted in creative bridge financing. My parents sold their first home for $47,000. Today, that little red brick rambler is valued at about $450,000. Though it seemed that they got stung on the purchase of their move-up home, it is worth approximately $1 million even after home prices started to fall. Without that broker's experience, marketplace insights, understanding of prevailing practices, and genuine concern for her clients, along with the help of the government approved mortgage lender, I do not believe that the American Dream would have been as easy for my parents to attain.

I share these experiences with you, the reader, to illustrate the power of commitment and planning, which is the primary lesson. There are, moreover, several other lessons. Another lesson is that most people will never be able to out-save the appreciation rate of real estate or the rate of inflation in the economy. Their experience underscores the adage that inflation is the homeowner's best friend.

Another lesson is that perception is reality. The difference between being in the best of times and the worst of times is that they are opposite sides of the same coin. My parents at the time seemingly bought at the worst moment. They paid almost double their expectations for their move-up home. If only they had taken the plunge a year or two earlier. If only the real estate broker had been more compelling when she delivered the appeal with a greater sense of urgency that *now* was the best time to buy. We can all kick ourselves for all the "could haves" and "should haves" in our lives. Only hindsight grants us 20/20 vision. The relationship between price and value is truly subjective whether we are in an economic cycle or a bubble. Although the hold up to trade up was to some extent due to my father's reluctance about making high monthly payments and wanting to save more in order to put down a larger down payment, their new mortgage payments ended up being much higher when all was said and done. After all, they paid so much more. But, why were they willing to do that? The value of that new home far exceeded the initial cost they were willing to pay. The higher cost they paid, however, was due to their perception that the value was greater than the new home's inflated sticker price.

Another key lesson learned is the principle of leverage. They put nothing down on their first home, and the value doubled in less than ten years. Similarly, they put 30 percent down on their next home and borrowed about $70,000. But, the investment basis rested on $100,500. In 30 years, that home's value increased more than ten-fold.

Finally, a crucial lesson is that real estate is a long-term investment. With a modest $30,500 down payment and a purchase money mortgage, my parents were able to significantly increase their asset base of $100,500 for long-term appreciation to reach in excess of $1 million. For most homeowners, the path to wealth is to take a long position: to buy and hold.

There are transaction-related costs associated with buying and selling, as well as with refinancing a mortgage loan. My parents represent a generation that was accustomed to saving and paying cash to the extent that they were able. In the time frame described here, credit cards were just being launched. Consequently, VISA and Master Card were the objects of consumer suspicion and under the careful scrutiny of Capitol Hill. As a result, my parents were never inundated by unsolicited appeals to refinance to a lower rate over a longer term in order to lower their monthly expenses. Direct marketing had not yet developed to the scientific art form that it is today. As a result, over the long term, they did very well by keeping things simple. They paid on time, and were careful about the purchases they made.

Today, my mother enjoys the park-like setting of her private back yard. In spring, daffodils bring color beneath the towering oak, locust, and elm trees where she enjoys life in the quiet and peaceable enjoyment of the fruit of her life's toils. She bides her time in retirement researching and investing in stocks that she believes are either undervalued or that will out perform the market. She ignores the experts in the mainstream media. Instead, she reads the papers. Her words of advice today are the same as that of the past: "Pay off your bills. Debt is terrible." The best mortgage is the one that is paid off. She represents roughly one third of homeowners, who have paid off their mortgages.

Preface

The central thesis for this book is that a lack of mortgage finance literacy in the general public coupled with underhanded tactics in the financial sector's mortgage industry sets up borrowers for repeated refinances, loss of wealth accumulation, and foreclosures. The first intended audience for this book is the homeowner considering a refinance, the landlord with rental properties, and the first time or move up homebuyer. These groups need to better understand the strategies and tactics of the mortgage lending industry as well as the government regulations intended to curb lender enthusiasm. In so understanding how the industry operates, mortgage borrowers and real estate investors will be better equipped to not be taken advantage of and to increase their net worth over time. The second intended audience for this book is the new generation of loan officers and their management teams. They may not fully appreciate what took place between 2001 and 2007, because they more than likely received a one-sided narrative from an industry trade association or from their corporation's communications and training departments. This audience needs to clearly understand that the financial sector undermined its right to deserve the public's respect and trust. Methods in regaining the public's trust should become evident with each chapter. The third intended audience is the nation's real estate agents and brokers. This group tends to be the first point of contact in a real estate transaction. For many real estate agents, the intricacies of mortgage finance are a mystery. This book was designed to make the various aspects of mortgages and the industry clear. The other intended audiences for this book include finance and economics academics and their students, who desire to better understand the relationship between failed text book theories that are still taught and actual business practice as well as the difference between the real economy and the synthetic economy. Finally, this book was written for those who believe that a political revolution is needed to produce widespread change and accountability. The public's response of fear and anger to the Wall Street bailouts was justified. Federal government intervention under an environment of panic and duress violated the rules of the free market, circumvented the bankruptcy courts, skewed asset price levels, and rewarded predatory and fraudulent behavior in the financial sector.

The core of this book is about the real estate and mortgage lending market with attention to the four P's of marketing—product, price, placement, and promotion. The analysis serves to contribute to mortgage finance literacy. Most people do not have the underpinnings to understand economics thanks in part to the monotone lectures about the supply and demand graphs in college many were happy to forget. None of those types of graphs are in this book. What are here are many of the core issues everyone needs to become familiar with to understand the relationship between credit as debt and real estate as both a home and an investment. Each chapter ends with Concluding Thoughts.

The United States housing and refinance boom that took place between 2001 and 2007 ended in the subprime meltdown, the collapse of the secondary market, a wave of foreclosures, a credit crunch, and a global financial crisis. Mortgage financing—not home values—were at the heart of the crisis. Leverage and securitization, misguided risk management measures, and investors failing to do their due diligence were at the heart of the international crisis. This book discusses predatory lending and mortgage fraud. This book was written to arm homeowners and would be home buyers to better understand how the mortgage lending and investment banking businesses work together in order to shed light on predatory practices that have always existed and will more than likely always exist.

The initial concepts for this book took place in 2005 when I was in a Masters in Business Administration (MBA) class and realized that MBA graduates in a finance sequence come out prepared at a minimum to become business strategists, investment analysts, and fund managers based on an understanding of theoretical models. There was very little attention given to mortgages or the day-to-day, consumer-related financial literacy and its connection with mortgage-related securities and bonds as investments. Moreover, by 2007, every MBA-level text book on banking, capital markets, and financial management was not only out of date but not even applicable to describe a dysfunctional market destroyed by both aggressive free market thinking and then government intervention.

Two things were obvious to me in mid-2007. First, all of the theories and financial models assembled to prop up the paradigm of free markets and Western finance had completely failed. Second, a 1960s-styled grassroots-driven revolution was needed to transform America. At the academic level, I observed that the best and brightest in any MBA program tended to memorize and master the many mathematical models. Almost none dared deconstruct, critically examine, and then challenge their validity. In other words, too many accepted mere theories and models as fact. Additionally, many of the newly published books addressing the crisis were written by economists, investors, or journalists with no hands on experience and too few spoke to real estate and lending with the consumer in mind. This book sought to avoid the pitfalls of other books that rushed to market, lacked in-depth discussion, and as a result lacked relevance. Consequently, by Labor Day weekend 2007 when FHA Secure was first unveiled, I felt that there was a need to write this book in order to meet a vacuum in the marketplace since FHA Secure was meaningless. At the pedestrian level, I sensed that in 2007 not enough Americans were paying attention to the corrupt relationship between Wall Street and Capitol Hill. By the Panic of 2008, it had become obvious to the nation—corruption was central to the problem and the nation took to the streets in protest.

My researching and writing focused on different aspects of the mortgage industry started in September 2007 as part of my academic work at Mount St. Mary's University. This book took one year to research, develop, and write, but I waited one and half years to release it to the public. When the Panic of 2008 occurred, I decided to not publish *Mortgaged and Armed* until later. I continued my research on the subprime meltdown, the credit crunch, American and banking history, the global financial crisis, and the political crisis that followed. As a result, other books will follow the release of *Mortgaged and Armed* since the original manuscript in three parts exceeded 800 pages.

My goal is readability. This book is not meant to be a dry academic text book, the kind that inspire so many college students to forever turn their backs on economics and finance. Instead, it is meant to be an engaging work to shake you free from your previously held conceptions about the interconnected world of finance, business practices, economics, the media, the legal system, and politics. In keeping with this, this book's writing style does not follow a tightly controlled rubric or syllogistic arguments. I knew that many of the books that would come out on the many interconnected topics tied to this book would be either journalistic, academic, too business oriented, or economic and tailored to justify government actions. This is an important point, because left to typical economists, academics, and policy makers this historic crisis would be reduced to a series of numbers and ratios. I reject that, because this crisis is fundamentally a people story. For the Internet generation reader, each chapter can be read as a stand alone piece. For the benefit of those where English is a second language and to my foreign readers abroad, the use of acronyms has been reduced to a minimum and avoided where possible. The last thing I want is a book that reads like document riddled with technical industry specific jargon that is further complicated by oddly abbreviated letters. The dates in parenthesis indicate the birth and death of a person and for American presidents and heads of state their term in office. For the researcher, there is well developed index that enables a topical approach into this book. My goal is relevance. What I want most of all is a book that will speak to those who are fearful and angry in order to help others make sense of what seems completely nonsensical.

At the back of the book is a glossary of mortgage, real estate, economic, and financial terms. I developed this and packed it with relevant terms. This is an important reference for readers and serves to complement this text. You may want to browse through the glossary so that you know where to turn while reading should you have questions like: "What is a fully amortized mortgage?" "What is a security?" or "What is "Ginnie Mae?" The basis for the glossary came from the Federal Reserve Bank of Boston, the U.S. Department of Housing and Urban Development, the Federal Trade Commission, the Federal Reserve Bank of San Francisco, the Federal Reserve Bank of Minneapolis, the Virtual Trade Mission, the Wisconsin Economic Education Council, and several academic texts books I use as an adjunct college professor of business.

In the beginning of this period, the economy had recovered from a failed hi-technology sector-based economy dominated by Microsoft. The action then shifted to a Home Depot economy during the boom. Investors tapped the equity in their own homes to invest in rental properties and to speculate. The economy moved ahead due to homeowners, who refinanced in record numbers and converted the equity in their homes to shop, pay off consumer credit, and make home improvements. Low rates, liberal underwriting, seductive advertising, aggressive marketing, and global investors happy to buy American debt securities made all of this possible. Homeowners on average doubled their debt balances. The average household income remained the same during the same period. This was the result of policy that mandated consumers drive the economy rather than corporations, which had gone overseas years prior in search of lower wages. Those corporate-driven actions drove American wages down. Following the bust in 2007, consumers drove the nation into a

Wal-Mart economy. Hardest hit parts of the country, however, could only support Dollar Store and Dollar Tree types of businesses—all in the United States, the leading G7 nation among the first-world economies.

The housing boom was orchestrated by policy makers and the financial sector. Some charge that Americans failed to manage their money. These critics, however, fail to take into account that the lack of cash necessitated borrowing since credit replaced money as the life blood of the economy. The fact is most Americans do not have cash due to wages that are not commensurate with the inflated cost of living. The Federal Reserve lowered the prime rate and kept it low for a long time. And, the Federal Reserve held true to the Bush Administration's economic philosophy that less regulation was better. Moreover, Federal policy mandated increased homeownership. The homeownership rate of 64 percent in 1994 increased to 69 percent at the market's peak. Fannie Mae and Freddie Mac, two government-sponsored enterprises that exist to provide a vibrant market for mortgages in the secondary market, lowered their underwriting standards, underwrote, and also invested in subprime mortgage loans. The Federal Housing Administration, the historic backbone of mortgage finance for first-time homebuyers as well as those in need of flexible underwriting, lost its market share to private labeled lenders from Wall Street's investment bankers, insurance companies, global banks, and hedge funds. At the market's peak, the Federal Housing Administration dwindled into an insignificant player with less than three percent market share. Private labeled lenders extended credit to borrowers with either little or no documentation of income and assets or those with unconventional means. Some of the borrowers were not credit worthy. Others had income sources and patterns of cash flow that did not fit into the underwriting standards of the government sponsored enterprises or the Federal Housing Administration. With each passing year, the increasingly liberal underwriting terms were the result of competition for market share as well as the desire to enlarge the size of the market in order to maintain the financial sector's earning targets.

Bubbles warp perception. Homebuyers and investors got caught up in the bidding warfare and frenzied mania as real estate agents delivered their perennial truism, "Now is the best time to buy." Homeowners got caught up in the refinancing frenzy, because lenders said, "These historic low rates may not last." Lenders in turn brought forth the full arsenal of shock and awe loan products, and in some cases carpet bombed communities using reverse redlining and aggressive marketing until the ironic line in the title of the Oscar-winning 1930 film *All Quiet on the Western Front* echoed in the modern day across many communities. Homes were left standing, but quiet and abandoned. In some parts of the country it was as if a neutron bomb went off—there was nothing left except row after row of foreclosure signs. Instead, auctions with a few insiders looking for a bargain while some of the former homeowners dealt with heart attacks, strokes, domestic abuse, divorce, suicide, and even mass killings that are by products of the smoldering ash of the American Dream—the end of the world as they knew it. A line from *The New York Times* here is poignant: "The shrapnel from the subprime explosion continues to scatter."[1] In some cases, homes were deliberately destroyed or burned to spite the lender exercising foreclosure. With this, it is not difficult to conclude that this battle in a greater war on the consumer has ended with many consumers as victims seeking to inflict damage on otherwise faceless institutions incapable of admitting wrong doing. Many of these problems, as we shall see, were not just the result of heavy marketing, but also the unintended consequences of prior government policy and financial engineers misreading risk and promoting "affordability" products that instead were just the opposite.

Fraud and predatory lending are at the heart of the crisis. Lenders, banking associations, and lobbyists pushed for lender-friendly legislation that was not balanced by the interests or long-term well being of homeowners. Consumer advocacy groups were no match for them at the local level as consumers and municipalities unsuccessfully fought back to stop the scourge of deceptive and abusive lending practices that were not designed to sustain homeownership or enable homeowners to build wealth. The primary part of this industry-driven problem is that it is systemic and deeply ingrained. The secondary part of this consumer-driven problem is the fact that financing is rooted in mathematics and economics. These two parts intersect with corporate attorneys, who wrote documents meant to be read by themselves, not everyday consumers. This major disconnect presents itself as an opening for predators to exploit, whether in banking or mortgages. But, at heart of the problem is the manner in which some of the loan products were engineered to operate and the manner in which they were underwritten. As troubling, the legal and penal systems have an inbuilt incentive for the criminally inclined to commit mortgage fraud rather than bank robbery.

The subprime meltdown was the result of reckless risk taking and negligence in the financial sector at the expense of the entire economy. The community of mortgage lenders and investment bankers pushed the risk envelope to the breaking point. Underwriters that issued mortgage backed securities over relied on financial models. Those models, which supported the paradigm in Western finance, failed. Rating agencies failed to more carefully examine the new issuances of securities prior to issuing a risk grade rating designed to alert investors. Investors failed to do their due diligence and failed to distinguish between mortgage, corporate, and government bonds. When subprime mortgage backed securities began to not perform in increasing numbers—an increasing number of homeowners were not paying their mortgages as agreed, investors stopped buying them when issued. The flow of global capital into this mortgage finance niche stopped.

The credit crunch was exacerbated by the Financial Accounting Standards Board with the support of the Security and Exchange Commission. Mortgage lenders and investment banks that could not sell new mortgage backed securities into the market suffered from a diminished balance sheet. Investors who demanded a refund also posed a financial risk to mortgage lenders and investment banks since these buy backs also diminished the balance sheet of the financial sector. The value of these mortgage backed securities that were no longer trading in the secondary market, however, posed another problem since their value became unknown. The accounting rule change that took place in the beginning stages of the crisis required those holding mortgage backed securities on their books to mark down the values from the modeled price to the market value price. These notational, not actual, losses further contracted the balance sheets of many firms. The Internal Revenue Service then permitted financial institutions that experienced a serious credit loss or write down to enjoy a serious write off that became a serious wind fall.[2] These ill conceived and ill timed set of regulatory rule changes resulted in the credit crunch that benefited the financial sector at the expense of the consumer and business sectors. The conditions were in place for the Wall Street bailout.

The wave of foreclosures was the result of two sides of the same coin: a lack of financial literacy and predatory lending products that were not designed for sustainable homeownership. Additionally, it was the result of over speculation. Fear of being left out of an appreciating market and desire for a return on investment motivated many to over leverage their income and assets. Moreover, those who financed their purchases or refinances with sophisticated financing were left to a promise note, written by lawyers, to understand the mechanics of a complex financial instrument. An inability to repay resulted in many foreclosures. Those foreclosures devastated communities and eroded the tax base of many municipalities. Several cities, as a result, sued numerous lenders to seek damages. One of the provisions of the Housing and Economic Recovery Act of 2008 reached out to an estimated 400,000 homeowners, to rescue them from foreclosure. By the end of 2008, however, only 100 households were helped. That bill was signed into law with the full knowledge that there were about 8,500 foreclosures per day across the nation against sub-prime borrowers, and that the numbers were accelerating. Alt-A, Option ARM, and 5/1 interest only borrowers will also lose their homes. The total number of foreclosures will reach between 6.5 million to 8 million by 2012, which at the higher end is 16 percent of all mortgages in the United States.[3] The problem never was due to pushing for increased homeownership. It was always about financial products and underwriting.

After the boom ended, home appreciation stopped, and then dropped. The collapse of housing prices was the result of prices that had reached unsustainable levels in many of the major metropolitan markets. Credit, not income, had sustained those absurd prices. When the financial products that had permitted borrowers to push prices up were pulled off of the shelf, home prices dropped. When lenders tightened their underwriting guidelines, the pool of potential qualified borrowers shrank. Extensive and in depth media coverage on the financial crisis sidelined would be buyers further shrinking the market. The intensity of the collapse of home prices, however, was due to mortgage lenders flooding the resale market with foreclosed homes that served as much to spook the market as it did to attract bargain hunters, who helped to drive values down. The market was also inundated with short sales that sat unsold due to the need for time consuming third party approvals. Moreover, lenders designating numerous communities across the nation as declining markets, which critics decried as redlining, served to propel home values downward even more. Finally, the Immigration and Naturalization Service and U.S. Department of Homeland Security in coordinated efforts with local law enforcement decided that it was time to enforce the nation's laws. As a result, many illegal aliens—those who bought homes that allowed others to move up to other homes—returned to their home countries. Some left due to round ups, and others left out of fear. More homes piled up in inventory and remained unsold. The imbalance between the number of qualified borrowers and the number of homes on the market was driven by the financial sector as well as the federal government.

A double set of financial losses hit homeowners: a loss in home equity tied to real estate and a loss in the value of stocks. Equity in real estate and stocks are needed for wealth building and retirement. For many Americans, social security income only covers prescription costs. Unlike corporations that can recapitalize after losses by appealing to investors, issuing more debt, or approaching the government for a bailout, no such equivalent exists for the American consumer and homeowner. Many homeowners could not refinance out of the financial problems that were in part of their own making but in large the result of the financial sector. In 2010, one third of all homeowners—21 million people—had negative equity in their home. Moreover, the sharp declines in the stock market wiped out $2 trillion in retirement savings over the 15 month period ending October 2008. These factors pose a threat to retirement planning. This book will address what homeowners planning for retirement can do to make sure that they retire in comfort, not poverty.

The global financial crisis resulted in the Emergency Economic Stabilization Act of 2008, which provides international investors a guarantee on the mortgage-related securities Wall Street sold them. Policy makers were warned by economists that the capital base of the most of the nation's financial base would be wiped out by 2009. In other words, the financial sector was certain to become bankrupt due to its own ill-conceived legislation that Capitol Hill had permitted and the business decisions that followed. Moreover, the Act went against economic history, which demonstrates that top down bailouts do not work. They did not work in the 1930s, and they did not work to lessen the crisis of 2008. The risk and cost of Wall Street's business practices were placed onto the United States tax payer. Investors reacted, which resulted in the Panic of 2008. Given that the manufactured credit crunch became global, a global solution—a Global Monetary Authority—was proposed. That in turn triggered fears of an impending New World Order where the G-20's finance ministers would through financial regulation do an end run around national sovereignty.

This was a man made crisis. Public policy, financial engineering, inflationary monetary policy, and consumer choice by default enabled the financialization of the economy. On the macro level, this is about Wall Street's *coup d'état* of the United States government with the American people held hostage for ransom—tax payer funded bail outs and socialized losses after years of having hailed the many wonders of financial innovation and the triumph of the free and unregulated markets.[4] On a micro level, the severity of each element of the crisis was intensified by human agency. Many have described the fiasco in the financial sector as "the perfect storm." But, that phrase blame shifts and describes an act of God, not the actions of men. There were no accidents, and there was no malfeasance in heaven towards mankind. Some of the issues discussed in this book prove to be provocative, because too many elements dovetail together to support the premise that the subprime meltdown and the foreclosure crisis that followed were orchestrated by careful design. At the most fundamental level, the financial sector used the corporate charter, lobbyists, trade associations, and legislative bodies as cover and waged war on the American consumer and defrauded foreign investors. Again, this is the central premise of this book. Among the collateral damages in this warfare were the nation's cities and neighborhoods as well as retired pensioners around the globe.

The wave of lawsuits against mortgage lenders and investment bankers is justified. Some of the issues addressed here fall under civil disputes if an aggrieved borrower or defrauded investor takes action. This necessitates heavy legal expenses, which denies the majority of injured borrowers and investors from obtaining justice. Fortunately, many complaints are class action claims. In some cases, it is simply a matter of injured citizens demanding and then securing a legislative solution to right the wrongs. Egregious offenses wielded by financial corporations against consumers and investors that are criminal in nature, on the other hand, result in legal representation by the state's attorney general or other government agencies on behalf of the injured. But, when victory does happen, the recompense comes nowhere close to making anyone financially whole. For the attorney general, victory on behalf of consumers is cause for celebration. For consumers, however, victory is more symbolic since it does bring a measure of closure, but never complete financial restitution.

The media plays a role. By informing and misinforming, the result for policy makers, investors, and consumers is a lack of clarity and confusion. Many take for granted the status quo. And, many do not understand how misinformed the general public becomes as a result of advocacy journalism, the sins of omission, and sanitized account of events consistently delivered by the mainstream media. This is an information shell game where the media becomes complicit in concealment and tells the audience: "Watch my eyes, not my hands." And, in the end, misinformation results through disinformation from unchallenged industry-generated press releases and interviews where some outlets serve as not the mouth piece, but the bull horn, to create the fog of war. If there is motive behind the control of the information flow and narrative it is due to some of the executives in the FIRE economy (finance-insurance-real estate) sitting on the boards of the major media outlets. At the end of the day, perception shapes reality. Whether it is from the media or a slick advertisement, the whole point is to get the American public to *feel* and not to think.

For many, the mortgage lending and investment banking industries are cloaked in mystery. They are riddled with obscure acronyms, financial ratios, and difficult-to-understand terms in legal documents. Moreover, that mystique is further shrouded by conflicting comments that come from Capitol Hill, Wall Street, the media, the local lender, the accountant, the stock broker, and the portfolio manager. This book was written to help you specifically understand the various aspects of the mortgage lending business, to help you to understand the role that accounting plays in determining stock prices, to help you to make more informed decisions, to understand the role of political and consumer advocacy groups, and to encourage you to become engaged in the legislative process, because wide spread change is needed.

Business schools, policy makers, regulators, and those within the mortgage lending and investment banking industries will study the Greenspan Era for years to come. I did not initially set out to examine regulatory negligence, a financial system that ran ahead of the regulators, product safety issues associated with some mortgage loans, or securities-related fraud associated with the sale of nonperforming subprime mortgages to pension fund managers responsible for retirement savings. Although each of these issues is addressed to a limited extent, I will leave the fuller analysis for others. This book instead addresses three interconnected narratives: one with the consumer (homeowners and tax payers), the second with financial institutions, and the third with policy makers and regulators. There are indeed several players: policy makers, consumers, financial institutions, central banks, rating agencies, investors, regulators, and the courts. These are the parties with a vested interest and each is a link in the financial chain.

On the book's related website www.MortgagedAndArmed.com, there are additional resources not found in this book. For example, there is a list of members of Congressional Banking Committees on Capitol Hill on both the Senate and House side. These public figures hold the keys to America's public policy when it comes to housing and banking regulations. I encourage citizens to engage their elected official, either as an individual or as part of one of numerous organizations that I am sure will welcome your participation, in order to help shape the discussion and the direction the legislative process takes. Tax payers who sit idly by as proposed bills are considered to become law have no basis to later complain that their taxes are being misappropriated if they do not agree with these bills that later become the law of the land. Yet, tax payers can demand amendments to right legislative wrongs. But, that requires becoming aware, staying informed, and becoming engaged. This book was designed to arm taxpayers for this purpose.

Also on the website is a list of banking regulators. These resources are there for the consumer to direct their concerns. Mortgage lenders, while fully cognizant of these entities, are not in the business of directing consumers in the finer techniques of filing complaints when another lender puts them into a loan that takes 70 percent of their gross monthly income for the mortgage payments.

Before and After the Boom

Before and during the housing boom, the best place to be was a mortgage broker if you were in this business. At the state level, regulations were lighter on brokers compared with mortgage bankers. In some localities, licensing was not even required. In contrast, mortgage bankers had capital reserve requirements as well as higher overhead costs that were associated with elegant marble, mahogany, and glass buildings in the high rent district of town.

After the boom, the worst place to be was a mortgage broker since the bankers and their trade groups had placed brokers under the scrutiny of Capitol Hill and the media. Bankers did not fare better. They pushed underwriting standards back 20 years and helped accelerate the inevitable collapse of housing prices. In fact, if not for the Federal Reserve—the lender of last resort, the backstop to the financial system—more of the major lenders probably would be bankrupt as a result of the financial decisions and investments they made.

Annual reports to the major lenders made forward-looking statements about the market and a company's business practices that investors relied upon. Class actions litigators across the United States ramped up the discovery process as they worked to prepare their case to represent borrowers and investors seeking to be made whole. And, the best place to be in the legal profession was in securities litigation, predatory lending and fair housing-related cases, foreclosure-related law, or the less glamorous bottom feeding practice of debt collections.

During the housing bubble and refinance boom's peak years of 2004 and 2005, most if not all mortgage lenders engaged in marketing practices that leveraged the unique benefits of product, price, placement and promotion. These elements—the four P's of marketing—are not radical in and of themselves. The industry's marketing practices, to the best of my understanding, were to a large extent in compliance with applicable laws and directed toward real estate agents for purchase loans and homeowners for refinance loans. As we take a closer look at the four P's of marketing in this book, however, it will become clear that aggressive marketing, liberal underwriting, and the overreliance on technology contributed to the many problems generically associated with the subprime meltdown, the wave of foreclosures, and everything else that followed.

Beyond Assigning Blame

When it comes to explaining the subprime and housing market meltdown, many insiders said there was plenty of blame to go around. Although this may be true, this type of response shrugs off individual and corporate responsibility onto an impersonal system of links in a large and impersonal financial chain. That response, moreover, is the equivalent of saying, "It happened." With two to three-and-a-half million homeowners who experienced foreclosure in 2008, we cannot just say, "It happened." And, we cannot dismiss this American tragedy, which will impact close to 5.4 million people, given 2.7 people on average per household, with the statement, "There is plenty of blame to go around." The problem is that "it" cannot be held accountable and be persuaded to change its practices so that the greater good can be served while also ensuring long-term sustainability for both the consumer and business community.

Many, like Senator Jim Bunning (R-Kentucky) and Senator Ron Paul (R-Texas), have laid the housing and lending industry's misfortunes at the feet of the Federal Reserve. Others, like U.S. Representative Marcy Kaptur (D–Ohio), correctly laid them at the feet of the banking industry.[5] Some have pointed the finger at Capitol Hill and various federal policies. Others have pointed to Fannie Mae and Freddie Mac for fiscal mismanagement as evidenced by bad accounting and poor judgment by investing in Alt-A loans and "affordability" products, which were the types of high risk loans underwritten by private labeled investors. And, others have laid blame at the feet of regulators, who failed to enforce existing rules. This list can go on and on. But, one thing is certain. Failing to identify the underlying sources and linkages will not permit solutions to come forward to address the many systemic risks that were deeply embedded in our nation's financial and regulatory apparatus.

This book was written for the many people who have privately complained to me during my research for this book that there was something very wrong in the United States with the inordinate amount of influence that wealthy individuals and financial institutions wield upon federal and state governments, as well as on tax-paying citizens, who happen to be consumers—the victims of those with corporate and political power. The common complaint I heard was, "Where are the prosecutions for the fraud we read about?" Throughout the debacle, there have been very few prosecutions for wrong-doing. There is a sense that there is no closure for the public that clearly sees an open wound in the collective psyche that it believes was inflicted by the mortgage lending industry and Wall Street's investment bankers, which were enabled by government regulators, who failed to perform their duties. The resulting fear and anger resting in the public needs to be transformed into action, which as you will see here justifies boycotting some financial institutions, limiting your losses, joining a consumer advocacy group, engaging in formulating policy, and becoming politically active. Yes, there should be accountability and liability, but it begins with the American tax-payer demanding accountability that results in prosecutions.

This book was written for the unknown person or group that put up the large banner on the median strip of a Maryland highway that read: Google "Money as Debt." Complaints about the Federal Reserve as a private banking cartel or central bankers as the leading cause of inflation and the boom-bust cycles are not new, and neither are the conspiracy theories or alternative historical narratives regarding how the Federal Reserve came into being. What may be new, or revived, however, is a popular awareness and anger directed at the Federal Reserve for its role in regulating interest rates and through that impacting the cost of goods that affect the standard of living—inflation through the devaluation of the currency that robs everyone of purchasing power and wealth.

This book was also written for the many vulnerable populations that became easy prey for predatory lenders. These include African Americans, Latino Americans, single women, the elderly, veterans, borrowers where English is not their native tongue, and tenants. They were vulnerable for many reasons, which I describe in this book.

David Dees of Dees Illustration

Chapter 1
Financing the American Dream

> *"Sell the sizzle, not the steak."*
> —An old advertising adage

The generals in financial institutions tend to be in marketing. They oversee the aerial support with an arsenal of advertisements on television, radio, the Internet, and direct mail that typically are associated with marketing campaigns to attract new customers while also retaining past customers. Of course, the more customers who respond to the ads, the better the odds are of generating additional new business.

The lieutenants in these organizations, however, are in sales. These are the troops on the ground. In the mortgage industry, loan originators are the boots on the ground. They handle customer inquiries, structure loans, and, when the numbers make sense so that there is a win-win scenario, originate loans. That, of course, is in the best of all possible worlds. History has shown, however, that a win-win approach in the lending business does not always happen. If, as a result of corporate strategy or office culture, the loan officer approaches the customer for the short-term as just another transaction, then there may be one outcome: the highest-margin loan requiring the borrower to refinance in a short period, or again and again and again. Though there are laws in some states against churning, there are ways lenders get around this while staying in compliance. In that scenario, that customer will eventually be "used up."[6] If, on the other hand, the loan officer seeks to build relationships for the long-term, then the best loan product will be originated. Since a referral base is essential for any loan officer thinking about sustained growth, those in the business for the long haul tend to take the long view. Those taking the short-term approach must continually advertise using costly direct mail, telemarketers, and placements on television and radio. Those costs of doing business are passed onto to the next set of customers.

Given the differences between short-term and long-term views of mortgage financing, those who direct marketing in mortgage companies are responsible for creating many of the adverse consequences in communities across the nation. Abundant media coverage, recent studies, and the increasing number of lawsuits across the country suggest that this is the case, as will be addressed later. These lawsuits, moreover, help explain the ambivalence in consumer behavior after the boom stemming from the adverse media attention on the lending industry.

Advertising is a "perpetual desire machine" that generates more and still more desire among those it targets.[7] In the realm of mortgage refinances, advertising is directed toward tapping stored wealth in the form of home equity for cash in order for the consumer to explore the possibilities of financial freedom. That financial freedom, however, translates into debt secured against real estate. In the realm of real estate sales, in contrast, the new or resale home is the focal point in advertising, where the mortgage is merely the financial instrument employed to leverage income and assets in order to make the acquisition. When financial products like mortgages are marketed using the creative art form, mortgage marketing focuses on benefits to the consumer rather than the features and mechanics of the loan. Therein rests much of the problem for the industry and the consumer. With the consumer focused on larger debt balances masquerading as financial freedom and homeownership as the embodiment of the American Dream, those immediate tangible benefits can eclipse understanding the terms and features of the loan that could result in long term consequences.

What is at risk, therefore, is a homeowner's immediate and long-term financial position. Whether purchasing or refinancing, building wealth over time through increasing equity more or less drives one of the reasons for homeownership. Aside from being the master of one's own domain with a sense of being a stakeholder in the community, equity develops through two means. First, reduction of the mortgage balance over time leads to equity regardless of the conditions of the real estate market. Second, even where there is no reduction of the mortgage balance, equity can either develop or diminish by market forces that affect home values. Of course, in the best of all possible worlds, a fully amortized loan coupled with a steadily rising real estate price levels slowly but surely builds enduring wealth for many homeowners.

Let's examine some of the nuances of mortgages, mortgage marketing, and the pay off for the industry. As we move forward, we will also briefly examine laws and regulations—and the legacy of past public policy—that demand a reexamination of what makes sense and what does not, as well as some of the targeted marketing that has caused serious problems in many communities across the nation.

Terminology

The first place to start is to define several key terms and reflect on history given the antiquity of the word *mortgage*. It is important to establish this foundation in order to clearly understand issues associated with home mortgage financing, homeownership, and foreclosure. The book's Glossary was designed to support the reader to better understand concepts that build on top of each other as the book unfolds.

At its most basic, a mortgage is a financial instrument, a contract. When used as a verb, it is an act that creates debt.[8] The word's etymological origin is from the Old French of the thirteenth century and is a combination of the words *mort* and *gage*, which were joined together to mean "dead pledge."[9]

A mortgage is a claim against real property assets. The borrower's pledge of his property as collateral comes with the provision that the pledge can be exercised by the lender for his benefit in the event of the borrower's default. When viewed in these simplest of terms, consumers looking at how mortgage products are marketed should hold some degree of sobriety. The actions of the lender can place borrowers at risk and, conversely, the consumer's act of borrowing can place the lender at risk.

A *note* or *promise note* is a contract between a lender and a borrower to repay a loan. This legal instrument binds both parties to various terms and conditions. Common to all notes are references to the loan amount, the interest rate, the terms under which payments are calculated, the term of the loan, the due date, and provisions for late fees. Some notes have an addendum called a *rider*, which more clearly describes how a loan operates, as in the case of an adjustable rate mortgage (ARM). The Fannie Mae/Freddie Mac Uniform Instruments for Fixed Rate, Balloon, and Adjustable Rate notes are standardized instruments.[10] Not all loan instruments, however, are alike. Typically, the *note* or *promise note* is one- or two-pages in length.

The *mortgage*, on the other hand, is the foreclosure instrument. The standard six- to eight-page document specifies the name of the trustee acting on behalf of the lender charged to initiate foreclosure under a provision that more or less says to the borrower: if you pay you stay, and if you don't you won't. The *mortgagor* is the borrower taking on debt and pledging the real estate as collateral, and the *mortgagee* is the lender extending credit secured by the real estate referenced in the contract. Many states refer to this document as the *deed of trust*. The difference between a mortgage and a deed of trust is based on the state in the country where the property exists given the different legal theories and laws concerning foreclosure. For a fuller overview on key terms associated with mortgages, finance, economics, and real estate see the Glossary.

Behind the Marketing

The role of marketing in the mortgage industry is to understand the size of the market, identify consumer demographic profiles and segment the market accordingly, clarify consumer wants and needs, and understand consumer behavior and trends. With this market intelligence, marketing efforts should result in raised consumer awareness of the firm and desire for the firm's financial products. In the best of marketing, efforts are pinpointed with precision, which in the lending industry results in matching specific mortgage products with specific borrower profiles. This saves everyone time and money and avoids the leave-no-tree standing campaigns that result in an avalanche of direct mail to all consumers. In the worst of mortgage marketing, there is sometimes a gross mismatch between the product and the consumer, which can be the result of either mass marketing resulting from a failure in strategic planning, or precision marketing that targets specific communities at a community's expense. The former example is costly and inefficient. The latter example can result in litigation alleging reverse redlining and the targeting of minorities.

Before any advertising takes place, mortgage companies work with an assortment of resources that include advertising companies and mail list brokers to make sure that they get the most for their marketing dollars. This is important for consumers as well, because in the end, the right company with, hopefully, the right mortgage product will be matched with the right consumer at the right time. By accessing information from the public records, list brokers can sell relevant data to mortgage companies for their marketing efforts. In theory, lower costs stemming from a better use of marketing dollars will lead to higher margins to lenders and lower costs to consumers by virtue of added competition. When properly done, the end result is win-win with the company and consumer benefitting in the open marketplace.

Data Mining

Through data mining, numerous companies cater to the unique needs of the mortgage industry. These entities are capable of identifying with pinpoint accuracy the size of a potential target market based on zip code, loan amount, loan type, credit score, and other relevant information with the help of technology and the public records. These fee-based services are offered in order to permit lenders to contact and match prospective borrowers who are most likely to be interested in purchasing or refinancing to either secure a better program or meet other needs.

To illustrate, some lending industry-driven marketing efforts during the boom targeted the 580-credit score population as possible government loan or subprime borrowers. In many cases, these credit profiles proved either better or worse than what originally was presented by the list brokers. As a result, lower-risk credit profiles with higher scores were steered into loan that conformed to Fannie Mae or Freddie Mac's guidelines without the risk-grade adjustments to the interest rate or additional points that result from risk-based pricing. The agency eligible A-minus borrowers paid a slightly higher rate and cost to get the rate. Higher risk credit profiles with lower scores either became government loan borrowers if they fit the underwriting parameters, or became subprime borrowers by default.

Similarly, marketing campaigns that went after the 680-credit score niche sought solid conventional borrowers. Since most borrowers do not always conform to fit neatly into the 28/36 debt-to-income ratios, or "the tight box" set by Fannie Mae and Freddie Mac for income qualifying, some borrowers were steered into Alt-A, which means alternative to agency, or Option ARM loans. Conforming to agency guidelines mean that no more than 28 percent of monthly household income should go to the monthly mortgage obligation. Similar to their lower-credit score counterparts, the lending industry as a whole found ways to match an array of products with the needs suggested by the different credit profiles and consumer demands. To illustrate, a 680-credit score permitted a borrower to apply for Alt-A financing, or a stated income documentation loan, which could also be coupled with a stated income home equity line of credit, or the HELOC. This over reliance on high scores that permitted liberal underwriting was a key factor leading to the run up on home prices, the increase in non-performing loans, and the loss of confidence among institutional investors, who stopped buying not just subprime mortgage backed securities, but other types as well.

One company specializing in potential mortgage borrower lists is Wall Street Media out of Coral Springs, Florida. On its Wall Street List website, the company states of its Federal Housing Administration and Veterans Affairs data:

> This database is compiled and updated monthly from county clerk and tax assessors' office in 38 states. [U.S. Department of Housing and Urban Administration] data used to target Government loans in urban as well as rural areas, is then appended quarterly. This compiling system allows [Wall Street List] to create mortgage lead files that are segmented by underwriting guidelines and estimated credit variables.[11]

Marketing representatives in mortgage companies that want a turnkey marketing solution can ratchet their marketing efforts up a notch by having companies like Wall Street List conduct a voice mail broadcast. Wall Street Media states that it complies with applicable consumer laws by scrubbing the data list against the Federal Trade Commission's[12] Do Not Call Registry.

Although this chapter does not seek to attest to the quality of service offered by Wall Street Media, it does point to the importance for mortgage companies having up-to-date data to turn into relevant and compelling information for their target market. To illustrate, within days of each other, it is not inconceivable to receive two direct mail pieces from different mortgage companies. One might reference a mortgage balance paid off many years ago. The other, however, might reference a current and accurate balance, and also reference a credit card balance in its offer for a cash-out refinance. The quality of the mined data to target a market speaks volumes about the convergence of public records, data mining, marketing, and matching consumers with the mortgage product that is right for them at the right time.

Trigger Lists

Lenders desire customer loyalty to the same extent that customers want the best product, service, interest rate, and cost to get the rate. Because many lenders secure capital from similar funding sources, rates should be fairly close with one another—assuming competitors have similar overhead cost structures.

A prospective borrower who has a general conversation with a loan officer about a mortgage company, market conditions, or loan products is not the same as a customer who is applying for a loan. An application permits a lender to examine credit, which serves to determine the program, note rate, and an accurate annual percentage rate, or APR. Once an application takes place, the credit bureaus make that information available to other lenders. This can result in consumers applying with several lenders at the same time, true to the LendingTree advertisement, "When lenders compete, you win^{SM}." But, lender and real estate groups have had issues with "trigger lists."

The three major credit bureaus, Equifax, Experian, and TransUnion, created "trigger lists" as a means to not only generate revenue for themselves, but also to permit households seeking an extension of credit to be solicited in order for them to competitively shop at the moment they are in the market. This is nothing short of intelligence built into the system. Trigger lists contain a list of recent mortgage applicants and include all pertinent information such as the applicant's name, address, phone number, as well as credit-related data. Within hours of an application, it is conceivable that applicants could be inundated with dozens of phone calls from mortgage companies hundreds of miles away. Moreover, it is equally as likely that third-party telemarketing firms in India, Ireland, Canada, or Panama calling on behalf of U.S.-based mortgage companies that out sourced the service will call in order to make a live transfer of the applicant to their client, the mortgage company.

In 2006, the 120,000-member trade group National Association of REALTORS® had brought up the debated issue of the "trigger list" with the Federal Trade Commission. That regulatory agency, however, saw nothing improper about the credit bureaus' practice of selling information to mortgage companies. As a federal agency tasked to be the nation's consumer watch dog, the Federal Trade Commission investigates deceptive and unfair trade practices that can harm consumers. Lew Sichelman of *Realty Times* reported, "National Association of REALTORS®'s main concern is that its members' deals could be put on hold or even short-circuited completely if a would-be buyer bites at an offer from another lender."[13] Real estate agent John Veneris of Downers Grove, Illinois, said that:

Suddenly the whole world descends on you. It could be a good deal for the consumer [by virtue of applying elsewhere], because it may be a better loan, but maybe not. People are always looking for a better deal.[14]

Veneris was the chairman of the National Association of REALTORS®'s Conventional Finance and Lending Committee in 2006 and added a caveat that his concern was that borrowers could become victimized by "the blood suckers of the lending industry."[15]

In 2006, the 27,000-member trade group the National Association of Mortgage Brokers wanted to put an end to trigger lists.[16] The association's executive vice president Roy DeLoach said, "There are very serious privacy, identity theft and bait-and-switch issues involved here."[17] As a result, National Association of Mortgage Brokers took a position seeking legal or regulatory controls regarding the use of trigger lists.

In *Realty Times*, Kenneth Harney reported that:

DeLoach and other critics of trigger marketing charge that they may violate federal privacy and credit statutes. DeLoach says that under the Fair Credit Reporting Act the bureaus cannot provide consumer financial data to third-party lead generators, because those firms have not obtained permission from consumers, and they're not in a position to make a "firm offer of credit" under the law.[18]

Critics have charged that the Federal Trade Commission under Platt Majoras' tenure gave the three major credit bureaus "too much latitude to profit from the sale of credit data to lenders and consumers."[19] Political commentator and author of *The Squandering of America: How the Failure of Our Politics Undermines Our Prosperity* Robert Kuttner stated that "Federal agencies that are supposed to be looking out for the consumer are really protecting the companies that do bad things the agencies were set up to prevent."[20]

Byron Acohido and Jon Swartz of *USA Today* reported, "These too-good-to-be-true [mortgage] offers came from brokers who skirted rules requiring traditional lenders to make firm offers only in writing."[21] In defense of the Federal Trade Commission's position, Majoras said, "We've been tough on the industry and strong in standing up for consumers."[22]

In her own self-defense regarding an appearance of impropriety, because her former law firm Jones Day, which had Experian as a corporate client, Majoras said that she recused herself from an August 2005 investigation that resulted in Experian paying a $950,000 fine for using deceptive sales practices. However, she confirmed she did not recuse herself from voting to approve a subsequent $300,000 fine Experian paid in February for a repeat offense.[23] Experian pulled in $3 billion revenue in 2006.

The credit bureaus' lobbying organization Consumer Data Industry Association run by chief operating officer Stuart Pratt said, "Mortgage triggers are like going to the mall, where you can shop for the best possible deal, easily and efficiently."[24] The Federal Trade Commission issued a consumer alert in February 2007 about the topic of trigger lists.[25]

There are numerous cracks in the trigger list system, moreover, that are wide open to those intent on committing fraud. One of the more troubling types is the bogus appraisal. After a credit report is pulled by a lender, one of the three major credit bureaus makes that information available on a fee basis to other mortgage companies. As noted earlier, the reasoning behind this practice is to permit competitive shopping. Where there is true competition, in theory, consumers benefit. That data, however, can and do sometimes end up in the wrong hands. Case in point: From time to time, after a credit report is pulled, a prospective borrower could immediately get a call from someone claiming to be an appraiser requesting to come out and appraise the home. The fee is collected, the inspection is done, and the so-called appraiser then disappears into the night. When the real appraiser contacted by the mortgage company shows up, the ugly truth becomes apparent to all: the borrower was scammed. Lenders can protect their borrowers by requiring the appraiser to mention the name of the loan officer or devise some other means to protect their customers. Borrowers can protect themselves as well by insisting that the alleged appraiser provide a full name, the company's name, and phone number in order to call back to schedule an appointment.

Controlled Business Arrangements

The issue that industry associations have against trigger lists may be associated with the loss of control over the transaction, increased competition that diminishes the likelihood of earning business, and repercussions from consumers regaining control of their decisions. The credit bureaus' and Federal Trade Commission's positions on trigger lists may have permitted a consumer end-run around the controlled business arrangement. A controlled business arrangement permits a real estate company to own or partner with a mortgage company, title company, builder, insurance company, and other affiliated businesses. By aggregating the array of services, fee income to the holding company escalates, as does partnership income to the affiliated entities. In other words, the controlled business arrangement is about regaining customer control and increasing fee income through up selling and cross selling.

In the hypothetical example in Table 1.1: Aggregated Fee Income, the fee income that comes under control in a controlled business arrangement can be significant. In just one $200,000 purchase transaction, a company that controls the real estate brokerage, mortgage lending, and title services may be able to extract $23,200. Consumer complaints about excessive lender or real estate broker fees are misplaced since they fail to take into account the actual business structure that exists in many firms. Similarly, consumer complaints about high closing costs that reach the state legislatures tend to die in committees since attorneys have a vested interest in maintaining the status quo. Earning commissions from selling title insurance—a point that is not disclosed to borrowers—is lucrative given the low overhead. Pay outs on these claims are as likely as getting hit by lightening.

Table 1:1 – Aggregated Fee Income in a Controlled Business Arrangement

$	200,000	Sales Price
$	190,000	Loan Amount
$	1,600	Title Fees (Attorney, Document Preparation, Notary, and Title Insurance)
$	1,600	Lender Fees (Processing, Appraisal, Underwriting, etc.)
$	12,000	Real Estate Sales Commission (6% of the Sales Price)
$	3,800	Loan Origination and Discount Point (2% of the Loan Amount)
$	3,800	Service Release Premium or Yield Spread Premium (2% Paid by Investor)
$	22,800	Total Fee Income to Controlled Business Arrangement

Source: Peter Hébert

Some may argue that controlled business arrangements, or affiliated business arrangements as they are also called, could be referred to as a legal monopoly that circumvents the spirit of the Sherman Antitrust Act of 1890 and the Clayton Act of 1914 since the business practice inhibits shopping, stifles genuine competition, restrains trade, and thereby keeps prices up. Others, in contrast, may argue that this type of arrangement is legal by virtue of consumer disclosures and benefits the consumer through the added convenience.

Towards the end of the Reagan Era, Long & Foster Real Estate ventured into affiliated and controlled business arrangements with title companies and its own mortgage company Prosperity Mortgage®. That did not sit well with several experienced real estate agents who left to either form their own companies or join companies like RE/MAX®. Long & Foster's website states that:

> Prosperity Mortgage joined Wells Fargo Home Mortgage in 1993 to form Prosperity Mortgage Company. As a result of this joint venture, Prosperity Mortgage has at least one mortgage officer in almost all of Long & Foster's 200+ offices.[26]

Over time, the once open-door policy to loan officers at regional companies like Long & Foster and its primary competitor Weichert Realtors® virtually closed to traditional loan officers. One Weichert sales manager made the closed door policy clear when he said, "Why should I let you in? Jim Weichert pays me bonuses on what this office produces overall, not on the loans you would originate here for your company. Sorry."[27] The closed-door policy to lenders continues to this day with many real estate brokers.[28]

As genuine competition fell by the way side, in its place, companies like Prosperity Mortgage® and Mortgage Access Corporation doing business as Weichert Financial Services of Weichert Realtors® took their place in many real estate offices across parts of the country in order to turn the offices into "'one-stop' destinations for the full range of real estate products and services."[29] From a strategic standpoint at the corporate level, the major shift in the real estate sales and purchase-driven mortgage financing made perfect sense. Real estate branch managers and agents directing customers to their in-house lender, however, inhibit competitive shopping. The now-fairly commonplace practice of controlled business arrangements goes against the grain of genuine competition, which only comes through businesses competing as customers actually comparison shop without restraints.

Baltimore, Maryland, resident Denise Minter filed a lawsuit on December 26, 2007, in Baltimore's U.S. District Court naming Wells Fargo Bank and Long & Foster Real Estate as defendants. Minter alleged that these companies created a sham company—Prosperity Mortgage—that "billed homebuyers for work that was never done."[30] The suit alleged that Prosperity Mortgage® brokered almost all of their loans to Wells Fargo, which then funded them. At issue was an alleged fee sharing arrangement. Rachel Sams of *Baltimore Business Journal* reported that:

> Wells Fargo allegedly funded Minter's loan and withheld $945 in fees for Prosperity Mortgage. Wells Fargo and Long & Foster allegedly split the fees paid to Prosperity Mortgage. The fee rewarded Long & Foster for referring the loan business to Wells Fargo, and is prohibited by federal law, which bars companies from accepting fees for the referral of settlement service business on a mortgage loan, according to the suit. [31]

Minter's 51-page complaint sought class action status. As Howard A. Lax, author of *The Mortgage News, A Mortgage Banking Newsletter* stated, "This is the latest in a string of Real Estate Settlement Procedures Act claims against Long & Foster that simply will not go away."[32]

During the boom, Long & Foster earned considerable fees not just from the commissions in selling houses. By May 2008, Long & Foster had finished building its $86 million, new 287,000-square foot headquarters in Chantilly, Virginia. It completely dwarfs Fannie Mae's 80,000-square foot "big house" at 3900 Wisconsin Avenue in upper northwest in Washington, D.C. Both facilities are modeled after Williamsburg's Governor's Palace. Long & Foster's mega, institutional-sized building has five floors. The company's president of Financial Services George Eastmant said, "Had we known [that the real estate market would have turned for the worse], we would have delayed the project."[33] "We're very proud and happy. But for the people who are unhappy, we don't want to rub their noses in it," said Eastmant in what appeared to be a reference to the company's 16,000 agents, who were struggling in a historically tough market that necessitate listing a record number of properties that require third-party approval for short-sales that more than likely will not happen in a reasonable period of time.

The Builder's Lender

Each year, new home sales make up a significant percentage of home sales and require mortgage financing. Surprising things can happen when a new homes sales agent places a phone call with a lender not on the homebuilder's "approved list." In one case,[34] the builder's lender was between one quarter to one half percent higher in rate compared with the prevailing Fannie Mae and Freddie Mac rates. She was not happy since the rates her customers were offered, she believed, were slowing her new home sales on the project. The problem she faced appeared to be three-fold.

First, the new home sales representative was locked into the builder's lender. It was likely that the builder's lender negotiated the construction-to-perm as well as the purchase money financing for the new homebuyer as part of the overall package between the builder and lender. On a business-to-business level, this made sense since the builder's goal is to minimize the cost of holding inventory. But, on a business-to-consumer level, this may have been short-sighted since the goal is to unload inventory.

Second, because the builder's lender was a small, local bank, the loan programs offered to customers were not only limited, but more expensive for the consumer as well. This small local bank just did not have access to many investors to offer the "outside of the box," or creative programs, nor did they have the volume to negotiate better pricing from their investors in the secondary market or other wholesalers to pass along to the consumer. In short, the builder's lender was overpriced and limited without enough variety in the mix of mortgage programs.

Third, many new homebuilders often offer attractive incentives to their buyers as inducements to purchase. That money, however, has to come from somewhere when it comes time to pay the cost of the "free" finished basement or some of the high closing fees commonly offered in competitive markets or high-closing cost areas. Higher interest rates, which produce a higher yield spread premium to the lender, can in turn be offered as a rebate to the consumer to cover some of the closing costs. There is nothing inherently wrong with the mechanics of this so long as there are timely and adequate disclosures.

In the end, it appeared that the problem that this new home sales representative faced was that the builder priced its target customers out of the market on total sales price, limited loan programs, higher interest rates, and, of course, higher cost of ownership via higher monthly payments. There were two underlying culprits: first, the controlled business arrangement between the builder and the lender that stifled lender competition and consumer shopping, and second, the builder's incentives that were priced into the interest rate offered to prospective purchasers. These two combinations worked fine in an overheated market where buyers stood in line to purchase homes sight unseen regardless of the price due to incredibly flexible financing. In a slowing market with more time for everyone including this new home sales representative to think, it was apparent that a lack of genuine competition helped slow sales.

The Latin phrase *caveat emptor,* "let the buyer beware," is ever true here. Whether looking at a new home, or a resale home, consumers tend to be better off when they shop around for mortgage financing. In this vein, the controversial trigger list comes to play at permitting consumers to secure competitive offers at their specific time of need.

Opt-In/Opt-Out Prescreen

Each time a consumer seeks an extension of credit or insurance, the credit report is pulled. The major bureaus own and manage consumer data, and they sell information to competing extenders of credit and insurance. This business practice cuts both ways for consumers: it can result in more competitive offers and it can also trigger an onslaught of unwelcomed phone calls and direct mail.

Here is the reasoning behind this: Equifax, Experian, and TransUnion (collectively the "consumer credit reporting companies") encourage consumers to make informed decisions about receiving firm (i.e., preapproved or prescreened) offers of credit or insurance. There are a few benefits from receiving firm offers. First, consumers are provided more product choices. Second, consumers learn about and have an opportunity to take advantage of offers that may not be available to the general public. Finally, firm offers help consumers to "comparison shop," which may increase a consumer's buying power and/or lower monthly obligations.

Under the Fair Credit Reporting Act, the consumer credit reporting companies are permitted to include consumer names on lists used by creditors or insurers in order for them to be able to make firm offers of credit or insurance even though it may not have been initiated by the consumer. The Fair Credit Reporting Act, however, provides consumer the right to "opt out," which prevents consumer credit reporting companies from providing a consumer's credit file information for firm offers.[35]

Financial Literacy

Financial literacy, or the lack thereof, is part of the problem that permitted lending abuses to flourish and for borrowers to self-inflict wide spread financial damage. The pervasive lack of financial literacy and predatory lending were opposite sides of the same coin. One cannot exist without the other. When the many types of mortgage fraud are thrown into mix, insult is added to injury.

In 2005, Consumer Federation of America and Fair Isaac Corporation, also known as FICO, engaged Opinion Research Corporation to conduct a consumer survey regarding the public's understanding of the role that a credit score has relative to mortgage rates and programs. The survey "found that 49 percent of respondents do not understand that credit scores measure a person's credit risk, while 45 percent think—incorrectly—that a higher income will result in a higher credit score."[36] FICO reports that a consumer with a 580 credit score is "likely to pay nearly three percentage points more in mortgage interest than someone with a score of 720."[37] In other words, a high credit score borrower taking on a $150,000, 30-year fixed-rate mortgage at 5.875 percent would have $890 per month principal and interest mortgage payments. In contrast, with a score in the 580s, that same loan amount at a subprime rate of 9 percent would run $1,200 per month in principal and interest mortgage payments. But, consumers knowing their credit scores does not equate to financial literacy.

A 2005 study that sought to assess the availability of mortgage finance-related courses directed to the consumer uncovered so little in the way of a formally organized series of classes.[38] The only relevant course was offered by the Mortgage Bankers Association of America. But, how many consumers shopping for a mortgage searched the archives of the Federal Reserve, the Federal Trade Commission, or the Mortgage Bankers Association for reliable information? These sources do, in fact, have good information. It is highly unlikely, however, that consumers go there first in order to make informed decisions. Journalists and researchers writing about these topics may go there, and those who read a newspaper will get the information they need—second hand, through an interpretive prism with omissions, and without the benefit of insight that comes from an industry insider or subject matter expert.

Consumer finance is first taught in high school home economics. Given that, it would stand to reason that American high school graduates would possess sufficient functional and financial literacy to understand the basics of consumer finance. But, that is not necessarily the case for many reasons.[39] First, promise notes, the addendums to them, and the riders to some notes are contracts that spell out the mechanics of a mortgage loan. These contracts are written by lawyers for lawyers. They are not written for the average American consumer to comprehend. Second, about 30 million adult Americans, or 14 percent of the population, are functionally illiterate and are below the basic literacy requirements to graduate from high school. Moreover, 63 million adult Americans, or 29 percent of the population, are only at the basic literacy level, which means they can perform only "simple and everyday literacy activities."[40] Given these factors and the statistics, assent to a legally binding contract written in legalese, not everyday language, becomes difficult. In other words, in some cases, customers may as well just place an X in place of their signature to acknowledge that they fully understand the terms and conditions when in fact they do not. These facts pose serious issues not just for customers, but employees within the financial sector who themselves may lack the skills needed to clearly communicate and to enhance a customer's comprehension of the many aspects of a mortgage obligation based on the different types of financial products. Even the most inexperienced and borderline incompetent bank employee has an asymmetrical relationship with the customer. The playing field is not level when it comes to comprehension and negotiating. Consequently, the cards are stacked against the customer, which is why the house almost always wins due to risk factors that that regulators failed to address.

During the housing boom, an increasing number of American consumers in the purchase and refinance realm demonstrated increasing signs of functional and financial illiteracy as compared with the early 1990s.[41] This is an anecdotal definition of functional illiteracy: a borrower with a 5.625 percent, fixed-rate, 30-year loan on a rental house called to refinance in 6.250 percent market. The general media reports the prevailing market rates, and they are published on numerous websites, including Freddie Mac's homepage. This is another anecdotal definition of financial illiteracy by way of example: a prospective borrower asked if it was a good idea to call back after he saved $10,000 from a second job so that he could buy discount points to get a lower rate, which translated into a half-percent rate drop. That person was told to put the hard-earned savings in the bank since unforeseeable events could occur and to only use equity to cover closing costs or take a premium rate when refinancing.

Headlines told countless stories about the real estate and lending business and, in the process, informed those who paid attention. Love them or hate them, the media did a remarkably good job in covering the warning signs and many problems during the refinance boom as they developed. The media got the story early and they got it right. Generally speaking, they did not make the news. They reported the news.

In some cases, however, the media got the story very wrong. When seasoned journalists report with shock and dismay that borrowers are actually capable of getting a No Income/No Asset (NINA) loan, the public is being subjected to enduring either amateurs of the first order given that this documentation type has been around since the 1980s, or tongue-in-check reporting to elicit shock value. Moreover, consumer finance reporters have covered mortgage lending with a voice of certainty and authority—yet have been completely mistaken about crucial facts. These points underscore both the importance of the media getting the story right, even when under deadline pressure, and the genuine complexity of the mortgage lending industry. Given that newspaper readership has been on the decline for decades, however, consumers getting news about mortgage loans would be left to television, radio, and the Internet. So, to some degree functional literacy, financial literacy, and media-driven misinformation as well were among the shortcomings that permitted consumers to become victims of loans with predatory features that would lead to the subprime meltdown.

Aside from periodic columns by industry experts and bloggers, financial literacy for the masses and popular culture may be summed up by three television personalities: Suze Orman, Dave Ramsey, and Jim Cramer. They each have shows, websites, and books to sell. But, at the end of the day, Orman and Cramer more so than Ramsey have achieved an almost cult-like status that they maintain through a parent-child relationship with their audience. They represent the next generation of "televangelists" promoting the good news of prudent spending, saving, and investing. Criticisms aside, all three bring something of value to the general public's table that may be summed up as the need to watch where the money is going, and the need to play to make it grow.

The *Suze Orman Show* is on radio and televised on *PBS, NBC,* and *CNN*. Orman's strength is a no-nonsense approach, and should be followed given that she is a certified financial advisor. Orman, moreover, has her priorities right: "People first, then money, then things." An on-line Resource Center at Orman's website is there to help consumers become more literate and savvy.[42] Suze, however, comes across as a lending industry lobbyist for tax deductible mortgages by making a distinction between "good debt" and "bad debt." Let's not fool ourselves or the audience, girl friend. Debt is debt. The best mortgage is the one with a zero balance. Even if there are tax credits to spur home buying and more tax deductions that go above the current limits, a home mortgage is the largest debt that most consumers have. Most lenders are friendly and concerned guides that aid consumers through the complicated and intimidating lending process. But, once the closed loan file has gone to the servicing arm, the friendly lender becomes the debt collector on behalf of a faceless bond holder, who will sue the lender if it does not foreclose if the borrower goes into default.

Dave Ramsey runs a syndicated talk radio show where he reaches three million listeners through three hundred fifty radio stations through a three-hour live format. He also appears on *FOX Business' The Dave Ramsey Show* where he offers "life-changing financial advice." Ramsey has a no-nonsense approach that can be summed as this: "You can never borrow your way into prosperity." Members of the White House Council of Economic Advisers would do well to pay attention. He is a critic of those who sell get-rich-in-real-estate courses since, as Ramsey points out, "Their schemes work great until a tenant moves out leaving the home vacant for six months or the 'simple cosmetic repairs' become a $100,000 money pit." Ramsey is old school—cash and carry. For those able to do so, as he noted, "Nothing has better cash-flow than a paid-for property."[43] Moreover, Ramsey is a step ahead of many consumers, who have been in bankruptcy. When asked how a previously bankrupt consumer should reestablish credit, Ramsey cut through the muddled thinking with: Why would you want to reestablish credit? Credit is how you got into the mess, and getting more credit to borrow more may get you back into the same mess. Ramsey suggests to approach lenders for credit as a last resort, but not as the first resort. Ramsey's fans are coached so that they can declare, "I am debt f-r-e-e!"

Jim Cramer of *CNBC's Mad Money* is the day trader's and investor's pick-me-up at the end of the day. His strength is that he is either a testosterone- or Red Bull-driven informative entertainer bringing the vitality

655370

CUSTOMER'S ORDER NO.		DEPARTMENT		DATE 8/21/20			
NAME Sean Donahue							
ADDRESS							
CITY, STATE, ZIP							

SOLD BY		CASH	C.O.D.	CHARGE	ON. ACCT.	MDSE. RETD.	PAID OUT

QUANTITY	DESCRIPTION		PRICE		AMOUNT	
1	1	Mortgage for Armul	50 00	50	cc	
2						
3		Maryland Taxes	Included			
4						
5				$ 50 00		
6						
7						
8						
9						
10						
11						
12						
13						
14						
15						
16						
17						
18						

RECEIVED BY

5805
6320/46350

KEEP THIS SLIP FOR REFERENCE

of the market into either the living room or the car through satellite radio. Cramer is a seasoned optimist, and he is right in believing that: "There is always a bull market somewhere, and he wants to help you find it."[44] Cramer's strength is in providing his viewers with business sector and market place analysis for reasoned decision-making. In this regard, he is superb and that is why he is respected. His weakness, however, is that he has sanctified the art of giving hot stock tips without providing his audience with a more thorough foundation in understanding decision making techniques like fundamental or technical analysis. If Cramer took the time to break down the Capital Asset Pricing Model for his viewers, for example, his ratings would probably drop.[45] Moreover, the weaknesses of the text book-driven model used by many portfolio managers would become apparent. Therein rests the dilemma of couch potato-based financial entertainment where marketplace hysteria and high drama are delivered to Americans needing direction with their investments. At the end of the day, viewers walk away with an inadequate understanding of the different business sectors, have little sense of bench marking, and do not understand the different types of analysis that should go into making a rational investment decision. Consequently, Cramer's got his share of fans, who have made money, and those who have lost since they do not have the academic foundation or did not do the due diligence necessary prior to intelligently investing.

One critic worth noting is *Comedy Central's* Jon Stewart of *The Daily Show*. On March 12, 2009, Stewart confronted Jim Cramer for *CNBC's* arrogant stance in the financial news industry towards struggling homeowners. Specifically, Stewart noted *CNBC's* Rick Santelli, who reports from the Chicago Mercantile Exchange, and his displeasure of government moves to stop foreclosures and to help homeowners. Cramer could not defend Santelli or himself. Cramer, according to Stewart, pulls "crazy bullshit every night." Referring to the economic crisis following the subprime meltdown, Stewart opened with, "How'd we get here?" Cramer responded with, "I don't know." Actually, Cramer does know. He was playing dumb. The investment houses and hedge funds with pension funds and an array of investments under management manipulated the market by driving the price levels. This is the classic pump and dump out of the play book from the Roaring Twenties. By moving price levels up or down, the market is manipulated and money is made. The general public goes long on investing in retirement plans. But, the big players create the movement by pushing values to unsustainable levels and then short sell-ing companies to force prices down through what is justified as financial free speech at the expense of retirement plans. Of course, the general public pays the price for this. Stewart said to Cramer: "It's not a fucking game." Wall Street "burned the fucking house down with our money and walked away rich as hell. And, you guys knew what was going down."[46]

Over-Draft Protection

Perhaps the easiest, least costly, and most often overlooked way for consumers to stay current on their obligations and safeguard their credit standing, especially then they experience tight periods, is to have over-draft protection.[47] Solid credit ratings are important since the lowest in-terest rates and the best programs are offered to borrowers with high credit scores. These are Fannie Mae and Freddie Mac programs, and the interest rates are reported on the news as the prevailing rate for the 30-year fixed mortgage, which is the industry benchmark.

Credit scores and mortgage histories tell lenders about a borrower's ability and willingness to repay obligations. The lowest rates are offered to borrowers with solid credit ratings and good mortgage histories, and higher rates are offered to borrowers with blemished credit and mortgage histories. In the worst of scenarios, no program or rate is offered due to the borrower's high credit risk.

Although the majority of homeowners have good credit and low fixed rates on their home loans, many do not. One of the reasons some borrowers fall into the subprime, or B-C-D rated, mortgages is simply because they have overlooked the cheapest form of insurance: over-draft protection.

Unforeseen expenses occur. Being between jobs, looking at major ex-penses beyond the monthly budget, or simply going from month to month is challenging for many families. When this happens, sometimes a check may bounce or a mortgage payment may be late. Late fees, nonsufficient funds fees, and mortgage lates then follow, which are reported to the credit bureaus.

Mortgage companies report late payments to Experian, Equifax and Trans Union, the three credit reporting agencies. Borrowers with "mortgage lates" on their credit reports may find limited refinancing or purchase options. Many 30-day lates will not hurt an FHA Streamline refinance since U.S. Department of Housing and Urban Development underwriting guidelines are liberal. But, many 30-day lates will shut the door on low rates for a cash-out refinance or a purchase. When this happens, borrowers are offered subprime rates, which generally are higher than the rates referred to as prime, triple-A, or agency—all of which mean Fannie Mae or Freddie Mac.

Subprime mortgages are not the end of the world, unless the loans were designed to make sustainable homeownership difficult if not impossible. Many subprime loans went to households that were in every income niche, but without over-draft protection. For many families this was avoidable. Avoiding higher mortgage rates can be done by planning ahead—regardless of whether a family is living month to month or quite secure with its monthly cash flow.

Over-draft protection can be set up with the bank or credit union that manages the checking account. The bank will charge a nominal rate of interest for advancing money each month when there are insufficient funds to cover the monthly expenses. The interest paid is nothing compared to the late fees and nonsufficient funds fees.

The Consumer's Perspective

Finding the right lender and the right loan can be a daunting task, because it is a fact finding mission. The first learning curve is recognizing that not all lenders are alike and all do not offer the same programs or rates. Moreover, just because two competitive lenders offer the same interest rate, it does not mean they are offering the same program—even if they are both 30-year fixed rate loans. The second learning curve is surveying the industry to see who has fallen and who is still standing. This requires some homework. Just because the last man standing in the lending industry can still take loan applications, it does not necessarily mean that this is the best choice for the consumer. When a major lender cuts back on staff and replaces it with an automated attendant guided by a series of questions for any of the customer relations functions, or has outsourced its back office functions to a third world country, quality customer service plummets. Moreover, competition tends to drive costs down and force competitors to compete on another playing field—quality service. Fewer competitors in the market place will ensure poorer service while keeping costs high. These factors make it all the more important to do some homework and carefully shop around.

The Company: Consumers should start their homework by conducting some due diligence on mortgage companies and then narrowing their search. The final selection may be due to the loan officer rather than the company's brand name since people tend to do business with people, not with corporations. Corporations are merely bundles of contracts and collections of strategic relationships. The law recognizes corporations as persons. But, anyone who has had a serious disagreement with a corporation has learned that they tend not to have heart, and that they tend to take a one-sided approach to negotiating. Moreover, should a complaint develop, the consumer may become viewed as a threat and the enemy rather than as a customer injured by the company's actions. While these points may not be pertinent if returning an item to Nordstrom, they certainly may be in a financial dealing where there is an irreconcilable difference where hundreds of thousands of dollars are in dispute. Therefore, start asking questions like: Would a lender agree to have Judge Judy hear and then decide on a dispute that requires arbitration? There is perhaps not a single lender that would simply because no lender wants to give voice to an aggrieved borrower in a public venue. Consequently, relevant questions are where to start.

Has the lender garnered adverse media attention, numerous lawsuits, or constant complaints from consumer advocacy groups? Love them or hate the, when social advocacy groups wage a campaign against Fannie Mae, a mortgage banker, or an investment banker it is for good reason. Therefore, ignore the media giving voice to criticisms of these types of groups as engaged in yet another "shake down," ignore the discrediting allegations of voter registration fraud, and look at the actual merits of the predatory lending complaints. A lender's reputation, credibility, and reliability should help determine the consumer's final choice. Consumers should ask many questions when they seek products or services.

How important is customer service during the application process and after closing? Has the lender severely cut back its staff? Follow the news. Many loan officers can tell you that they have unwittingly served as the "complaint department" for other companies that cut staff, increased advertising, but failed to make the connection between their marketing and other departments that deal directly with consumers. Consumers pay the price for this: it results in poor to nonexistent customer service. Moreover, inadequate staffing can also result in the inability to approve and fund a loan. In other words, do not be deceived by lenders that aggressively advertise since they may not be able to deliver according to expectations.

Is the lender strictly a broker, a mortgage lender, or a depository institution that also does mortgages? Each has pros and cons. Ideally, the selected company has a full product line up that includes government, conventional, portfolio, jumbo, Alt-A, and subprime loans. What type of charter does the institution have? Are they regulated by the state or a federal agency? If there is a dispute with an institution with a national charter, the efforts of the state on your behalf may prove futile due to preemption. Do they have a policy of referring the customer up to the best possible product and with better rates and terms? Ask what the company's polices are, and get it in writing.

Also, what kind of loan officers does the company hire? During the boom, countless help wanted advertisements primarily sought candidates with strong sales skills in order to ensure that the sales department was a cash cow driven by customer transactions rather than relationships. While there is nothing inherently wrong with someone with good sales skills, it should cause pause given the loan officer's background. Therefore, ask questions tied to the educational, prior employment background, and company training. Some lending operations provide extensive employee training. Others do not, but instead are sales- and transaction-driven sweat shops where management offers new hires with a phone and a desk and views customers as "used up" if they are unable to refinance them again. In this regard, one question to pose might be along the lines of asking for a description of the company's policy on business ethics.

Borrowers can further protect themselves by doing a thorough background check on the loan officer and the management team by conducting an online inmate locator search at the Federal Bureau of Prisons website at www.bop.gov. Many states that issue licenses do not bar convicted felons from obtaining a mortgage lending license. In many states, if the felon was not convicted of a financially-related crime, he or she can obtain a license. While that may make sense for those who believe that prison time rehabilitates character, it may provide pause for others given that the loan officer may make a house call to collect copies of tax returns and other sensitive information. Car theft and home invasions are not crimes like embezzlement, which is a financial crime. Additionally, the same level of self-protection should be conducted at the state and county levels. While this may come as a shock to some, be forewarned that some of the nation's major lenders had no problem looking the other way on background issues so long as the loan officer made money for the firm.[48] Given that many states and corporations do not deem the background issue a matter of risk for the public, the burden is on the consumer.

Finally, managers, not loan officers, set the tone for the culture in an office irrespective of corporate policy. With this point made, it should be noted that management comes in all varieties. At one extreme is the type that is forthright and bears the liability of a rogue loan officer in order to make their customers whole. At the other extreme is the type that views injured borrowers as legal liabilities rather than their rogue loan officers. Similarly, there are those who are educated, trained, and experienced to be a credit to the industry and then there are those who had start up money from former ventures and opened up a mortgage brokerage. In some of the latter cases there are those who have no idea what it means to act as a fiduciary and what it means to exercise due care towards a customer. As a result of these points, mortgage borrowers should do thorough background research and ask more questions before applying. In other words, turn the tables: ask them to submit their application and credentials, and then check them out.

Finally, lenders typically do not extend mortgage financing to those who have been bankrupt. Borrowers should carefully reconsider extending their trust and confidence of doing business with the many financial corporations that became insolvent and then raided the U.S. Treasury as an alternative to going through the humiliation of Chapter 13 bankruptcy proceedings to liquidate the mismanaged firms. Many of the leaders in the financial sector during the market's peak were recipients of the $700 billion Wall Street bailout. Rather than face humiliation, these firms instead chose to accept fear and anger as the public's response. Credit unions and small local banks did not create the financial and economic chaos or the foreclosure crisis. Just because the government has rewarded bad behavior, there is no reason for the public to reward irresponsible corporate behavior unless there is a desire for more of the same in the future.

The Applicant: The homework continues with consumers collecting documentation about income, employment, asset, mortgage, and insurance, as well as getting an update on their home's current market value if refinancing. Lenders will not accept copies of credit reports coming from the credit bureaus or a third party due to fraud concerns. Borrowers should be prepared, therefore, to provide their social security numbers. If seeking the opinion of more than one lender, consumers should do so within a few days of each other. Lenders who advise customers that a second opinion is not necessary do not want them to competitively shop, but shopping is a customer's right. Excessive inquiries can lower a credit score, but that will not be the result of speaking with two or three lenders within a few days.

If there are credit issues, consumers can get a free copy of their credit report.[49] Some lenders may help consumers understand and resolve issues.[50] But, consumers should be mindful of the fact that most loan officers are not economists or certified financial planners, though that often is what the public assumes and expects. Typically, only a high school education is required for entry into different facets of the lending business.

The Product: If competitively shopping, consumers should only compare identical loans with each other, and always use the annual percentage rate, or the APR, on the Truth in Lending disclosure as the comparative benchmark. If considering a nontraditional loan—an Alt-A loan, a subprime loan, or an Option ARM—consumers should insist on a copy of the program disclosure at application. If it is "against company policy," consumers should remind the lender that they are the customer. If the lender does not budge, regulators and the media can be brought in to bring the matter to light.

Borrowers should never borrow on terms that they do not understand or under terms that they do not feel comfortable with. They should make every effort to understand how the loan works prior to closing based on the contract, and not verbal assurances from anyone in the transaction. Consumers should retain the services of an unbiased professional—someone who has no vested interest in the transaction—in order to fully understand the nature of the obligation. Consider the reasons for this:

Real estate agents will tell buyers: "now is the time to buy." Translation: do it now. These are perennial adages that are industry-driven. Additionally, real estate agents represent the client, who pays the fee for services, which historically has been the seller. If the buyer does not have a buyer agent, the agent has fiduciary obligations to the seller. Moreover, how is a borrower to know if he is being steered in the right direction for a mortgage loan? Real estate agents are not loan officers, nor should they be.

Loan officers represent the interests of their employers, not borrowers. Consequently, a loan officer's fiduciary obligations are towards the corporation, and not the customer. A loan officer's obligation is to exercise a standard of due care. That standard of care does not necessarily mean any obligation to offer a fully amortized 30-year fixed rate loan if a higher fee can be derived from the customer for the corporation's benefit if an alternative loan is offered and accepted by the borrower.

Title agents are not lawyers, and the borrower at closing is not the client if an attorney conducts closing. Their job is to follow lender instructions, which includes preparing the HUD-1 settlement statement. The burden of the terms of the loan is on the consumer, which necessitates that borrowers read and understand the closing documents, specifically the promise note and rider to the note.

Consumers should clearly understand the exact nature of the business relationships. Each third party has a vested interest in the transaction, which means they may not derive any compensation unless the transaction closes and funds. The opinions of third party service providers, while valuable, may be biased, or self-interested, and should be seen as such. Even when every party exercises good faith and is above reproach in ethical conduct, there is still plenty of room for misunderstanding.

Concluding Thoughts

I conclude this chapter with a series of discussions. These address the rules of the road. Some may force you to think outside of the box. Please, therefore, consider this as your check list.

Consumers have been too trusting. Lenders, whether mortgage or consumer credit-related, have historically held the upper hand over consumers in financial transactions for several reasons. One reason that consumers have been at a disadvantage is because knowledge of the lending industry, its procedures, and regulations is asymmetrical. An average consumer is no match for the seasoned lender when it comes to these factors. Consumers can, however, take steps to balance the playing field. By following certain steps, consumers can protect themselves from rogue lenders and lenders in compliance with the law yet engaged in predatory behavior. Moreover, they can protect themselves from making poor choices through lack of careful planning.

Return the favor. One means of changing this asymmetrical relationship between households and lenders is by engaging in like-kind behavior. If, for example, a lender discloses that the telephone call may be recorded, disclose the same in turn. By recording calls, whether in electronic, tape, or written form, consumers take a small but significant step in achieving parity with lenders. The recorded information will not only contain critical facts concerning a course of action, but will also indicate who is less than thorough or forthright as comparisons among lenders are made. Moreover, by making and keeping contemporaneous records, should a dispute arise that may be cause for complaint or legal action, consumers will be better positioned to have any wrongs suffered taken seriously and equitably remedied either by the corporation's management or its regulators.

You *think* you have rights. Americans believe that they have a constitutionally protected right to privacy found in the search and seizure clause of the Fourth Amendment. And, this right does indeed exist when it comes to curbing governmental encroachment, but it does not exist in the public and commercial spheres of life. The three major credit bureaus are the *de facto* Big Brother of the United States. They in fact know more about every American than what some Americans fear the Central Intelligence Agency, the Federal Bureau of Investigation, the National Security Administration, or Homeland Security may know. The bureaus collect data on everyone, which then becomes information, and in turn can be transformed into actionable intelligence when in the right hands.

Yet, too few stop to consider what the implications are for being on the electronic "credit grid." The secretive nature of the power and sources of this data is such that even former Federal Reserve Governor Edward Gramlich would not say how the Federal Reserve had obtained consumer data regarding credit cards during the May 17, 2005 testimony before the U.S. Senate Committee on Banking, Housing, and Urban Affairs.[51] When pressed by Senator Chris Dodd (D-Connecticut), Gramlich said:

> We [the Federal Reserve] have purchased private credit card data. ... uh, I'm, I'm, uh, it's from a private company, and I'm not sure whether I should say that, and I'm not sure.... Let me ... let me ... let me check with our lawyers, and I'll get you the information on it.[52]

Gramlich was nervous. He did not want to go on record with the *C-Span* camera on him before the American public to name the organization that sells the personal data on Americans for a price. The bureaus collect, manage, and sell the data they own. James D. Scurlock's 2006 documentary film *Maxed Out* suggests that companies like Choicepoint, which as of September 19, 2008 was owned by New York City based LexisNexis®, are among the private aggregators of personal information and may have sold the consumer credit data to the Federal Reserve.

The immediate easy solution for all American is greater individual responsibility and offensive action. It never occurs to Americans to just say no and to opt-out of this intrusive system whenever possible. The bureaus own the personal data. No one should pay a third party to monitor or fix their credit report. These offers in the mail and advertisements on television and the Internet are scams that rob Americans out of millions of dollar. Americans are led to believe that they should personally bear the cost for updating faulty data or paying for a third-party credit monitoring service while not understanding that the bureaus extend preferential treatment and care to members of Congress. Push the burden and hassle back onto the provider of credit and the credit bureaus to fix *their* errors. When possible, initiate and participate in class action claims for faulty data collection and data management that deprives Americans of credit, costs consumers more in over priced credit, or even bars qualified applicants of employment.

A job offer may be based on the contents of a credit report. An economic downturn can lead to financial challenges. These challenges, reversals of good fortune, and impaired credit have nothing to do with academic preparedness, technical skills, or work experience. They have nothing to do with a credit score, which is used as a metric for determining an ability to repay a debt. What is needed is a nationwide refusal to participate in this absurd intrusion into privacy that has been perpetrated by the banking establishment onto Americans. The appropriate consumer response should be class action lawsuits directed against those who violate privacy rights.

The other course of action that is needed is a change in legislation that tilts towards consumers. Consumers should request a copy of the credit reports of loan officers and their management team. That would permit the customer to preempt themselves from doing business with deadbeats. This may sound outrageous and even funny. It is not. That after all, is the same logic these people use. They want to size you up. Size them up. They want the job. Determine if they deserve to be hired. The same logic holds true in employment circumstances. If no one is willing to have an even playing field, then the best solution is for a constitutional right of privacy to be extended to both the public and commercial spheres of life. Americans need to petition Congress to have their rights truly protected. If Congress will not listen, use these directives to level the playing field and force change. Leverage the power of social networking, and the tables will gradually turn. Once the tables turn, you will have privacy rights and more personal dignity.

Consumers should invest in themselves. Become more financially literate while also understanding how the extension of credit works and how debt calculations operate. Each industry has a unique vocabulary, and this is certainly true of mortgage finance. While understanding key terminology is a starting place, understanding one's own financial position is as important. A simple arrangement like over-draft protection separates prime borrowers from subprime borrowers. During the boom, countless borrowers who did not have this protection in place had late payments on their mortgage obligation, which barred them from the best loan programs. While the entertaining programs of Orman, Ramsey, and Cramer have their place, these are no substitute for an adult education course at a community college, an online course offered by a career school, or books written by these or other subject matter experts. At a minimum, households can better manage the day-to-day issues and plan ahead by preparing and living according to a budget. In accounting or corporate finance, the simplest of budgets would be called an income statement and the balance sheet. The household income statement should list what is coming in and subtract what is going out to derive at net income to be saved, invested, or spent. This tool can protect households from needlessly falling into the consumer credit card trap to finance the day-to-day living expenses since over time consumer debt balances can grow due to fees, accrued interest, and changes to terms that end up robbing households of financial freedom. Similarly, the household balance sheet should list assets like real estate, stocks, bonds, cash value life insurance, and other assets that can be converted into cash. This tool permits households to understand their current financial position as well as make net worth forecasts for retirement. Finally, households can avert financial catastrophe by investing in a life insurance policy to at a minimum cover the mortgage balance. Leaving a spouse or heirs with a mortgage free property in the event of death will not mean that they will become rich. On the contrary, it will mean that loved ones can live life free of debt and sleep at night without the worries triggered by the financial sector that can destroy important relationships.

Marketing exists to connect lenders and borrowers and facilitate activity in the market. Data mining companies exist to provide a legitimate service, reduce cost, and allow greater efficiency. This level of marketplace intelligence, when properly executed, results in win-win relationships. Moreover, the Federal Trade Commission permits consumers to either Opt-In or Opt-Out when it comes to receiving competitive offers for the extension of credit. Taken together, these factors can be powerful consumer tools.

Save the "junk mail." Refer to the solicitations when needed.[53] There is a lot to learn about different companies when comparing one offer and approach with another. The amateurs and less than ethical companies will stand out as their promotional pieces are compared with those from the professionals. In the end, however, all marketing material is designed to make the phone ring. Here are a few things to look for:

Dismiss considering a company if the solicitation says that no credit check is required. What lender would lend $200,000 without first examining a borrower's credit and understanding what the contents imply?

Dismiss offers designed to look like a federal government notice from either the Internal Revenue Service or any other state or federal agency. Any company that cannot rely on its own corporate reputation and that stoops to this type of gimmick is resorting to slight of hand chicanery.

Dismiss considering a company offering interest rates that are far below market rates. This is a possible sign of baiting and switching. A few things may be happening here: the lender assumes several points need to be charged, an adjustable rate mortgage is being offered, or they sent a market sensitive piece that is out-dated by the time it reached the mailbox—a sign of incompetence.

It matters not if the direct mail piece is signed by the executive vice president of the north east region or the loan officer working in town. The million dollar title typically appears on bank letter head with ten point font written by a corporate communication officer, who knows little about mortgages on a day in and day out level. That type of piece appeals to ego: you are a vice president, and so is your loan officer, a vice president. This is about peer-to-peer business. The marketing from the loan officer in town may be signed with the first name and a slogan like "your local FHA expert." At the end of the day, each more than likely has access to the same money at the same cost. With FedEx and facsimile as a common means of delivering documents, the consumer may never know whether the vice president or the loan officer was working from home in a bath robe and slippers when the mortgage application was negotiated.

Complain when necessary. Consumers should write a letter of complaint and send a copy of any direct mail piece that raises an eyebrow of suspicion to elected officials, the Federal Trade Commission, the state's attorney general, the Better Business Bureau, consumer advocacy groups, and post to blogs as well. Consumers have the power to stop abusive and deceptive lending practices by creating a body of consumer complaints against rogue lenders and then applying as much pressure as possible until the insults directed at American consumer stop. There is plenty of shame to go around. Shaming lenders into compliance with better business practices starts with consumers exercising greater individual responsibility and taking far more control in their relationships with lenders.

Make the system work for you. When shopping for a mortgage, borrowers should use the system to work for them. If an application is made for a mortgage, borrowers should expect phone calls if not registered with the Do Not Call list. Those are opportunities to comparison shop. Those who have made an application should keep a pen and notepad nearby to record the contact information along with the offer if one is made by anyone making a competitive offer. Financial corporations often record phone calls with customers. Again, do the same for quality assurance with the proper disclosure. A verbal competitive offer is 100 percent meaningless unless supported by a Good Faith Estimate and a Truth in Lending Disclosure at a minimum. Ideally, the lender will also provide a preapproval letter that stipulates terms and conditions. If a solicitation comes from a company, and the caller cannot offer a website address, a company address, a phone number, or anything to help with conducting a background check, assume an attempt at fraud and contact the state's attorney general, the Federal Trade Commission, and the Federal Bureau of Investigation. Get them involved so that the rogue actors are shut down. This holds true for debt consolidation and credit card interest rate reduction offers as well. If opted-out, there will be no calls offering financing. Therefore, comparison shopping needs to be self-initiated within a few days of the first loan application. The customer is always right. Customers have a right to shop. And, they should especially if dealing with a major real estate firm or builder that has a controlled business arrangement in place. Lenders violating a consumer's wish to not be contacted can be subjected to a fine as high as $10,000 per instance.

Rate shoppers need to be smarter. Consumers, who are rate shopping for a loan that conforms to Fannie Mae or Freddie Mac guidelines, should go to the Freddie Mac home page to get a sense of what interest rates are doing for the week. Their Primary Mortgage Market Survey® discloses the average interest rate and cost to get the rate for a given week for both the 30 year and 15 year fixed mortgages.[54] This is a wonderful place for consumers to get a reliable benchmark as they start shopping.

Borrowers need to better understand risk. Historically, lenders have incrementally encouraged borrowers to take on greater risk while failing to increasingly and adequately warn of the many real hazards inherent in leveraged borrowing. This came about gradually as a result of competition at the retail level and the misplaced assumption that risk could be insured at the secondary market level. Borrowers need to be mindful when risk is layered, the potential for problems are compounded. These risks include a high loan-to-value mortgage, a high debt-to-income qualifying ratio, an adjustable rate mortgage, and a limited documentation mortgage application. When two or more of the risk factors are layered, borrowers can be set up for a greater likelihood of financial failure. Consider the facts. Home values do not always go up. Therefore, a 95 percent or 100 percent mortgage could end up with a negative equity if consumer confidence, the unemployment rate, and the real estate market changes. This may be fine if the goal is to never retire the debt. But, just this factor alone contributes to a greater likelihood for foreclosure. High housing costs relative to actual income can be a set up for financial catastrophe, because life happens. More credit is not the right answer when those unanticipated financial events take place. The reality is few households should consider an adjustable rate mortgage, because few truly understand them and few have the financial means to handle significant changes in payments. Finally, limited documentation loans are suitable for some, but not all. This niche is the open door for predatory borrowing, predatory lending, and mortgage fraud directed by the lender coaching the borrower through the process. Borrowers who foolishly set themselves up for failure by lying about their incomes may have worked the system to their short-term advantage, but more than likely it was aided and abetted by an insider, who contributed to a long-term problem.

The loan application process is backwards. Financial products, such as mortgages, are complex for many people and due to the mathematics and calculations associated with them, are abstract and therefore difficult to comprehend. Yet, the industry has resorted to lawyers to describe them in obtuse English so that other lawyers can understand the contractual nature of the note, but not necessarily the financial ramifications of what is described. The promise note and product disclosure are given to borrowers at closing, not at application. This is 100 percent backwards and perpetuates widespread rushed closings with out truly adequate informed consent. Regardless of the loan, those two documents should be read at or immediately after application, not at or after closing. Always ask for a product disclosure at application. If anyone is told they do not exist or policy bars release of such a disclosure until settlement, consider applying elsewhere if the goal is to be fully informed and armed.

Understand lending regulations. This is the means of maintaining an upper hand with mortgage lenders. These regulations exist to define acceptable and unacceptable conduct, curb lender behavior through sanctions, and protect consumers. Lenders know where the holes are in the array of regulations and which violations amount to a slap on the wrist. It does consumers no good to complain about the last lender, who never sent the Good Faith Estimate or Truth in Lending Disclosure—a common violation of the law, if the regulatory authorities and attorney general are not notified. Consumers have the power to keep lenders honest and even weed out the bad players, who have caused harm. Complaints need to be put into action. By creating a body of evidence regarding a regulatory violation, the business character of a financial corporation not worth doing business with will become public knowledge. In the end, the marketplace that is made up of consumers armed with information will reward good rather than bad conduct.

The Telemarketing and Consumer Fraud and Abuse Prevention Act became law on August 16, 1994 since telemarketers defraud Americans of $40 billion each year. This Act defines and prohibits deceptive telemarketing, prohibits telemarketers from making unsolicited telephone calls that are coercive and invasive of privacy, restricts the hours when unsolicited telephone calls can be made, and requires telemarketers to disclose the nature of the call. The Federal Trade Commission established telemarketing sales rules to include the Do Not Call program through an online registry at https://www.donotcall.gov, which is an outgrowth of the Do-Not-Call Registry Act that became effective on March 31, 2003. Telemarketers violating a consumer's wish to not be contacted can be subjected to a $10,000 fine per violation.

The Fair Credit Reporting Act was originally passed into law on October 26, 1970 and amended many times over the years. Credit reporting forms play a vital role in society. The fate of each household insofar as credit is concerned hangs in the balance due to the contents of a credit report and credit scores. Yet, not everyone is aware of their rights or how to understand a credit report. The Fair Credit Reporting Act "promotes the accuracy, fairness, and privacy of information"[55] in the credit files of the credit bureaus and the third-party reporting agencies. Companies that report to the reporting agencies are required to investigate consumer disputes. Creditors are required to inform consumers if derogatory information in the credit file has resulted in an adverse decision. Consumers have the right to sue creditors in state and federal court for Fair Credit Reporting Act violations. More information is available at the Federal Trade Commission.[56]

The Fair and Accurate Credit Transactions Act amended the Fair Credit Reporting Act on December 4, 2003. Among its many provisions, this amendment allows consumers to receive one free credit report each year from each of the bureaus. This can be done by contacting the Annual Credit Report Request Service.[57] The free report can be requested by telephone, mail, or through the government-authorized website, annual-creditreport.com. Moreover, the Fair and Accurate Credit Transactions Act requires the bureaus to provide fraud alerts for consumers, who have demonstrated that they have been a victim of identity theft. More information is available at the Federal Trade Commission.[58]

The Equal Credit Opportunity Act is Title VII of the Consumer Credit Protection Act. The Equal Credit Opportunity Act became law on March 23, 1976 and prohibits discrimination on the basis of race, color, religion, national origin, sex or marital status, or age unless there is no legal capacity to enter into a contract. Moreover, the Equal Credit Opportunity Act, bars lenders from discriminating against applicants on the basis of their income sources. Finally, a lender cannot turn prospective borrowers away if they have exercised any consumer protection rights against that lender under the Consumer Credit Protection Act. In other words, borrowers can file a complaint against a lender with the appropriate agency or regulator if they suspect that they may be a target of a discriminatory action and a lender cannot refuse their application or loan approval on the basis of their preemptive action for regulatory oversight. More information about the Equal Credit Opportunity Act is available at the U.S. Department of Justice[59] and at the Federal Trade Commission.[60]

The Real Estate Settlement Procedures Act is a federal law that came about on December 22, 1974 in order to protect consumers undertaking a purchase, refinance, home improvement loan, or a line of credit by helping them to be better informed about terms and costs as they shop. The reason for the Real Estate Settlement Procedures Act, however, was to prohibit kick backs, fee splitting, and referral fees among parties, which can lead to higher consumer costs. The Real Estate Settlement Procedures Act is implemented by Regulation X under the U.S. Department of Housing and Urban Development (HUD). The Real Estate Settlement Procedures Act requires lenders to provide borrowers with timely disclosures and informational booklets. In a purchase transaction, lenders are required to provide a "Special Information Booklet" that describes real estate settlement services. For all transactions, lenders are required to provide borrowers with a Good Faith Estimate of settlement costs. This disclosure itemizes the estimated costs associated with the loan that the borrower pays at settlement. Conscientious lenders will provide their borrowers with "The Consumer's Guide to Mortgage Settlement Costs," which is a publication of the Federal Reserve Board that is also available online.[61] If the lender requires the borrower to use a specific settlement company, then this fact must be disclosed on the Good Faith Estimate. Lenders are also required to provide their borrowers with a Mortgage Servicing Disclosure Statement, which describes if the lender intends to service the loan or to release servicing rights to another lender. The Real Estate Settlement Procedures Act also requires lenders to provide borrowers with an Affiliated Business Arrangement Disclosure prior to referring the customer to other entities within a controlled business arrangement. The Real Estate Settlement Procedures Act permits borrowers to review the HUD-1, or settlement statement, one day prior to closing. The settlement statement should be fairly close to the Good Faith Estimate since that estimate should have been made in good faith. The Real Estate Settlement Procedures Act also provides borrowers with the right to receive a copy of the appraisal within 30 days of closing.

Borrowers have recourse. Borrowers can take action against a lender's, or another service provider's, failure to comply with the Real Estate Settlement Procedures Act through three courses of action. A federal banking regulator may at its discretion impose a penalty on a lender for not providing a borrower with a Special Information Booklet. For other Real Estate Settlement Procedures Act violations, aggrieved borrowers can sue in civil court. They can also contact the U.S. Department of Housing and Urban Development, their state's attorney general, or their state insurance commissioner depending on the nature of the lender's violation of the Real Estate Settlement Procedures Act. The Real Estate Settlement Procedures Act requires that the lender pay the legal fees, and damage awards can be three times the amount of the claim. In any of these cases, there are statutes of limitation. More information is at the U.S. Housing and Urban Development website.[62]

Controlled business arrangements are a fact. Knowing this, therefore, consumers may enter into a contest of wills as to who retains control over the transaction. While these arrangements are legal, that does not mean consumers should not shop for lower costs, better terms, and better service. Some may be perfectly delighted with the real estate agent doing the hand off to the in-house lender and then to the in-house title agent due to the convenience without taking into account the cost. There is after all, value in service and convenience, and many recognize this. Others, however, should shop, compare, and look for savings since the costs can add up. This should especially hold true when looking at a new home. There is so much excitement that comes with purchasing a new house, but it collides with the confusion that comes with so many choices and options that can significantly add to the total price tag. Given that a home is such a major investment, it really pays to comparison shop for financing since people tend to buy on emotion and justify through rationalization after having signed the purchase contract and the mortgage application. When that process fades, the loan amount, the loan type, the cost for the loan, and the mortgage payments remain. As a result, some consumers will look for a basis to level complaints against companies for alleged Real Estate Settlement Procedures Act violations. It pays, therefore, for consumer to know their rights and carefully shop for financing since, after all, an ounce of prevention is better than a pound of cure.

The Truth in Lending Act is Title I of the Consumer Protection Act that requires creditors to meaningfully disclose financing terms. It came into law on May 29, 1968 and became effective on July 1, 1969, and is implemented by the Federal Reserve Board of Governor's Regulation Z. Over the years, the Truth in Lending Act has been amended several times. Some of the key consumer safeguards under the Truth in Lending Act are that lenders must disclose in a standardized manner on the Truth in Lending Disclosure the annual percentage rate, which is often referred to as the APR. Also, under the Truth in Lending Act lenders must provide applicants with the Consumer Handbook on Adjustable Rate Mortgages if they have applied for an adjustable rate mortgage and must disclose the total of payments if the borrower makes the minimum payments over the life of the loan. One key point is that the annual percentage rate discloses the actual cost of securing credit and should be used as the reference point for comparison shopping. The Truth in Lending Act provides a three day right of rescission on owner occupied refinances. More information about the Truth in Lending Act is available at the Federal Deposit Insurance Corporation and Comptroller of the Currency.[63]

Curbs on lenders fall short. The Board of Governors of the Federal Reserve and U.S. Department of Housing and Urban Development in July 1998 said in joint testimony before Congress that for consumers, the Real Estate Settlement Procedures Act and the Truth in Lending Act rules "may fall short of meeting their intended goals."[64] Advance payment of fees to a lender and untimely delivery of disclosures by the lender to the borrower can make comparison shopping difficult. Additionally, significant differences between a Good Faith Estimate and the settlement statements do not mean there are remedies or restitutions for aggrieved borrowers. Moreover, financing costs and the annual percentage rate may not be fully understood. Consequently, neither the Real Estate Settlement Procedures Act nor the Truth in Lending Act protects consumers from predators and abusive lending practices since all that is required are disclosures, not limitations on charges or interest rates.

The Home Equity Loan Consumer Protection Act, enacted November 23, 1988, amends the Truth in Lending Act and requires creditors to provide disclosures on open-ended credit lines when a home is the security. Congressional hearings had uncovered that the growth in home equity loans from $40 billion in1986 to $75 billion by October 1988 required better consumer protection laws.[65] This law applies to the home equity line of credit, which is a non-purchase mortgage. Lenders are required to disclose the terms, interest rates, conditions, and information about the variable rate—the adjustable rate feature that is associated with a home equity line of credit. Consumers are entitled to a refund of application fees if a lender delivers a home equity line of credit not consistent with what was disclosed in the application. In spite of this law, many consumers do not realize that a home equity line of credit is an adjustable rate mortgage that amortizes as a simple interest loan.

The Home Ownership and Equity Protection Act of 1994 also amends the Truth in Lending Act. In 2001, the Federal Reserve Board of Governor's Section 32 of Regulation Z was amended to enforce the Home Ownership and Equity Protection Act. This last act was intended to define the limits and curb the adverse impact on consumers receiving high-cost, that is, subprime loans that had some of the many predatory lending features. The Home Ownership and Equity Protection Act established a boundary on securitized loans that were sold into the secondary market, and investors would not buy some loans sold with recourse due to the Home Ownership and Equity Protection Act provisions that laid liability on investors rather than the originating lenders. So as the holder in due course, the Home Ownership and Equity Protection Act could hold the ultimate bond holder liable for the actions of originating lenders. But, the Home Ownership and Equity Protection Act and the Federal Reserve did not stop a practice that instead became nationwide in scope and defined the culture of many leading lending institutions.

At its most fundamental level, which is to protect borrowers refinancing and taking home equity loans, the Home Ownership and Equity Protection Act was designed to:

Limit the annual percentage rate to no more than 8 percent above rates on Treasury securities for first mortgages;

Limit the annual percentage rate to no more than 10 percent above the rates on Treasury securities for second mortgages; and

Place an 8 percent cap on the total fees and points that borrowers can be charged for the total loan amount, or $583—which ever is higher.

An 8 to 10 percent mark up over the index is a high interest rate, and 8 percent in closing costs are also remarkably high. Yet, the Home Ownership and Equity Protection Act was the best that the Federal Reserve could do at the time to curb the appetite for high margins at lending institutions. Lenders are required to comply with a high rate and high cost test, which takes place in underwriting prior to loan closing. The Home Ownership and Equity Protection Act does not, however, prohibit lenders from permitting borrowers to have a 50 percent debt-to-income ratio, which not only results in a hand to mouth existence, but also means that the borrower is just one pay check away from default given the difficulty to set aside reserves. The Home Ownership and Equity Protection Act does not address requiring borrowers to have cash reserves as a safety net. Those borrowers, who did a sated income loan and overstated their income where the lender did not do the due diligence to prevent fraud, permitted borrowers to be set up for financial failure and then foreclosure. More information is available about the Home Ownership and Equity Protection Act at the Federal Trade Commission.[66]

In a Federal Trade Commission *Facts for Consumers* alert, the Home Ownership and Equity Protection Act appears to prohibit true hard money lending. The alert states creditors may not, "Make loans based on the collateral value of your property without regard to your ability to repay the loan."[67] The Federal Trade Commission states that:

> You may have the right to sue a lender for violations of these new requirements. In a successful suit, you may be able to recover statutory and actual damages, court costs and attorney's fees. In addition, a violation of the high-rate, high-fee requirements of the [Truth in Lending Act] may enable you to rescind (or cancel) the loan for up to three years. [68]

The Mortgage Disclosure Improvement Act came about as part of the overarching Housing and Economic Recovery Act of 2008. The Mortgage Disclosure Improvement Act took effect July 30, 2009. This law requires lenders to transparently disclose yield spread premiums and service release premiums, which are used to buy up an interest rate in order to enhance lender compensation. These two pricing mechanisms are oftentimes respectively referred to as YSP and SRP. The Mortgage Disclosure Improvement Act, on this specific issue, is silent on the federally regulated banks which use overages to achieve a similar end result. Consequently, comparative shopping among a broker, a state regulated bank, and a federally regulated bank will not be equally transparent. Moreover, the Mortgage Disclosure Improvement Act requires lenders to issue an updated Truth in Lending Disclosure with an accurate Annual Percentage Rate within three business days when an interest rate or loan program has changed during the loan application process. Moreover, closing cannot be rushed since another provision of the Mortgage Disclosure Improvement Act is to assure borrowers with an additional three business days to review the revised documents.

The Secure and Fair Enforcement for Mortgage Licensing Act (the SAFE Act) also came about as part of the overarching Housing and Economic Recovery Act of 2008. One of the purposes of the SAFE Act is to ensure a minimal level of standardized knowledge across the lending industry to make sure that all loan officers know the difference between the Real Estate Settlement Procedures Act and the Truth in Lending Act and to understand why the Equal Credit Opportunity Act exists. To ensure this, a mandatory 20 hour continuing education course followed by a closed book test with a 75 passing score requirement. Moreover, the SAFE Act mandates the creation and management of a federal level data base of licensed loan officers. This means that in theory the system could be used to identify and bar a rogue loan officer given the ability to track an originator's lending behavior over the course of a few years. Nothing in the SAFE Act, however, bars a person with a criminal conviction or a felony record from becoming a licensed loan officer unless the crime was financial in nature. That level of added protection for the public is left to the states that have different licensing standards; and to corporations, which have different hiring standards. It is up to the consumer to provide the added layer of safety should this issue pose a concern given who may be handling a copy of tax returns, a driver's license, and a copy of the credit report given that everything is fully disclosed.

Real estate and lending regulations are inadequate to arm and protect consumers. The laws that do exist came about to protect consumers from lenders. Yet, they still fall short. There is nothing in any loan document, any legislation, or any regulation to protect a household from what could be the most deceptive loan in existence: the fully amortized simple interest loan. These loans function like credit cards, not like traditional mortgages. On a $200,000 mortgage where the payment is posted on the 15th of every month, where there are no late fees and no damage to credit for being late, after 30 years the loan balance is not zero. It is approximately $100,000. Nothing in the Real Estate Settlement Procedures Act, the Truth in Lending Act, or even the Mortgage Disclosure Improvement Act adequately discloses and warns consumers about the mechanics of how a simple interest mortgage loan amortizes. Reading the promise note on this loan and comparing it with a fully amortized agency or government loan may not clear up the difference either. The same issues hold true for comparative shopping among agency, government, and private sector mortgages. The disclosures are inadequate due to one simple reason: the financial sector does not want mortgage loans to be too easily reduced to the level of a commodity, because if that happened costs would drop as consumers became more empowered through better understanding.

The problems are not rooted in financial mismanagement. Most consumers struggle to maintain their foothold in the economy. That struggle is due to inflation that devalues the purchasing power of the dollar, globalization that ships jobs abroad, the trend among employers to contract rather than employ that drives wages down while stripping families of benefits, and consumer credit that is used to finance shortfalls in the household budget. Those in upper management of the financial sector know these factors as well as others that set American households up for the perceived need to borrow more in order to solve debt-related challenges. Nothing, however, could be further from the truth. More debt will not solve the challenges of unserviceable debt. And, oftentimes, restructuring debt will not benefit a household's financial position either. The financial sector's remedy for households is perpetual financial servitude and tenancy. The most important economy of all is that of the household. If cash and carry through the use of a debit card limits purchases, the household will be better off in the immediate and long term. Those who claim that the use of consumer credit is patriotic since it stimulates the entire economy speak on behalf of creditors, who are all too happy to extract predatory interest rates in the neighborhood of 30 percent from unsuspecting households. Wall Street reform includes embedded regulators.

Chapter 2
Loan Officers Originate for Underwriting

"If you think no one cares you're alive, miss a couple of house payments."
—Real Estate Humor from Tom Antion & Associates

The mortgage loan officer is on the front line in the mortgage loan underwriting process.[69] As such, that role, which is to originate good loans, will remain constant. Matching the consumer with the right product at the right price is the loan officer's chief responsibility. Product knowledge applied to each borrower's unique position will mean that underwriting approval and funding likely will follow. Many loan officers do not realize, have forgotten, or, due to changes in business practices driven to extract higher margins through greater efficiency and scale, have compromised these fundamental facts.

Mortgage underwriting at its simplest is divided into four components: assessing credit, verifying income, verifying assets, and confirming the property value. On behalf of the lending institution, the loan officer as the primary point of contact with the consumer has a lot of control over:

Detecting and stopping mortgage fraud;
Educating the consumer about loan programs, repayment terms, and conditions;
Explaining how interest rates are priced in the marketplace and determined at application;
Determining the loan program and negotiating an interest rate; and
Ensuring that the originated loan produces a tangible net benefit to the borrower.

This latter issue of being required to produce a loan that provides a net benefit to the borrower is debated and controversial within the lending industry since the standard for determining a net benefit can be subjective, limit consumer options, and deprive a firm of revenue.

An example of this is the hard money, or equity-based, loan. The loan is made regardless of a borrower's employment circumstances or ability to repay. A scene in Tony Gilroy's film, *Michael Clayton,* alludes to a hard money loan with the borrower asking for more time since he cannot repay as agreed. As with all loan transactions, a lender places the money at risk to produce a return on investment. The borrower has a need that the traditional channels will not accommodate. Private parties come together on the basis of collateral that is roughly 70 percent loan-to-value, which concludes the transaction. Many would argue that the hard money loan is clearly predatory. Given the high rate, the probability that it is an adjustable rate mortgage, and no demonstrated ability to repay, the risk of foreclosure is high. Therein lies insight on the rightfully debated question: What constitutes a net benefit to the borrower? The majority of lenders, in contrast to this example, adhere to objective standards and underwriters do stop loans dead in their tracks if they fail to produce one borrower benefit.

The loan officer's initial task in the preliminary interview and application process is to determine whether a loan should be originated. Two lending industry approaches prevail. One approach is to write as many applications as possible and let it get sorted out in processing. That produces a bottleneck in processing, however, and delays truly qualified applicants from getting their loans approved and closed in a timely manner. The other approach is to only focus on ready, willing, and able customers—in other words, those who are truly qualified. The difference between one approach and the other is training and experience within different lending institutions. Regardless of the approach, the loan officer's role is to be the consumer advocate within the underwriting guidelines. Loan officers should know which direction to take: whether to stop the application or to originate a loan that produces a tangible net benefit for the borrower.

Loan officers accept *prima facie* the forthrightness, accuracy, or thoroughness of the applicant's background and financial position as stated on the mortgage application. This may come across as naïve, but there are fraud detection measures built into the loan application process when lending operations take the time to do the due diligence. The burden of caution due to risk of loss is on borrowers, whether purchasing or refinancing, because they will have the burden of being responsible for keeping the mortgage payments current. Moreover, the process assumes that borrowers accept individual responsibility, which means that they can read and do indeed understand prior to signing. Customers never place an "x" to designate the signature of an illiterate person.

If customers borrow up to 50 percent of the debt-to-income ratio, which the lending industry may permit, then borrowers will live paycheck to paycheck or may need to access assets like savings, or even credit, to sustain the cost of living. They are, in theory, only a broken leg away from going bankrupt, assuming that they do not have adequate disability insurance. Consequently, borrowers should not overly depend on the mortgage lender to remind them of other bills. Loan officers do not know whether customers are paying for a boat slip, have a child at a private school, or own property abroad with taxes and maintenance fees due from time to time. These types of items may not appear on a credit report, which forms part of the basis for the interview during the application process.

The loan officer may approach a prospective applicant along general guidelines associated with different loan programs. A more careful analysis, however, takes place with the help of an automated underwriting system, which unveils the fluid nature of *black box technology*. Simply put, "black box" alludes to the secretive or proprietary criteria built into the programmed matrices in software programs that seek to balance numerous borrower risk factors in order to render an underwriting decision.

Freddie Mac's automated underwriting system, Loan Prospector®, looks at the three C's of underwriting and at the borrower's credit reputation, capacity, and collateral as a basis in underwriting.[70] If the borrower's profile matches Freddie Mac's guidelines, an automated approval follows. Sometimes, underwriting guidelines may make reference to a fourth C for character, which looks at job stability or length of time in the property.

Many people believe that Fannie Mae and Freddie Mac require a credit score of 620 or higher and a qualifying debt-to-income ratio of 28 percent for housing.[71] But the underwriting criteria established by the agencies are more involved than that, and they are fluid given market conditions. For example, in one automated underwriting scenario during the boom, a purchaser proposed to put down 25 percent, and would have $75,000 in the bank after closing. The purchaser's credit score was in the high 700s, but, the debt-to-income ratio was 65 percent. Was this borrower approved or denied? One of the agency's automated underwriting systems approved this credit profile using a 5.500 percent fixed-rate fully amortized for 30 years. There was barely enough income left at the end of each month to pay Uncle Sam, let alone enough for groceries and so forth. How was this possible? The system looked at the assets in reserves and calculated that there was enough set aside at $1,000 per month withdrawals for six years if this borrower needed the cash. Since the borrower was not comfortable, however, he instead elected to finance the purchase with a 5/1 interest only loan since the payments would be significantly lower for that five year period, which was long enough to help him reach retirement.

The Federal Housing Administration's automated underwriting engine relies on the Fannie Mae's system and uses a Technology Open to Approved Lenders (TOTAL) Mortgage Scorecard for reaching a decision.[72] Though FHA's Total Scorecard approach is not credit score driven, lenders that underwrite and fund Federal Housing Administration loans will indeed use credit scores in order to mitigate the risk of default and the risk of a buy back on a government loan. The 100 percent purchase money programs available through both Fannie Mae and Freddie Mac during the housing bubble years also used automated underwriting to reach a final decision, and, they too were not credit score-driven programs. Underwriting using technology permits flexibility. Due to the possibility of strong compensating factors in a borrower's overall credit profile, weaknesses in one area can be overcome by strengths in another area of a borrower's overall profile.

In the early 1990s, it was an industry wide practice to qualify borrowers who had applied for a one-year adjustable rate mortgage at two percent above the note rate. From a lender's perspective, that was "common sense" underwriting. After all, an adjustable rate mortgage interest rate moves with the underlying index. A prudent lender would mitigate risk by assuming the worst-case scenario, which would be an upward rate adjustment. The tug of war between the lending community and real estate agents advocating on behalf of homebuyers, coupled with the competitive pressures of the market, caused the risk and reward balance to shift with the greater risk placed upon lenders. Over time, common sense underwriting shifted and borrowers qualified at the start rate. After all, the customer is king, and he can apply elsewhere if the first choice for a lender proved to be too difficult to work with. A prudent borrower would mitigate risk by taking into account either a worst-case scenario for the second year or the possibility of a refinance to a fixed rate.

Oftentimes, a borrower may be better suited for or qualify for several limited or alternative documentation programs, which have been around since the 1980s. These Alt-A loans, which is abbreviated for Alternative-A, means that a Fannie Mae- or Freddie Mac-eligible borrower may be able to obtain one of the following limited documentation type loans:

SIVA (Stated Income, Verified Assets), SISA (Stated Income, Stated Assets), or NINA (No Income, No Assets). These at one time were private labeled loans that were alternative to agency loans, which Fannie Mae and Freddie Mac would not underwrite or invest in. The difference between these three—SIVA, SISA, and NINA—is typically the underwriting standards that set the middle credit score requirement, loan-to-value limitations, and risk-based cost adjustments for the program's rate. Alt-A, or stated income, loans required fairly high credit scores. They naturally did not go to credit-impaired borrowers. As the mortgage industry grew and a secondary market opened for subprime borrowers, Alt-B and Alt-C mortgages became more universally available. Like any other business, the customer base can grow if terms are granted under more liberal terms. And, this is indeed what happened across the stated income spectrum.

Finally, subprime automated approvals were readily available via the price engines available to retailers from the numerous private-labeled wholesalers representing either the major lenders or Wall Street investment banks. The loan officer's role was simply to plug in the borrower characteristics. The price engine, in turn, rendered not only an approval but from the better-designed systems, numerous programs to finance the transaction.

Underwriting matrices come in numerous variations based on the investment banker and wholesaler (see Table 2.1). These matrices reflect what is programmed into different underwriting engines. They come in countless varieties reflecting what can be underwritten for the consumer given that the loan can be securitized and sold on Wall Street or held as a whole loan and kept in portfolio. When market conditions are robust, terms are liberal. When a market is in contraction, terms are conversely tighter or even nonexistent. In other words, lenders have the power to stimulate an economy to growth or contract it into a recession or even worse.

Processors and underwriters to a great extent serve as due diligence backstops for the loan officer. Some loan applications die in the processing stage. And some die in the underwriting stage. An application that makes it through processing means that the borrower's application is complete and ready for underwriting. Traditionally speaking, that means the following documents have been gathered and verifications have been made in four areas: income and employment; assets in reserves; a tri-merged credit report; and an appraisal that confirms the subject property's value in the current market. Self-employed borrowers may be required to submit a letter from a certified public accountant that speaks to the accuracy of the tax returns as well as a year-to-date income statement. Higher priced homes may require a second appraisal.

Table 2.1 – Underwriting Matrix
Full Documentation

Credit Grade	Mortgage Late	Credit Score	Loan-to-Value			
			85%	90%	95%	100%
		700	6.65%	7.00%	7.22%	7.85%
		680	6.75%	7.10%	7.30%	7.95%
		660	6.85%	7.20%	7.40%	8.05%
		640	6.95%	7.30%	7.50%	8.15%
A +	0 x 30	620	7.30%	7.55%	8.00%	8.85%
		600	7.40%	7.75%	8.20%	9.05%
		580	7.65%	8.10%	8.60%	
		550	8.05%	8.40%		
		525	8.50%			
		500				

Source: Peter Hébert (for illustrative purposes only).

If the loan officer's processing team uncovers material facts that compromise the borrower's application, then the application process could end. Some elements detrimental to an application may include identity verification (either fraud or lack of supporting documentation); income and employment (either fraud or lack of supporting documentation); assets (either fraud or lack of supporting documentation); deterioration in the applicant's credit after application; and low property appraisal or material defects to the property that the borrower is not willing to remedy.

An underwriter's role is to ensure that the borrower's application meets the program guidelines, quality control check the application and ensure that the loan is in compliance with various lending regulations. Some elements detrimental to an application in underwriting may include an inability to verify the borrower's employment; the program guidelines tied to a specific investor significantly changed due to changes in market conditions; the appraiser used unacceptable comparables to derive a value; the appraiser has the same last name as the borrower, the loan officer, or the real estate agent (may not be an arm's-length transaction, hence the presumption of fraud) in which case a new appraisal may be required; and the borrower made a major purchase, like a car or boat, after application, pushing the debt-to-income ratios beyond the program's guidelines.

Either way, there are three backstops to ensuring that the borrower is truly qualified for the loan. When the system properly works, loan officers may originate fewer loans due to better initial screening. Processors weed out fewer loans in processing due to better originations. And underwriters approve more given that quality control measures on the front end are followed.

When all the elements of the loan come together as they should, the chosen loan program produces tangible net benefits to borrowers, including:

Cash after closing used for home improvement, which enhances the property's functional use, economic life, and resale value;

Cash after closing for other investments such as a mutual fund, a retirement fund, or other real estate investments here or abroad;

Consolidated consumer credit card debt to improve monthly cash flow, which often leads to a higher credit score, given the lower debt utilization on charge accounts;

A reduction in the interest rate that leads to 10 percent or $100 lower monthly payments;

The ability to recover closing costs within 36 months; and/or

A change in the term to extend payments over a longer period or to compress them for an earlier payoff.

Self-Employed Borrowers

Self-employed business people are entrepreneurs and they come in all shapes and sizes. In fact, America runs on small businesses. As a result of their unique needs, loan officers are challenged with sorting through the straight-forward purchase and refinance applicants with those who need help in getting their financial house in order so they can go to the next level.

Many borrowers, who applied for a loan during the boom, have expressed surprise since after having made application for a loan with several lenders no one returned phone calls. In some cases this was due to poor customer service stemming from too many customers. In other cases, this was due to customers making four applications and then being dropped by all four lenders since no lender wanted a 25 percent chance of closing a loan that required 100 percent of their attention. The adverse action letter is the lender's out since in these scenarios, oftentimes, the file is incomplete. In other scenarios, however, the reason for putting a customer on ignore was different. After interviewing borrowers and examining credit, it is quickly apparent if a lender has a high-maintenance borrower—and a contributing factor to the lending crisis. For example, a self-employed and his wife ran a cash only business. Neither had any supporting documents. Their high debt-to-income ratio was the result of alleged income factored against actual debt. The primary borrower's middle credit score was low and the loan-to-value ratio was too high. As a result, the borrower would be denied any extension of credit on the objective facts that income on the business could not be verified through tax returns and bank statements, and the credit score was not high enough for a stated income loan for a self-employed borrower.

It was clear that no lender was willing to be a party to fraud in order to accommodate this borrower type, who was part of the Alt-A and subprime stated income documentation phenomenon across the United States during the refinance and housing boom. The classic lender response was: "I will be delighted to work with you. Fax the last two year federal tax returns with all schedules, and your business account's bank statements for the last 12 months with all pages in order. If you do, I will do everything in my power to help you within the underwriting guidelines." Calls are not returned, and "deals" like this die, since there are no supporting documents. Loan scenarios like this that closed and funded, however, were plentiful and more than likely laden with fraud. This fraud ran from application with the borrower, through the lender for knowingly originating a loan with no means of repayment, in processing for not engaging in adequate due diligence, and in underwriting for funding a loan when they could have and should have known better. The ultimate victims were the communities, when the foreclosure eventually occurred, and the investors, who lost their capital investments. The blow back came onto the reputations of the lending community, the investment banking community, the rating agencies, and the regulators—all of which could have and should have done better in order to avoid incompetence on one hand and malpractice on the other.

A Fitch Ratings[73] study released in November 2007 examined 45 mortgage loan files due to early payment default, and stated that "there was the appearance of fraud or misrepresentation in almost every file."[74] At the height of the boom, some investors only required a business card as evidence of self-employment. Anyone intent on committing fraud could have easily had phony cards printed for next to nothing and then used that as "evidence of employment" in order to secure a mortgage loan for hundreds of thousands of dollars. It's incredible as everyone reflects on the greed that clouded the better judgment of lenders desirous of more fee income and global investors desirous of high returns on subprime loans from the United States market.

After the boom, many loan programs were pulled off the shelf, and underwriting guidelines tightened on those that remained. That placed many self-employed borrowers who took out loans during the boom in a precarious situation. Hardest hit were self-employed borrowers tied to the construction and home improvement industry. High income Alt-A borrowers fared no better since they too overleveraged their income and in some cases overstated their income in order to qualify for more home as a larger investment base for a larger future return.

To secure the lowest possible mortgage interest rate under the best terms requires the highest possible net income that can be fully documented. That means that self-employed borrowers should expense less or find other strategies to produce a higher net income. Moreover, that also means keeping federal tax returns with all schedules, year-to-date income statements, and all business bank statements in order from a two- to three-year period. Failure to do these things may result in unintended consequences to borrowers that include either a higher interest rate, or not having credit extended at all—the consequences for not planning ahead.

The advice of a tax preparer or accountant may undermine the ability of self-employed borrowers to have credit extended when needed most. Loan officers qualify self-employed borrowers based on net income, not on the gross to the business. More often than not self-employed borrowers are stated income borrowers. The traditional logic when dealing with the Internal Revenue Service is to shield as much income as possible by expensing as much as is permitted within Internal Revenue Service regulations. Lowering taxable income produces a lower net income on the tax returns. This makes sense if the sole concern is to pay as little tax as possible. But, that only makes sense if the self-employed businessperson is living debt free and has no need for the extension of credit. The reality is that self-employed business people probably have mortgage and consumer credit card debt tied to both personal and business-related expenses. In short, the accountant's advice may be at odds with the advice of a mortgage lender. Finally, self-employed borrowers should regularly file and pay their estimated quarterly taxes in a timely manner since failure to comply with the law results in penalties and federal tax liens placed against real estate. Following these guidelines will make not only the self-employed borrower's life much easier, but the loan officer's as well.

Over expensing and not reporting income are not only criminal conduct and a serious problem for the borrower with the Internal Revenue Service, but undermine borrowers when they seek an extension of credit, which tends to be at moments of great need. The actions of the past can result in self-inflicted wounds in the future.

There is an almost fatal logic with some business people, who brag about not paying taxes due to aggressive expensing. The goal of any business is profitability.[75] If a business shows a low net income, that means the margins are low relative to their expenses. The other fatal logic comes to play when a business owner tells his accountant, "Unfortunately we don't have any other expenses to claim." Self-employed households should be thankful that there were no medical catastrophes or other expenses that could undermine the financial integrity of their personal lives or businesses.

Many businesses are sole proprietorships where personal funds are commingled with those of the business. This may not be an issue of concern where legal liability and overhead are minimal. Due to the low costs and many benefits, many businesses, however, are incorporated in one form or another. Although that is a step in the right direction, many business owners need to go to the next step and retain either a bookkeeper adept at financial records management and tax filing, or a certified public accountant to guide the business as it grows. Generating quarterly year-to-date profit and loss statements not only is a great way of benchmarking the company's financial performance, but also is required when submitting papers to a lender when seeking an extension of credit.

The best thing to do if running a cash business is to open a bank account in the business' name, and run all business through that account. This way, should there be a need to secure credit, the bank statements will serve as evidence of income. Moreover, the lending community in general prefers seeing three major credit accounts in the credit file with two years history since this tends to be a good indicator of a consumer's ability and willingness to repay obligations. Some underwriters, however, specialize in programs that do not require trade lines, but there is a cost for this, which usually appears in the form of a higher rate or less favorable terms.

Many self-employed borrowers tend to hang on to their own unique cultural values, which includes hoarding cash.[76] Entrepreneurs should legitimate their savings. That means a mom-and-pop operation doing a cash-and-carry business should get the money out from under the mattress and put it in either the bank or have it placed under professional management. Whether we call this a paper trail or compliance with the Patriot Act,[77] getting the money into the financial system legitimates the assets. Verifiable assets mean an improved chance for being eligible for a better loan program. Cash is legal tender. Under the Patriot Act, however, stockpiling cash and transacting business in cash implies that the cash is not legitimate since it cannot be traced.

On a mortgage loan program level, some investors withdrew their stated income and bank statement programs for self-employed borrowers after the boom. This resulted in all self-employed borrowers being required to be self-employed for two years or at least have filed as self-employed for two consecutive tax years. Cash flow is the key. In some cases, this necessitates that the loan officer do the corporate income tax analysis in order to identify the net income, taking noncash expenses like depreciation or amortization and add them back in. Once that is done, borrowers typically will have two year's of net income averaged as the basis for qualifying. If they have not yet filed, then an up-to-date profit-and-loss statement for the tax year will suffice with some underwriters. Moreover, while others still have conforming products that will allow self-employed borrowers up to 90 percent loan-to-value, they do not believe that those programs will survive past the first quarter of 2008. Portfolio investors, on the other hand, may underwrite a stated income self-employed borrower up to 80 percent loan-to-value. Generally speaking, tax returns do not paint a pretty enough picture depending on the type of business. Consequently, more often than not, most self-employed borrowers use bank statements, which underwriters consider as a means to fully document and verify income and assets. Borrowers have to weigh their options and decide how much risk they are willing to take while doing anything to get out of an adjustable rate mortgage and into a loan with a fixed-interest rate. Turning a blind eye to the possibility of volatility in market conditions is what brought about tightened underwriting and lack of programs that really hurt this segment of the market. Continuing to not become conversant with changes in the lending environment and ignoring the facts are only going to prolong problems for some self-employed borrowers well into the future.

Concluding Thoughts

I again conclude this chapter with a series of discussions. These should force you to think about the loan application process in a new manner. Please, again, consider this as your check list.

Everything boils down to trust. Trust and reputation are among the most cherished assets in any business, and yet so easily squandered by poor judgment. If a household has a good loan officer, borrowers would do well to stay loyal. That loan officer probably had the customer's best interests at heart. More than likely, the customer knew it and felt it. That person, like the real estate agent who helped buy or sell a home, is part of the team for counsel. If on the other hand, this was not the case, then as consumers learn more about the lending industry, asking friends for recommendations or asking the credit union for some names for the contact list would be in order.

Purchase below what lenders will permit. First time homebuyers tend to be payment sensitive and short on cash. These households should take into account the possibility of making ends meet on just one income, especially if buying a home in an economic downturn. Consequently, first time homebuyers should consider the possibility of not purchasing up to their qualified limits.

Entrepreneurs need to build their team. Self-employed individuals should look to the attorney, certified public account, and certified financial planner as members of their personal "board of directors." The value derived from their services will far out weigh the costs as their counsel is followed. Keep a paper trail of key documents. After the financial house is in order, there should be far less need to apply for a loan with less favorable terms than what would otherwise be obtained.

The bar may be raised for investors. Investors requiring financing more than likely will be placed under greater scrutiny for income and asset verifications. Moreover, the agencies have scaled back on the number of investor property loans that they are willing to purchase. Some loan officers specialize in working with investors due to an affinity and knowledge of the program guidelines as well as knowledge of Starker Exchanges and trusts.

Have the paperwork ready and have the financial house in order first. Those looking to purchase or refinance should have their documents in order prior to loan application. Lenders need to see originals on some documents, but primarily work with copies when building the loan file. Documents should not be folded, stapled, or mutilated since everything is run through a copier for either a hard copy file or conversion to portable document format (PDF). Avoid mailing originals at all cost. Most loan officers have pricing control. High maintenance borrowers will more than likely pay more for their loan than borrowers who have their documents and financial house in order. If the loan officer has to handle a loan file ten times as much as another file, the chances are pretty good that the borrower tied to that file will pay more for the loan. That extra cost will be due to a lock extension that expired and a movement in the market that was passed onto the consumer plus a little more for good measure. The quickest and easiest loans to close come from low maintenance borrowers, who are forthright and communicate, and they tend to get the lowest rates and the lowest costs.

In the next chapters, I will deconstruct mortgage loans in order to help you better understand how each element dovetails in origination and underwriting and to appreciate how unintended consequences can arise.

Chapter 3
The Product

"The great virtue of free enterprise is that it forces existing businesses to meet the test of the market continuously, to produce products that meet consumer demands at lowest cost, or else be driven from the market."
—Milton Friedman

When it comes to product, most consumers in any industrialized nation have many loans to select from. This is largely due to mortgage capital coming from many sources across the globe. Seen in this light, the availability of mortgages in any nation with a developed secondary market is the result of global savings seeking higher rates of return with real estate as the security collateral.

Mortgages products fall into either purchase money or refinances. These products come in several forms including but not limited to: the fully amortizing loan; the simple interest loan; the non-amortizing interest only loan; the adjustable rate mortgage, or ARM; the balloon; the hybrid adjustable rate mortgage; the Option ARM with a negative amortization feature; the home equity line of credit, or HELOC; the offset loan; and the reverse mortgage. These products will be on and off the shelf based on the regulatory mood of an administration and the needs of the marketplace as defined and dictated by the financial sector. These products are not simple to understand, even after a careful reading of a promise note or rider to the note, which is intended to carefully describe the loan's mechanics. These product descriptions were written by lawyers for lawyers, not the general public. Sorting loans by category, therefore, helps to better understand the different types of mortgages since there are significant differences that should not be taken for granted.

Lenders do not provide the note, deed of trust, or mortgage to consumers in advance though they should. The borrower's first exposure to the mechanics of a loan and the repayment terms of the note for which he has been approved is at closing, not at application. As difficult as it may be to believe, the role of the real estate settlement attorney, or the title agent closing the transaction, is to follow lender instructions—not to read, analyze, interpret, and then explain how the loan actually works. Lawyers are not financial analysts. Yet, for a purchaser, that burden of comprehension is done at closing since the loan funds at closing. For the person refinancing, the right to review the closing documents is three days from the date the closing documents are dated, not necessarily the date the loan closes. This consumer protection provision is designed to give consumers a cooling-off period—time to stare at the ceiling for a few nights in a row to see if buyer's remorse kicks in. However, it should be noted that the three-day right of rescission only applies to owner occupants. It does not apply to landlords, speculators, or purchasers. In a purchase, typically, time is of the essence. With landlords and speculators, they should know what they are doing.

Legal review may not be entirely adequate for providing consumers the extra level of safeguard since attorneys may not be mortgage experts. Law schools do not prepare attorneys to understand complex financial instruments when it produces a new graduating class of attorneys. They are schooled in legal theory, contracts, and court decisions. And, those who conduct settlements make their money selling title insurance for which they earn a commission though that is never disclosed to the customer. Moreover, financial planners and consumer debt counselors are not mortgage experts, either. So, that leaves the experienced mortgage loan officer to attend closing and explain the documents, which may pose a conflict of interest since the loan officer's motive is to close the deal. Like it or not, these are some of the built-in ambiguities and short comings that borrowers should be cognizant of as they consider mortgage financing. This systemic problem built into the transaction could easily be resolved if the mortgage lender was a fiduciary, the borrower was treated like a client rather than a customer.

Government Loans

Government loans include those products from the Federal Housing Administration, the Veterans Administration, and the United States Department of Agriculture's Rural Development. The Federal Housing Administration has three dynamic programs worth noting given that this government agency was the horse that dragged the United States economy out of the Great Depression and more than likely will rescue housing from the aftermath of the twenty first century housing collapse.

At the height of the Vietnam war in 1968 when Fannie Mae was privatized in order to help balance the federal budget, the U.S. Congress created the Government National Mortgage Association, or Ginnie Mae, as the guarantor of government-issued mortgage bonds. Its mission is to "expand affordable housing in America by linking global capital markets to the nation's housing markets."[78] As such, Washington, D.C.-based Ginnie Mae is a federal government agency within the U.S. Department of Housing and Urban Development to ensure adequate funds primarily for government loans insured by the Federal Housing Administration and those guaranteed by the Veterans Administration. Moreover, Ginnie Mae also accepts loans from the Department of Agriculture's Rural Housing Service and the U.S. Department of Housing and Urban Development's Office of Public and Indian Housing.[79]

In 1970, Ginnie Mae introduced mortgage pass-through certificates that allowed individual investors to have a pro rated share of principal and interest payments from an underlying mortgage pool.[80] Ginnie Mae states, "Ginnie Mae securities are the *only* mortgage-backed securities to carry the full faith and credit guaranty of the United States government, which means that even in difficult times an investment in Ginnie Mae mortgage-backed securities one of the safest an investor can make."[81] What are mortgage-backed securities? According to Ginnie Mae:

> Mortgage-backed securities (MBS) are pools of mortgages used as collateral for the issuance of securities in the secondary market. MBS are commonly referred to as 'pass-through' certificates because the principal and interest of the underlying loans is 'passed through' to investors. The interest rate of the security is lower than the interest rate of the underlying loan to allow for payment of servicing and guaranty fees. Ginnie Mae MBS are fully modified pass-through securities guaranteed by the full faith and credit of the United States government. Regardless of whether the mortgage payment is made, investors in Ginnie Mae MBS will receive full and timely payment of principal as well as interest.[82]

Ginnie Mae securities come in two types: Ginnie Mae I and Ginnie Mae II. Ginnie Mae I issuances need to come from the same lender, have the same fixed interest rate due within 20 to 30 years, and be a $1 million pool. Ginnie Mae II securities, in contrast, permit adjustable rate mortgages, a wider geographic dispersion of loans, and multiple lenders issuing $250,000 pools that are later aggregated into larger Ginnie Mae II securities.[83]

Borrowers shopping for government loans can identify the difference between the two by the interest rate. A Ginnie Mae I rate is incremented by one half percent while a Ginnie Mae II rate is incremented by one quarter percent. When a Ginnie Mae I and Ginnie II rate is compared for the same loan product, the Ginnie Mae II will be higher.

All types of financial institutions involved in government mortgage issue Ginnie Mae securities. The lion's share, however, has been issued by mortgage bankers that made up over 43 percent of issuances. In contrast, mutual savings banks and credit unions each issued roughly 1 percent of the Ginnie Mae securities as of December 2007.[84]

Ginnie Mae has a consumer-friendly section on its website called Your Path to Homeownership. There are three homeownership calculators. The "Buy Versus Rent Calculator" permits renters considering homeownership to weigh the pros and cons through charts and calculations to aid in decision making. The Affordability Calculator helps homebuyers estimate how much they can afford to pay for their home. The Loan Estimator Calculator does estimates for the Federal Housing Administration, Veterans Administration and Conventional loans based on a hypothetical home sale price.[85] Moreover, Ginnie Mae provides an in-depth explanation of the loan application and home purchase process.

The Servicemembers' Civil Relief Act requires mortgage lenders to charge 6 percent for active duty military personnel, members of the National Guard, and reservists. If the market rates are higher, then this amounts to an interest rate subsidy. Ginnie Mae reimbursed issuers for the interest shortfall when borrowers were called to Bosnia, Kosovo, Southwest Asia, Afghanistan, and other areas tied to Operation Enduring Freedom.[86] Ginnie Mae estimated that in 2008 alone, it saved its issuer community about $7.5 million in lost interest.[87]

Federal Housing Administration: FHA's core programs are the FHA 203(b) loan, the FHA 203(k) loan, and the FHA Streamline loan. The general qualifying guidelines for income and debt tend to be 29 percent front ratio for housing and 41 percent back ratio for housing and consumer debt combined. But, black box modeling in automated underwriting can produce different ratios due to the borrower's compensating factors. The Federal Housing Administration limits lender fees, so closing costs are lower as compared with Fannie Mae, Freddie Mac, and private-labeled lenders. Mortgage insurance premiums are required, and they are added to the loan balance as well as to the monthly payments.[88] These borrower-paid and financed premiums serve to manage the collateral risk in the event of foreclosure and also to ensure on time payments to the bond holder even when the borrower does not pay on time. Moreover, lenders can offer borrowers a premium interest rate in order to permit lenders to provide the borrower with a lender credit in order to lower the impact of closing costs.

Federal Housing Administration mortgage loans are not credit-score driven. Since these loans are sold into the secondary market with recourse, which means sold with a return policy, lenders may impose a minimum credit score requirements in order to manage their risk of future loss. This being the case, it should come as no surprise, therefore, that after the collapse of the secondary market Federal Housing Administration mortgages became the new subprime source of financing. With subprime borrowers refinancing in droves to get out of faulty loan products and into safer government loans, it stands to reason that the same competitive dynamics that shaped the broader lending environment will shape Federal Housing Administration lending. The big banks and private labeled firms on Wall Street will compete for market share by incrementally lowering the bar on credit scores. Those accepting lower scores will capture market share that will need to be balanced with managing the risk that comes with an increase number of non-performing loans.

FHA 203(b) Loan: The loan is used to finance the purchase of new or resale one- to four-family home. The initial investment for the purchaser is roughly a 3 percent down payment. In high-cost areas across the country, the figure drops to 2.25 percent. On a cash-out refinance, the Federal Housing Administration moved from 85 percent to 95 percent loan-to-value—a stunning attempt at competitive placement in the market and reason to further the refinance boom.[89] During the boom, borrowers were permitted to have 30-day mortgage lates within the prior 12 months when they refinanced, but the mortgage must have been current by closing. But, a 60-day late limited a cash-out refinance to 85 percent loan-to-value. Though Federal Housing Administration mortgages are not a credit score-driven program, in late 2007 lenders became more cautious since these government loans are sold with recourse. This means that if the borrower does not perform, a loan could be forced back onto the originating lender, which would mean a refund for the investor and a huge liability for the lender. Consequently, major lenders will add a layer of protection to mitigate their own risk by using the credit score not only as a basis for underwriting, but also as a basis for interest rate mark-ups. By April 2009, the Federal Housing Administration lowered the cash out limits to 85 percent loan-to-value financing, which was due to the higher nonperformance rates on higher loan-to-value loans done during the boom.

The Federal Housing Administration's potential marketplace power lies in the fact that there are no bumps or hits to pricing for the higher loan-to-value loan ratios as compared with private labeled investors. Risk-based pricing instead is built into the mortgage insurance premium, or MIP, that borrowers pay to insure against their own possible delinquency (so that investors get paid on time no matter what) and against their own possible total default. Should the Federal Housing Administration incur a loss, the agency's auditors will conduct their due diligence to determine if there was lender-related fraud, and if so, pin the loss onto that originating lender.

However, many lenders impose credit score minimums, thereby effectively curtailing the Federal Housing Administration's viability for consumers. This was due to the post meltdown environment to lenders seeking to mitigate risk at all costs given that Federal Housing Administration loans are sold with recourse. This means that if a marginally qualified borrower is approved and then fails to pay as agreed, the lender could be forced to repurchase the loan. That loan would be pulled out of the Ginnie Mae security, handed back to the lender on a platter with a due-on-receipt invoice in the amount of the loan balance. The buy-back business is financially painful for a company. The underwriter who approved a bad loan more than likely is asked to clear out his desk. That underwriter was the victim of management applying pressure to get more loans closed.

In a *Realty Times* article, syndicated columnist Ken Harney reported that with "HUD's 'Credit Watch' program, auditors scour FHA lenders' default rate statistics, and discipline those whose rates substantially exceed regional averages."[90] That discipline amounts to a two-year revocation of their ability to originate government loans. Moreover, Harney further reported, "HUD intends to extend the same statistical reach to appraisers—identifying those who appear to work frequently for lenders with high default ratios. Those appraisers could then be targeted for either disciplinary action or termination from the FHA program if their appraisals appear to contribute to a lender's high default rate."[91]

FHA 203(k) Loan: The loan is for rehabilitation and can be used for either a purchase or a refinance of a property in need of serious work. This loan is the ultimate alternative to the home equity line of credit. When work around the home is done, the borrower has a single mortgage that is fully amortized at a relatively low interest rate.[92]

A variation on the FHA 203(k) is the streamline version for both purchases and refinances. If it is a purchase transaction, the sale is subject to a licensed contractor putting together an estimate and an appraisal subject to the work being completed. But, there is one catch: no structural work is permitted for the streamline version of the 203(k). Up to $35,000 in home improvement funds are available.

FHA Streamline Loan: This is the one loan in the lending industry that violates the "if it seems too good to be true, it probably is" rule. Homeowners occupying their homes with Federal Housing Administration loans are entitled to refinance their loans to lower rates without using the full contents of their credit report to determine credit worthiness, without an appraisal, and without employment or income verifications. The reasoning is simple: If the borrower can afford to make payments at 6 percent on their Federal Housing Administration loan, they more likely will be able to afford making timely payments if they save $100 per month at a lower interest rate in a new Federal Housing Administration loan when a lower interest rate is available.[93]

Government loans do not have a prepayment penalty, though the Truth in Lending disclosure may say that it does. This discrepancy exists, because government loan payoffs are calculated on a monthly basis. This means that a closing on the first day of the month may have 29 to 30 extra days of interest added as part of the payoff. The U.S. Department of Housing and Urban Development describes that monthly interest added to the pay off as a penalty, but in the broadest sense of the phrase "prepayment penalty," it is not quite the same as what can take place with some subprime loans when they are paid off early.

Veterans Administration Loans: Veterans Administration mortgages are for eligible veterans of the United States armed forces. Once eligible, qualified borrowers can obtain 100 percent purchase money for owner occupancy that is fully insured by the government. Cash out refinances are limited to 90 percent of the home's value. There is a 3.5 percent Veteran Administration funding fee that is higher than the Federal Housing Administration's mortgage insurance premium. Disabled veterans, however, are exempt from the funding fee. In many ways, the Veterans Administration loan is similar to the Federal Housing Administration loan with the exception that the lack of mortgage insurance and the fact that it is guaranteed loan does not necessarily mean what veterans may think. The government's guarantee of Veterans Administration loans is for the investor, not the borrower. In the event of default or foreclosure, the bondholder will be made whole by the United States government.

Agency Loans

Conventional products that conform to Fannie Mae and Freddie Mac underwriting guidelines are known as agency loans. Fannie Mae and Freddie Mac are the secondary market for what are known as conventional conforming loans. Loan types cover the entire mix of adjustable rate mortgages, fixed rate loans, and balloon mortgages where the balance becomes due in full after a specified time period like five or ten years. Agency loans do not have prepayment penalties, and pay offs are calculated on a *per diem* basis. While underwriting standards are conservative, they can become surprisingly liberal when significant assets can be documented. One key element in a conforming loan is the loan limit. In 2000, the loan limit for a single family home was $252,700. By 2006, that loan limit was bumped up to $417,000. The conforming loan limit goes up to $801,950 for a four-unit home. The Economic Stimulus Act of 2008 temporarily permitted the loan limit in "high-cost" areas to be as high as 125 percent of the area median home price not to exceed $729,750 for a single family home.

Jumbo Loans

A jumbo loan is larger than the mortgage loan limit that conforms to agency guidelines. These are loan amounts over $417,001. Historically, qualifying ratios permit 33 percent of the monthly household income to go towards housing, and an additional 5 percent to go towards long term obligations like student loans, car payment, and consumer credit. Like an agency loan, underwriting standards are conservative, but can become surprisingly liberal when significant assets can be documented. Mortgage bankers and brokers sell these loans into the private secondary market to investors specializing in these types of loans for investment. During a normal financial market, every lender had access to jumbo financing. After July 2007, it became increasingly difficult to place jumbo loans since investors shied away from these loans. Santa Fe-based Thornburg Mortgage was a specialist in this lending niche, and reported a $3.3 billion loss for the first quarter of 2008. Close to half of that loss was due to the loss in market value of the mortgage-backed securities in it own holdings.[94] The irony is that these may have been perfectly fine loans within the securities though the underlying asset—the value of the homes—had lost value. But, since the market for these securities virtually died, so did the value of the security—even if the loans were performing.

Portfolio Loans

Portfolio products tend to be adjustable rate mortgages and are not sold into the secondary market; rather, they are kept on an institution's books. Prudent portfolio lenders follow Fannie Mae and Freddie Mac guidelines and throw in a few exceptions to differentiate the product to match a perceived borrower profile that is underserved. At the other end of this spectrum is the true subprime portfolio lender looking for the case-by-case deal that makes sense to underwrite. In either case, either a depository institution or an investor-based institution makes the mortgage capital available.

Private Labeled Lender Loans

Prior to the general availability of subprime loans, the very rare and hard-to-find subprime, or B-C-D, lender may have been referred to as "the prince of darkness."[95] In the early 1980s, the label seemed appropriate since it was assumed that the borrower would be dealing with a mysterious, if not an altogether shady, character. As it turned out, those private B-C-D investors were area doctors and lawyers with excess capital in search of higher returns than was available through other means. Since most borrowers had no direct contact with "the prince of darkness" given the several layers of people to go through that concealed his identity, the label stuck—and for seemingly good reason. The loan terms were onerous: a high interest rate adjustable loan, the deed held in lieu of foreclosure, and plenty of required equity.

Subprime lending originated in the private-labeled lending market with finance companies. Television advertisements from some companies featured scruffy-looking characters wearing black shirts, white ties, and dapper-rimmed hats. It was the mafia look, completely the opposite of the pin-stripe banker suit of the bank loan officer. But, when others like Fannie Mae or the Federal Housing Administration said no, these lenders said yes. And, over time, that permitted this underserved lending niche to significantly grow. Wall Street caught on, and Bear Stearns, Goldman Sachs, Lehman Brothers and rest became active participants. So, what was once in the shadows and in the periphery of America's credit-based economy— the loan shark and hard money lender—came in to the spotlight and mainstream with the full backing of Wall Street's most prominent firms.

Subprime products do not conform to either government or agency guidelines, tend to be private-labeled offerings, and are, therefore, non-agency loans. In the annual reports of the publicly traded banks and investment houses that specialize in this lending niche, they refer to these as nonprime loans. Consequently, nonprime, or subprime, denotes B-C-D paper, whereas prime lending denotes A-paper. Interest rates for subprime loans tend to be priced differently as a result of the risk grade distinctions, but this was not always the case.

As difficult as it may seem to believe, during the refinance and housing boom the best subprime loan products were better priced than Fannie Mae's A-minus risk graded loans. Consequently, when it came time for a lender and borrower to make a decision as in this type of scenario, the subprime loan was often selected since all other factors were equal. This, however, was the exception rather than the rule.

At the higher end of the credit profile spectrum is the high-income borrower with a demonstrated ability to repay, but with needs that went beyond what Fannie Mae or Freddie Mac were willing to underwrite. Examples of this included the need for a higher debt-to-income ratio, 100 percent financing, or loan amounts exceeding the $417,000 conforming loan limit.

At the lower end of the credit profile spectrum, there were borrowers with a demonstrated inability or unwillingness to pay as agreed as reflected in their credit reports. Examples of this included numerous 30-day lates on the mortgage in the last 12 months, a recently discharged bankruptcy, or an active Chapter 13 bankruptcy. In addition, self-employed borrowers not adept at record keeping had little choice in the market when it came to lending options.

"Subprime lending" and "the crisis in the housing and credit markets" are phrases often found together in the same sentence. Typical subprime loans were the hybrid adjustable rate mortgage: the 2/28 or 3/27. More sophisticated variations were hybrid adjustable rate mortgages amortized for 50 years, ballooning in 30 years, with interest only payments during the initial two or three years and then becoming fully amortizing and adjusting thereafter resulting in multiple payment shocks. Mortgage default and foreclosure process starts rose as a result of originating these types of loans to borrowers, who with each passing year, had weaker credit profiles.

Some subprime loans were structured with prepayment penalties. These were designed for three reasons: First, to enable a lower rate and not trigger a violation of the Home Ownership and Equity Protection Act; second, to incentivize secondary market investors that the income streams would likely continue; and third, to compensate the servicer in the event of early payoff since high turnover in a servicing portfolio is a major market place risk challenge for lenders in an environment where rates are on the decline. In his book, *Greed, Fraud & Ignorance*, Richard Bitner[96] said that "Most investors built their pricing models around the sweet spot, the two-year adjustable mortgage with the three year prepayment penalty, because it maximized revenue for everyone in the food chain."[97] Every link in the financial chain benefitted except the borrower, of course.

Consumer advocates complained to regulators about prepayment penalties, which vary between two and as many as six months' worth of interest depending on the lender. The central arguments have been that this onerous feature robs homeowners of equity, locks them into less than desirable loans, and are predatory in nature. As onerous was the task of understanding how to calculate the early payoff penalty, which is not described in plain English in the note or rider to the note.

Borrowers experienced low rates during the initial fixed term and then often experienced a payment increase due to the movement of the loan's index plus its margin. By the second quarter of 2007, "the number of borrowers behind on their payments hit a five-year peak."[98] Of the 450,000 subprime borrowers with adjustable rate mortgages, the delinquency figures increase within this borrower pool.[99]

According to Federal Reserve chairman Ben Bernanke, "Subprime mortgage borrowing nearly tripled during the housing boom years of 2004 and 2005."[100] Since Wall Street's investment bankers did not deal directly with the public, they made products available to a network of mortgage brokers through wholesale lending subsidiaries. Between 2003 and 2006, *Inside Mortgage Finance* estimated that, of the entire mortgage origination market, mortgage brokers originated 29.4 percent of all origination volume with the balance going to retail and correspondent lenders. In contrast, Access Mortgage Research & Consulting (formerly known as Wholesale Access Mortgage Research & Consulting, Inc.) estimated that mortgage brokers originated more than half of the overall market share, as shown in Table 3.1.

Table 3.1 – Mortgage Broker Market Share

2003	68% market share
2004	63% market share
2005	61% market share
2006	58% market share
2007	50% market share
2008	35% market share
2009	23% market share
2010	13% market share

Source: Wholesale Access Mortgage Research & Consulting, Inc.

By 2005, Wall Street's appetite for high-yielding subprime-backed securities peaked. As a result, 81 percent of subprime loans originated that year were securitized and sold to private-labeled investors in the secondary market. By 2006, mortgage brokers grew their subprime market share to 63.3 percent, with the retail channel taking 19.4 percent, and correspondent lenders (brokers with a large line of credit from a bank) originating the remaining 17.4 percent of the subprime market.[101] In a study on the subprime lending crisis, Senator Charles E. Schumer (D–New York) and

Congresswoman Carolyn B. Maloney (D–New York) stated that the significant growth in subprime market share by mortgage brokers was due to the weak regulations governing them.[102] This is not true at all. The significant growth in subprime market share by mortgage brokers was do to the speed with which every Wall Street firm was able to set up or acquire an existing wholesale lending operation that existed to funnel product to consumers through a low cost channel, the mortgage broker. Moreover, at the big banks, individual loan officers did not have to be licensed since they could originate under the company's license. The statements of Schumer and Maloney only served to advance the interests of the financial sector—shift the blame, the adverse media attention, and the legislative risk onto mortgage brokers

Schumer and Maloney were further mistaken since the data they relied upon underestimated the broker share since brokers originated half of the correspondent loans as well.[103] Moreover, their understanding of brokers having a large broker share of the subprime market does not take into account the fact that this was due to the investment firms as well as the major lenders wholesaling and pushing subprime products through the wholesale channel for brokers to in turn retail. Some of these lenders and investment firms had no retail presence due to cost. So, they pushed subprime product through the existing broker channels with the existing retail storefronts or Internet presence.[104]

Former Federal Reserve Governor Edward M. Gramlich, who died September 5, 2007, believed that subprime lending was an important development to extend credit to an underserved market niche. But, he also believed that some of these loan products were mismatched with the borrower's repayment abilities given how these loans were designed to operate. Consequently, the birth of subprime lending took place in a predatory environment in terms of how these loans were designed to operate and who they targeted.

After the subprime meltdown got under way, subprime loans could no longer be securitized and sold on the secondary market. As a result, some investors filled the vacuum by keeping their subprime originations in their portfolios. These loans, however, were fixed-rate loans and the rates were between two to four percent higher and sometimes more compared with subprime rates from 2005. The fixed rates were the result of a lending guidance issued by banking regulators than banned short-term hybrid adjustable rate mortgages. Though many consumer groups had clearly described the inherent risks posed to borrowers by short-term adjustable rate mortgages with pre-payment penalties, the nation's banking regulators waited to see the mounting evidence in the form of a foreclosure crisis for this to be finally clear to them. The higher interest rates, or widened credit spreads, were the result of risk-based pricing due to a more uncertain lending environment.

Being all things to all people can undermine branding opportunities and differentiation in the marketplace, which are needed in order to stand out from the crowd. Consequently, though a lender may have access to every product, lenders astute at marketing tend to focus on the benefits and features of one product at a time in marketing communications given the changes in market conditions. Given that an increasing number of consumers were more often than not short on income and cash, lenders increasingly matched consumers with products designed to meet their needs. Consequently, 100 percent financing in one shape or form became prevalent across the industry at the peak of the bubble.

The Fully Amortizing Loan

A fully amortized loan means that money goes toward principal and interest with each payment. These loans feature 30, 25, 20, 15, or 10-year terms with fixed interest rates and fixed payments of principal and interest. The benefit to the borrower is predictability in monthly payments as well as a zero balance over time as the borrower fulfills the loan's terms. If rates fall, however, the borrower is stuck with the fixed rate unless they chose to refinance to a lower rate. Moreover, borrowers with short-term housing plans may find themselves paying more in interest.

With the simple phrase, "Interest will be charged on unpaid principal until the full amount of principal has been paid,"[105] it is understood without doing calculations that less interest will be due as the principal balance declines, as illustrated in Figure 3.1. In fact, reducing the balanced owed can be hurried along. For anyone desiring to more quickly build wealth, this is the most important concept, because mortgage debt can be more quickly paid off.

On a $100,000 mortgage at 6 percent, monthly principal and interest payments are $599.55. With the first payment, $500 is interest and $99.55 is principal. The Truth in Lending disclosure for this hypothetical scenario shows $215,838.45 in total payments repaid over 30 years: $100,000 in principal plus $115,838.45 in interest. After the first year, the mortgage balance drops to $98,772, the equivalent of about two monthly mortgage payments. Over time, more of the monthly payments go toward principal. By the 223rd month (18.6 years), $301.24 goes toward principal and $298.31 goes toward interest. By the 256th month (21.3 years), the mortgage balance drops to $49,938.84.

Figure 3.1 – Monthly Principal and Interest Repayments

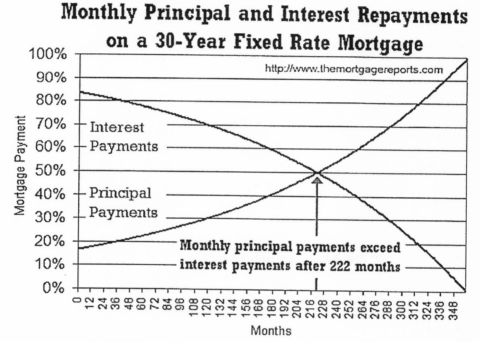

Source: TheMortgageReports.com

A fully amortized loan with no prepayment penalty permits the borrower to pay off early. To illustrate, adding just $93.86 extra per month earmarked toward principal from the first monthly payment will retire the debt in 256 months (21.3 years). Those extra principal payments equal $24,028. That in turn cuts interest payments to retire the debt by $25,910.84.[106]

The fixed-rate mortgage is the loan that became mainstream after the Great Depression and prevalent during Eisenhower's Great Society program. The predictability of monthly payments is perhaps the key benefit of this loan since homeowners have considerable control over their budget. Moreover, equity builds gradually even if there is no appreciation in real estate prices. Another important point is that when the economy evidences inflation, the effective monthly payments essentially drop given the rise in wages.

The Non-Amortizing Interest only Loan

The interest only loan comes in many forms. The first three, five, seven, or ten years of the loan may be interest only, with the remaining term fully amortized or a balloon. The 30-year fixed, 10-year interest only mortgage, for example, has an interest only period for ten years. On year eleven, it becomes a 20-year fully amortized loan. This recasting of the term means there would be a payment shock even if the rate remained fixed. Another variant of this loan is that on year eleven, the loan becomes an adjustable rate mortgage. Moreover, at the end of the interest only period, the original amount borrowed would still be owed unless the borrower paid extra toward the principal balance.

In the purchase money realm, the 5/1 interest only mortgage may have been the leading loan of choice in the Washington, D.C. metropolitan area, for example. The reason was simple: the interest only loan is a leverage tool that permitted marginally qualified borrowers to qualify for larger loan amounts than they would had they chosen a fully amortized loan. Not only were the 3/1 and 5/1 adjustable rate mortgage interest rates lower than the 10/1 adjustable rate mortgage interest rates, but the interest only feature produced a significant borrower benefit: much lower payments and greater leverage. Consequently, these loans, especially when coupled with higher debt-to-income allowances in underwriting, were among the so-called "affordability" products. Given these facts, what applied in the Washington, D.C. market more than likely applied to other major housing markets.

Many economists suspect that interest only mortgages, adjustable rate mortgages, and other complex mortgage products helped people buy homes that they could not otherwise afford during the boom.[107] Loan products that permitted borrowers to qualify at lower rates and in many cases with higher debt-to-income ratios together permitted purchasers to qualify for larger mortgages. When these two underwriting features are coupled with stated income documentation due to a borrower's high credit score, we have what June Fletcher in her 2005 book *House Poor* refers to as a "mortgage on steroids."[108] This was nothing short of financial alchemy on the retail lending front, which paled in comparison with what took place in the secondary market when these loans were then pooled, securitized as mortgage backed securities, and then re-securitized as collateralized debt obligations.

In 2004, the interest only mortgage certainly was popular. A Loan-Performance study indicated that 40 percent of the originated loans that were more than $360,000 in high-cost housing areas were interest only mortgages.[109] These high-cost areas included places like San Diego; Washington, D.C.; Seattle; Reno; Atlanta; and much of northern California.

The interest only loan presents a problem for borrowers where home prices fall, because it is unlikely that they repaid principal during the initial term—which is the reason they took the loan in the first place. With the possibility of a diminished equity position, we see here the flip side of leverage. Just as corporations come unraveled from over leveraging, so too do mortgage borrowers, who made bets on the wrong side of the real estate appreciation curve. When leverage works in your favor, it is like riding a surf board on the tip of a wave. When leverage goes against you, it is not just wipe out, but a crushing blow by the wave, a force much greater than yourself, pushing you onto the ocean floor for some scrapes and bruises thrown in for good measure.

The Balloon

Prior to the Great Depression, the prevalent mortgage was a short-term interest only loan with the balance due in full in five years or renewable for another five year term. In the modern era, the typical balloon mortgage might feature a slightly below market rate on a 30-year fixed loan with the remaining balance due in 15 years. The balloon feature, needless to say is a source of anxiety that is overcome by either a refinance or sale of the property.

Though prevalent during the refinance boom and housing bubble years, the interest only loan with the balloon feature dates back to the 1920s.[110] At the top of the Fannie Mae/Freddie Mac Uniform Instrument for the fixed rate balloon note, it states in bold, all cap letters, that a future refinance is not guaranteed and that the balance is due in full at maturity. The top of the Multistate Balloon Note reads:

This loan is payable in full at maturity. You must repay the entire principal balance of the loan and unpaid interest then due. The lender is under no obligation to refinance the loan at that time. You will, therefore, be required to make payment out of other assets that you may own, or you will have to find a lender, which may be the lender you have this loan with, willing to lend you the money. If you refinance this loan at maturity, you may have to pay some or all of the closing costs normally associated with a new loan even if you obtain refinancing from the same lender.[111]

Clearly, it is incumbent upon the borrower to carefully consider this type of obligation given the placement and manner of the disclosure.

The Adjustable Rate Mortgage

The adjustable rate mortgage came into the marketplace after the savings and loan crisis of the late 1980s and early 1990s. The crisis resulted in part from savings and loans holding low-rate fixed-rate mortgages on their books. As interest rates in the market rose, their cost of funds did too. This meant that capital tied up in low-rate mortgages eventually could not offset the higher rates required to pay customers for their deposits. The imbalance in the cash flows led to financial disaster when more than 1,000 savings and loans failed. Adjustable rate mortgages were designed in response to the savings and loan crisis so that interest-rate risk would be shared by the lender and the borrower.

Adjustable rate mortgage interest rates are tied to a marketplace index plus a margin. As the index moves up, down, or sideways, so does the interest rate the customer pays. Safety features to mitigate payment shocks are built in to the product. An initial rate cap and a lifetime cap are designed to protect the consumer from any dramatic upward movement in the underlying index. Conversely, a floor is designed to protect the lender from any steep move downward in the index. Periodic adjustment caps exist for consumers to be able to plan ahead for the worst case scenario and plan ahead accordingly.

Some adjustable rate mortgages come with a conversion feature, which means that after a predetermined number of years, the borrower can elect to convert the adjustable rate mortgage to a fixed-rate loan without refinancing. This is an important feature with the benefit to the consumer being some measure of peace of mind given this built-in flexibility. One of the conversion feature criteria in the market place is that the new fixed rate would be based on the prevailing Fannie Mae or Freddie Mac fixed rate plus one half percent for a small fee in the hundreds of dollars.

The hybrid adjustable rate mortgage has an initial fixed rate for a two-, three-, five-, seven-, or ten-year term. There are exotic variations on the theme as well. The 2/28 and 3/27 adjustable rate mortgage has garnered quite a bit of attention, because it was the prevalent loan among subprime borrowers. But there are other adjustable rate mortgages that push the envelope for complexity in an attempt to deliver lower payment while thoroughly confusing the customer in the process. For example, one exotic adjustable rate mortgage was created as a three-year adjustable rate mortgage, the first five years interest only, 50-year amortization, with a balloon in 15 years. At the top of the Fannie Mae/Freddie Mac Uniform Instrument for the Adjustable Rate Mortgage tied to the 1-Year Treasury Index it states in bold all cap letters that the interest rate is adjustable. The top of the Multistate Adjustable Rate Note reads:

> This note contains provisions allowing for changes in my interest rate and my monthly payment. This note limits the amount my interest rate can change at any one time and the maximum rate I must pay.[112]

The prominent placement of the disclosure should call attention to the borrower regarding the nature of the obligation.

There is nothing arbitrary about the mechanics of an adjustable rate mortgage. The benefits to the consumer include lower monthly payments and, as a result, the ability to qualify for a larger loan amount. Moreover, in a declining interest rate environment, there is no need to refinance. Conversely, because some indexes lag behind the market, even in an environment where rates are gradually moving upward, the consumer can still come out ahead. The key for the consumer in exploiting the advantage of an adjustable rate mortgage, however, is some degree of financial literacy, familiarity with indexes, and an understanding of the markets that comes from following the business and financial media.

The Option ARM

Option ARMs permit borrowers to have four payment options each month. These loans are 30-and 15-year fully amortized, interest only, and the minimum payment, which is less than what is owed to service the interest. If the fully amortized payment is made, money goes to both principal and interest. Since the loan is an adjustable rate mortgage, the rate can adjust during the initial period depending on the loan's specific terms. These loans are sensitive to rising rates, because their rates adjust each month.

With an Option ARM, the interest only payment is just that: Make that payment and the balance remains the same. Calculating that payment is as easy as taking the loan amount, multiplying it by the interest rate, and then dividing that by 12. The minimum payment option, however, is more subtle to understand. The minimum payment is less than the interest required to service the loan, so the difference each month is deferred by being added to the loan balance. At the end of each year, the payment could increase by 7.5 percent. So if the payments are $1,000 per month for the first year, they could increase to $1,075 for the second year. This gradual increase to the payments would occur during the option period, which could be three or five years depending on the loan's specifics.

When the interest only and minimum payment option ends, the loan becomes fully amortized and recasts over the remaining term. These cause a payment shock, because principal must be repaid along with interest and over a shorter period. For example, if the initial term was for 30 years and the payment option period was for the first five years, then the reaming term would be 25-years. If only the minimum payment was made over the first five years, then the balance could increase to 125 percent of the original loan amount due to deferred interest, a third factor in a payment shock. This may be one of the most difficult loans to understand not just for borrowers, but some loan officers as well.

The benefits to the consumer, who understands the features of the loan, are flexibility and leverage. And, there are no penalties for making a minimum payment. Given that many homeowners move every six years on average, this loan may have made sense for some provided that the equity position does not erode from both deferrals of interest and declining market conditions, which would result in a double whammy in losses. There are several variants of the Option ARM, thus mandating a careful reading of the program disclosure prior to application, not at closing.

The Option ARM came out in the 1980s. Herb and Marion Sandler are reported to have invented the Option ARM when they ran Oakland, California-based Golden West Financial Corporation.[113] When they were first introduced by World Savings Bank[114] loan officers these loans were said to be intended for the high-level executive, who was well compensated and even more handsomely compensated in bonuses. The apparent thinking behind this loan was that it was not only a leverage tool for the high-income buyer looking for the ultimate estate, but it also permitted that homeowner to maintain the appearance of a high standard of living that could be fully covered as the quarterly bonuses came in throughout the year.

Prior to 2003, very few borrowers used Option ARMs.[115] At the height of the housing boom in 2004 and 2005, however, Option ARMs became a mainstream loan.[116] Option ARM origination volume across the industry increased in 2005 due to greater borrower leverage and more securitizations followed.[117] Mortgage strategy analyst David Liu with Union Bank of Switzerland in New York stated that 40 percent of mortgages of more than $360,000 were Option ARMs that were originated for homeowners with good credit during the first quarter of 2005. At the peak of the bubble in 2005, Option ARM flyers were tucked under the windshield wipers of a parking lot full of cars in front of Wal-Marts, not at Nordstrom's where more affluent consumers shop. In other words, the Option ARM had come from the periphery into the mainstream.

The key changes that took place were the introduction of a fixed rate feature that allowed Option ARMs to resemble hybrid adjustable rate mortgages while retaining the payment option feature. One of the problems with the Option ARM is frequent borrower complaints about not understanding the mechanics of the loan and regulator concerns over increased risks.[118] While these loans were intended as cash flow management products for a sophisticated borrower profile, Option ARMs instead became ticking time bombs for some mainstream borrowers. Of course, this vintage of Option ARMs taken out in 2004 and 2005 would adjust with much higher payments and balances than borrowers thought. With declining home prices coupled with rising loan balances, these borrowers increasingly could not refinance. Those who were caught up in the real estate mania either ignored or failed to appreciate the many risks.

Charlotte, North Carolina-based Wachovia Corporation became synonymous with Option ARM loans after its $25 billion acquisition of

Golden West Financial Corporation in 2006. Wachovia holds in excess of $122 billion in Option ARM loans. On June 30, 2008, however, Wachovia announced that it would no longer originate Option ARM loans due to rising loan balances secured against declining real estate values. In addition, Wachovia decided to waive the prepayment penalty so that those borrowers who could refinance would be free to do so.[119] As of mid-July 2008, nearly six percent of Wachovia's Option ARM loans were nearing default with expectations that default rates could hit 12 percent. In response, Wachovia set aside $5.6 billion to offset anticipated losses.[120] More than 18 percent of the Option ARMs originated industrywide in 2005 and 2006 were 60 days past due in 2008, according to London-based Barclays Capital, which analyzed securitized Option ARMs.[121]

The Home Equity Line of Credit

The home equity line of credit, or HELOC—pronounced "he lock," is a line of credit tied to real estate. It is a mortgage, and it is an adjustable rate mortgage. If there is an existing mortgage on real estate and a home equity line of credit is placed against it, then it becomes a second mortgage. If the real estate has no debt against it, then the home equity line of credit becomes a first mortgage. There are three key points to this loan type.

First, some home equity line of credit products are structured as simple-interest loans. If payment is just one day past due, one additional day of interest could accrue and be added to the loan balance. Although this is not negative amortization, it is due to calculating payments based on a simple-interest formula. Professor of Finance Emeritus at the Wharton School of the University of Pennsylvania Jack M. Guttentag said, "The more aware I have become that my previous articles on the subject understated the risks [that simple interest mortgages] pose for borrowers."[122] This risk is because interest accrues daily instead of monthly as with conventional and government mortgages. In this regard, Guttentag cautioned borrowers about this risky loan on two points:

> One, since interest on a [simple interest mortgage] is charged daily, there is no rationale for a late charge, but lenders impose one anyway—because they can. A late fee on a standard mortgage is completely reasonable, but late fees on [simple interest mortgages] are

an abuse. And two, borrowers are credited for payments when the payments are posted by the lender, not when they are sent by the borrower. Every day of delay generates another day of interest income, and if the lender delays posting the payment past the penalty-free period, the borrower will be billed for a late fee as well. This means that borrowers who want to avoid the slippery slope have to adjust their payment practices to the posting procedures of the lender. This is difficult to do unless they receive monthly statements. Not all servicers provide monthly statements.[123]

Second, typically, the home equity line of credit has an initial draw period where the property owner can write checks—no questions asked—unless the line of credit is closed at the lender's discretion. Repayment of the home equity line of credit during the initial draw period is interest only.

Third, when the draw period closes, the loan becomes fully amortized for the remaining term. Consequently, the monthly obligation will be higher since both principal and interest will be required to retire the debt over the remaining term. With these points made, there are countless variations on this home equity line of credit theme that requires a very careful reading of both the promise note and product disclosure. Guttentag noted that:

> The possibility that a standard mortgage with an ambiguous note can be converted to simple interest is scary. Truth in Lending is no help because lenders are not required to identify loans as simple interest mortgages. [124]

As a result of these issues, home equity line of credit products should be approached with the same level of due diligence in approaching an adjustable rate mortgage or an interest only loan with a balloon feature.

The Offset Loan

The offset loan comes from Australia, and is based on the premise that a household's deposits should be permitted to offset the accrued interest due on an outstanding mortgage balance. Interest on the mortgage is calculated on a daily basis. The savings on deposit offsets the mortgage balance. Periodic deposits like paychecks and bonuses also offset the mortgage balance. The benefit to the financial institution offering the offset loan is that customers are incentivized to place all of their funds under the firm's management. The potential benefit to the customer is that if there are significant assets and large periodic deposits, the amount of interest paid could be less and the time to retire the debt could be reduced when compared against a traditional mortgage. The potential risk to the customer, however, is that the mortgage balance could increase due to the simple interest rate calculation. That reversal of expectations could take place if the periodic deposits are not consistent, if the deposits are made at a later date in the month, or if the savings are drawn down due to the anticipated or emergency needs of the household.

The Reverse Mortgage

Most working Americans believe that the golden years should be leisurely and without care. Nothing could be further from the truth, however, without good health and adequate income. Two thirds of Americans own their homes, and one third of those have no mortgage debt. But, a staggering one third of Americans retire in poverty. Yet, many in poverty have untapped equity in their homes. Sadly, long term disability is more likely as Americans get older.

The reverse mortgage was pioneered in the 1980s in recognition that social security is inadequate for retirement and in anticipation that the Baby Boomers would retire with equity in droves. The Home Equity Conversion Mortgage, or the FHA-insured reverse mortgage, can be used by homeowners with about 50 percent equity or more and who are 62 and older to turn their home's equity into monthly income or a line of credit. There are other equity-based formulas to calculate eligibility, so borrowers should comparison shop. Although there is no immediate repayment obligation, the borrowed funds plus accrued interest have to be repaid when the homeowners either no longer occupy the home or die. The reverse mortgage is an equity-based loan that does not take into account income or credit score.

Borrowers are required to secure counseling from a third-party provider prior to entering into a reverse mortgage. The counseling serves to provide an in-depth overview of the program as well as to offer ample time for questions and answers. Importantly, the counseling serves to protect older homeowners from the potential of predatory lending practices that target older Americans, among other groups.

The Federal Trade Commission notes that there are three types of reverse mortgages: single-purpose reverse mortgages, which are offered by some state and local government agencies and nonprofit organizations; federally-insured reverse mortgages, which are known as Home Equity Conversion Mortgages and are backed by the U.S. Department of Housing and Urban Development; and proprietary reverse mortgages, which are private loans backed by the companies that develop them.[125]

It is crucial for homeowners considering this loan to shop and carefully compare the costs given the implications to the estate's value after death should there be a concern for heirs. The key point to remember is that the loan balance on a reverse mortgage will grow over time and diminish the equity in the house. The Federal Trade Commission suggests contacting www.eldercare.gov concerning loan programs for home repairs and improvements, tax deferrals, or property tax postponements as an alternative in order to keep costs down.[126]

Eligible homeowners have five options in accessing their equity without an immediate repayment obligation:

Tenure—equal monthly payments as long as at least one borrower lives and continues to occupy the property as a principal residence.

Term—equal monthly payments for a fixed period of months selected.

Line of Credit—unscheduled payments or in installments, at times and in amounts of borrower's choosing until the line of credit is exhausted.

Modified Tenure—combination of line of credit with monthly payments for as long as the borrower remains in the home.

Modified Term—combination of line of credit with monthly payments for a fixed period of months selected by the borrower.[127]

With the aforementioned points made, it is critical that borrowers considering a reverse mortgage do their due diligence and carefully consider all of the implications. Since each prospective borrower has a unique circumstance, the solution for one may not be a suitable solution for another. The following is a sampling of experiences with reverse mortgages.

Avoiding Foreclosure: A person called to discuss debt consolidation and the challenges facing his mother-in-law. She was on fixed income for retirement, had deferred home maintenance, was in Chapter 13 bankruptcy, was in a stay of foreclosure due to the protection provided by bankruptcy, and had a low credit score. The tide seemed to be completely against this borrower. But, she had two things that turned the tide in her favor: She was over 62 and she had equity in her home. So, a reverse mortgage was suggested.

The son-in-law had power of attorney for his elderly mother-in-law, and he followed through with the required counseling as a prerequisite for the reverse mortgage. He said that he had some hesitations when he first heard about the reverse mortgage. So the required counseling was a good thing. "A lot of people are misinformed about reverse mortgages, because they think or have been told that the government is going to take their house. That is not true," he said after he went through the required reverse mortgage counseling session.

The homeowner's son-in-law was then counseled about next steps, and once he understood the risks of moving forward, the application proceeded. He petitioned the court to come out of the Chapter 13 bankruptcy. Once that was granted, the homeowner's then current mortgage company resumed foreclosure proceedings. This meant a race against time. The appraisal was immediately done, but the report indicated that the floors had termite damage and the roof also had serious problems. The son-in-law immediately had the termite problem addressed. Fortunately, the reverse mortgage program guidelines allowed for a roof repair escrow, which would be set aside at closing. Next, getting a payoff from the lender proved to be a challenge since we were dealing with a less than cooperative and forthright trustee, whose job was to initiate and then execute foreclosure on a scheduled date. That meant that if there was a failure to perform in a timely manner, the homeowner, a legally blind person and a widow, would be thrown out onto the streets. The thought tormented everyone who diligently worked on the loan.

From processing to closing took eight days. Closing took place five day prior to the scheduled foreclosure. Every step of the way was handled with great efficiency and precision to avoid oversights and mistakes. Everyone involved went above and beyond in their efforts to ensure a timely closing.

At loan closing, money was set aside and held by the title company for the roof repair. Once the repairs were done, the bills were paid from that escrow account, and the difference was sent to the homeowner. Also at closing, the homeowner received a check to do with as she pleased. And more importantly, the homeowner received a monthly check for the rest of her life. No more payments, just income. The monthly check to the homeowner will supplement her monthly social security and pension income checks.

Regretting Prior Decisions: A retired couple called to refinance and consolidate their consumer credit bills. Given their age and equity, a reverse mortgage was suggested. They secured the required counseling. They also discussed their plans with their daughter, who was in graduate school at the time.

The customer is always right. They decided against the reverse mortgage after having discussed the loan, its features, and benefits together as a family. All the debts were then consolidated, and the mortgage was refinanced resulting in a higher balance, but with better cash flow as a result of spreading out payments over a 30-year term.

Several months later, the borrower called back and asked if it was too late to do a reverse mortgage. After writing more mortgage payment checks and having had time for the counseling to sink in, a change of mind took hold. But, it was too late—the borrower no longer had enough equity. Even after having made the wrong choice, the initial choice sealed her fate. The loan officer's role in this troubling account is neutrality: present the information in as clear and thorough a manner as possible, and then let the customer decide what is best.

Removing Misconceptions: Another couple called about a reverse mortgage. They had no mortgage balance, had some credit card debt, and wanted to access their equity to invest in certificates of deposit. They were led to believe from their tax preparer that the income was free and that there was no repayment obligation. That was partly true. "There's no free lunch," the loan officer said. "That reverse mortgage is a loan and will need to be repaid one day." That clarified the first misconception.

The discussion then shifted to the number of heirs in their estate, the size of their estate, and the potential financial impact to their heirs given a diminished estate. If they drew equity to pay off credit cards, over several years, they could owe double the amount of the cards thus diminishing the value of their estate. Given their obligations to one of the heirs, that was out of the question. That clarified a second major misconception.

The conversation then turned to using cash from the reverse mortgage to investing in certificates of deposit. Even if the interest rate were fixed at six percent on the reverse mortgage, the couple drew $10,000 and earned four percent if they were lucky, that means they would lose two percent, because the cost of funds exceeds the rate of return. Then, there are negligible tax issues due to interest income. Since the debt balance would grow at a faster rate than the certificates of deposit, this would be a losing proposition. That clarified the third misconception.

Underlying the motive behind this call, however, was credit card debt that had become unserviceable due to interest rates that approached a predatory 30 percent. Exploring a Chapter 7 bankruptcy and getting the unsecured consumer debt discharged would be a far better alternative to doing a reverse mortgage since at the end of the day the goal is to preserve wealth and leave a legacy.

Final Thoughts: Reverse mortgages can serve those who are asset-rich but income-poor, and should be used as a last resort. Henry Hebeler, author of *Getting Started in a Financially Secure Retirement,* warned:

> Once [a reverse mortgage] is executed, people are left with practically no alternative but to stay in the home—even though other things may have happened, such as the only helpful, caring child has moved to another city, or the house is now ill-suited for some disability.[128]

Borrowers considering a reverse mortgage should carefully check out costs, beware of pitches, weigh options, and think long term.[129]

Reverse mortgage lending may be the hottest lending product on the shelf as Baby Boomers born between 1945 and 1960 increasingly come into retirement age from 2007 and beyond. Borrowers should be aware that predatory lenders perpetrating mortgage fraud tend to take advantage of vulnerable groups. Yesterday's once-sharp-as-a-whip consumer may be tomorrow's not-so-sharp borrower. This chapter, therefore, closes with words of caution from the Federal Trade Commission:

> Be cautious if anyone tries to sell you something, like an annuity, and suggests that a reverse mortgage would be an easy way to pay for it. If you don't fully understand what they're selling, or you're not sure you need what they're selling, be even more skeptical. Keep in mind that your total cost would be the cost of what they're selling plus the cost of the reverse mortgage. If you think you need what they're selling, shop around before you buy. No matter why you decide to take a reverse mortgage, you generally have at least three business days after signing the loan documents to cancel it for any reason without penalty. Remember that you must cancel in writing. The lender must return any money you have paid so far for the financing.[130]

In addition to the U.S. Department Housing and Urban Development and the Federal Trade Commission, the American Association of Retired Persons (AARP) is an excellent source of consumer-oriented information for those consider a reverse mortgage.

Concluding Thoughts

I again conclude with a series of discussions. These address how the industry views mortgages and how you in turn should respond. Some of the ideas may force you to see the negotiation process in a new manner. Please, again, consider this as your check list.

Policy makers are not financial experts. Legislators on Capitol Hill can only understand and then formulate proposals based on the information that comes before them. Controlling that flow of information, perception, and understanding of a problem is where subject matter experts and lobbyists representing special interests come to play. Consequently, access to legislative power is important in shaping not just the narrative, but in understanding a complex problem, and then formulating a legislative solution that is equitable to all parties with a vested interest. Financial corporations have to a great extent controlled the narrative in the media and have shaped self-serving policies in the legislative process. In the case of Schumer and Maloney, they were victims of the garbage in and garbage out rule since they over relied on information that came from the big banks and Wall Street firms. The result was the shifting of responsibility from themselves by placing it onto others. The prevailing public narrative that followed the Capitol Hill hearings of 2007 and 2008 as it focused on the subprime meltdown was that mortgage brokers were to blame. This is partly true. Those brokers, however, were the strategic partners and business customers of the big banks and Wall Street firms, which did the predatory product design, loan underwriting, and securitization.

The financial sector does not want a mortgage to become a commodity. In every other business sector, commoditization leads to standardization, ease of comparison shopping, and inevitable price drops. In that paradigm, the consumer wins. The opposite is true with the lending industry. By introducing complexity, the financial sector rendered consumer safeguards like the Truth in Lending Act to become obsolete since the goal of the truth in lending disclosure is to permit genuine comparison shopping by benchmarking costs and interest rates. Moreover, when loan officers check off "conforming loan" on the first page of the standard loan application, but originate a private-labeled loan there is no way for consumers to know until after the fact that they did not receive a Fannie Mae or Freddie Mac loan or understand if the loan is fully amortized or a simple interest loan. The appropriate response is litigation and adverse publicity.

Mortgages are financial products. Those who engineered the products, sold the servicing rights, securitized loan pools into bonds, and then sold these securities have many liabilities. Product liability certainly is one and speaks to the issue of the suitability standard. Matters dealing with fraud and criminal negligence pull the state in to take action. Private contracts, in contrast, are civil matters and privately negotiated. Because of this, mortgage borrowers may want to think twice about agreeing to settle a dispute in arbitration rather than pursing a complaint in a court of law. If enough consumers refuse to sign arbitration agreements, and instead work with the state and federal elected bodies, this practice among some lenders will stop. That can happen when consumers simply say no. Consumers may be able to balance the playing field insofar as the financial burden of litigation is concerned by working with consumer advocacy groups. Identifying onerous lending practices and successfully petitioning legislative bodies could result in the criminalization of objectionable products or practices. While this would result in a contest of will with financial corporations, this type of high-stakes fight should be undertaken in order to better protect consumers.

Understand that not all loans are alike. Mortgage loans that are presented as "affordability products" whether by the government, an agency, or a lender are not affordable. This double-speak comes from the Orwellian school of lending designed to encourage leverage and ultimately perpetual financial servitude. They are not only the opposite, but part of the cause for making home prices unaffordable and responsible for pushing them to unsustainable levels. The end result of these "affordability products" was temporary financial tenancy, and in many cases, foreclosure that followed. These products do not lead to out right homeownership, and therefore should be avoided. Some of those "affordability" credit props, now pulled out from under housing, are in part the reason for falling home prices. Home prices will stabilize and even rise when incomes rise and home inventory drops. Consequently, the problem in the economy is not tied to falling home prices. Prices must fall. The problem with home prices is rooted in "affordability products." There is only one true affordability product: the 30-year fixed rate mortgage. Do not be afraid to keep shopping, because there are better and truly affordable programs that will enable households to pay off the debt over time, which means that in the end, homeowners will actually own outright rather than forever pay interest to bond holders in other countries.

An ARM is not for everyone. A short-term adjustable rate mortgage is a leverage product that is not suited for most households. When combined with an interest only feature, stated income documentation, a prepayment penalty, and a high margin, this type of loan can make it costly to maintain as well as difficult to refinance if a borrower's credit standing and property value declines. Due to the high incidences of foreclosure associated with this loan, regulators required lenders to stop offering the product. Borrower recourse against lenders, investment bankers, and bond holders should start with forensic loan auditing. Where the like kind complaints have merit, they can result in participating in class action claims, which will more than likely rest on Section 5 of the Federal Trade Commission Act.

The Federal Reserve is a negligent mortgage regulator. The Federal Reserve, after more than two years (between 2007 and 2009), never produced any consumer-friendly set of mortgage applications and closing documents that explain to average Americans the difference between a 30-year fixed rate fully amortized loan and a 30-year fixed rate simple interest loan though it repeatedly assured Congress consumer-oriented documents were on the way. Those promise notes, contracts written by lawyers for lawyers that explain mortgages, are handed to the borrower at closing. This process is completely backwards. Consumers should review these contracts at application not at closing. The importance of this is about understanding the obligations well in advance of closing.

Do not wait for a consumer friendly law to drop out of the sky, because it will not happen. It will only happen when the next civil rights leader comes along demanding fair housing and equal access to credit, and is then assassinated. That is, after all, how this nation got its fair housing and lending laws. Congress reacted to the assassination of Martin Luther King, Jr. In the lender play book, there is only one rule and that is it's my way or the highway. In the consumer playbook, there is only one rule and it's the customer is always right. Therefore, take control. Take the initiative, and do not be afraid to push against the prevailing wisdom.

Legalese is part of the problem. The lack of plain English in a mortgage loan contract, the promise note and rider to the note, was to some degree at the heart of the lending crisis. These documents amount to an intellectual brow beating of consumers delivered by corporate attorneys representing financial firms. Bear in mind that during the boom the average loan officer had three years of experience, and only a high school diploma was sufficient to gain entry into most lending institutions. Yet, a person with a law degree drafted a promise note, which describes the mechanics of the loan in the most obtuse form the English language is capable of expressing for the general public. Moreover, the degree of sophistication and complexity of some of the financial products left many loan originators ill-equipped to understand and then in turn communicate the mechanics of the loan to their own customers. Finally, title agents and settlement attorneys, who serve as the last contact in the lending transaction, are there to follow lender instructions, not provide legal counsel to borrowers at settlement. If you do not understand the documents, ask them to resubmit them in plain English, or walk away.

Be intellectually honest. Respect the English language and understand its many subtleties. When a real estate agent, loan officer, title agent, or a settlement attorney uses the word "agreement," understand that they mean "contract." These words are not psychologically synonymous. A contract is enforceable in court. An agreement implies a handshake, or consent without the implications of legal ramifications. Yet, the agreement in question is a contract with legal consequences. The softening of the bluntness of the English language, or dumbing down, took place in earnest throughout the 1980s under the guise of neuro-linguistics and professional selling in seminars across the nation. Yet, it not only undermines the consumer's understanding of the binding nature of the transaction, but it also disarms the parties from being highly attentive to the many important details to the transaction. There are two choices. Repeatedly correct those loan officers and real estate agents who were taught to play this game. Or, walk away from those who engage in this form of professional selling, because it is meant to be deceptive. Look for those industry professionals who say, "It's a contract. You could get sued for not performing." That is honest straight talk.

Borrowers need to retain counsel. With these points made, borrowers should not be penny wise and pound foolish in the next mortgage transaction. Spend a few extra dollars, and have the documents reviewed by outside counsel. Retain an experienced financial advisor and planner or industry insider where compensation for the service is not tied to whether or not a closing takes place. This person should understand tax law and forecasting so that the real estate asset and mortgage debt can work to help the household meet the tax shelter needs, wealth building, and retirement planning goals. If considering an attorney, stick with only those experienced with mortgages—not just contract law. While this may be more challenging, it is not impossible. Require that these counselors communicate in plain English without over relying on industry jargon. Treat them exactly in the same way you would treat any other service provider. Consumers should read the closing documents themselves and make sure that they not only understand them, but that they are also consistent with both verbal representations and the written application. The role of the outside counsel should serve to address questions as they arise not to make the final decision.

Real estate is an asset. It is one of the three asset classes alongside stocks and bonds. Building wealth takes place by retiring debt. As an asset, real estate affords homeowners with remarkable financial flexibility given the ability to tap equity during the working years and during retirement if needed. Homeowners should take advantage of the financing programs that exist to ensure that their investment is maintained and in keeping with market place expectations. But, that does not mean repeated refinances are advisable. Given that the economic life of a house is 20 years, it should stand to reason that the most appropriate mortgage would be the 15-year or 20-year fixed rate loan. Additionally, age should be taken into account. A 45-year-old homeowner should avoid looking at a 30-year term mortgage unless the plan is to have mortgage payments until the age of 75. If at all possible, take a shorter term loan that can be paid off prior to retirement. Moreover, respect the equity in the home, and understand how prior generations viewed that trapped savings. It was viewed as forced retirement savings or for the purpose of leaving it to heirs. Those who overindulge by too frequently accessing their equity may find that there is not enough left for retirement. Everyone is responsible for their own actions. What looks like a good decision on the face of things today can have devastating consequences years down the road.

It's time to get real. Those who find these financial concepts to be too provocative or even radical may have been victimized by the indoctrination from real estate agents, mortgage lenders, tax planners, and stock brokers who only knew how to parrot the prevailing wisdom of their respective industries. They should consider seeking out the services of a deprogramming clinic.[131] Remember: the best mortgage is the one that is paid off.

MORTGAGED AND ARMED

Chapter 4

The Price

"If you live by the price, you will die by the price."
—The Seasoned Loan Officer's Adage

Consumers need to better understand that all products have prices. The same holds true for mortgages. Publishing mortgage interest rates in marketing materials can be a costly mistake since rates fluctuate daily. If rates rise, then marketing collateral published with lower rates can be seen as evidence of incompetence and generate consumer mistrust. The best example of this is the Saturday ads of published rates that were phoned in to the paper on the prior Thursday before 5 p.m. These ads make the phone ring, but they generate bottom feeders, or more politely put, price shoppers.

Astute loan officers and consumers know that true price comparisons are best done by getting a price quote from several lenders, preferably the same day, and then using a Truth in Lending Disclosure Statement—provided that comparisons are of the same product. The Truth in Lending Act requires lenders to disclose an annual percentage rate in order to permit prospective borrowers to have a benchmark when comparison shopping. Leading with price not only wastes marketing dollars, but also creates a situation where customers may feel misled. After all, disappointment is a function of expectation. Customer retention becomes more difficult given the need for follow up amidst competitors doing the same while driving prices and margins down.

United States mortgage interest rates typically are priced in one eighth, or .125 percent, increments. Mortgages associated with the London Inter Offered Rate, or the LIBOR, are priced in other increments. As the rates move up, the cost to get the same interest rate tends to move down. Conversely, as the rates move down, the cost to get the same interest rate goes up. That cost is translated into discount points, which are a percentage of the loan amount.

Pricing an interest rate produces a dynamic impact on both purchasing and borrowing power. To illustrate, just a 1 percent rise in interest rates from 5.5 percent to 6.5 percent on $200,000 results in about an 11 percent increase in payments, or a about a 10 percent decrease in borrowing power. This interest rate dynamic moves principal and interest payments of $1,136 at 5.5 percent to $1,264 per month when the rate is 6.5 percent. If there is a need to hold payments at $1,136, then a 5.5 percent rate on a $200,000 loan translates into a $179,728 loan if the rate is 6.5 percent

In any given market condition, a range of interest rates is available—at a price. Pricing is determined by the loan's underlying index as well as the margin to the lender. Another important factor in pricing a loan is the role that yield spread premiums, service release premiums, and overages play in determining an interest rate. Let us examine these important elements: indexes, yield spread premiums, and interest rate constituents.

Indexes

The Federal Reserve is an independent agency comprised of privately owned corporations authorized by the United States government to help shape and manage the nation's monetary policy. According to the Federal Open Market Committee:

> The term "monetary policy" refers to the actions undertaken by a central bank, such as the Federal Reserve, to influence the availability and cost of money and credit to help promote national economic goals. The Federal Reserve Act of 1913 gave the Federal Reserve responsibility for setting monetary policy.[132]

Congress, however, is responsible for shaping and managing fiscal policy. Simply put, fiscal policy is: "The federal government's decisions about the amount of money it spends and collects in taxes to achieve full employment and non-inflationary economy."[133] The economy, in contrast, is controlled by the private sector.

The general public mistakenly assumes that when the Federal Reserve announces a rate cut that it means that the 30-year fixed mortgage rate was cut or that the government has cut rates. Nothing could be further from the truth. That misconception about the Federal Reserve may stem from what could be the misleading abbreviated phrase "the Fed." The Federal Reserve only drives short-term rates by setting the Fed Funds rate, which impacts second mortgages. The Fed Funds rate in turn sets the prime rate, which determines the rate for the home equity line of credit, and the Fed Funds Rate determines the lending rate offered to commercial banks that may need to shore up their cash position to satisfy fractional reserve requirements.

The Prime Rate

The prime rate is the most frequently used index for home equity line of credit products. Many consumers do not realize that not only is a home equity line of credit a mortgage, but it is also an adjustable rate mortgage that is tied to the prime rate. This prime rate has no relationship with prime mortgage rates borrowers are offered by Fannie Mae and Freddie Mac. The prime rate is the rate that banks charge their best customers for short-term unsecured loans. Determining the prime rate is a function of banks building on the Fed Funds rate, which is determined eight times per year when the Federal Reserve Board of Governors meets in Federal Open Market Committee. As the Fed Funds rate moves up and down per the Federal Open Market Committee's estimation of the economy's needs, so does the prime rate. In this regard, the Fed Funds rate and the prime rate serve as the gas pedal and brakes for the economy. If the Federal Open Market Committee sees inflationary signs, then the Fed Funds rate will move upward to slow economic activity. Conversely, if the Federal Open Market Committee sees signs of stagnation, then the Fed Funds rate will drop in order to encourage borrowing. These factors impact the movement of the prime rate.

The Bond Market

The free market for borrowed funds drives long-term mortgage interest rates. This takes place in the auctioning of U.S. Treasury bonds in the capital markets. All 10-year U.S. Treasury bonds become the index for the 30-year fixed rate mortgage. Why is this? Most people do not keep their mortgages for ten years either due to trading up or refinancing.

The 1-year U.S. Treasury is the index for the 1-year adjustable rate mortgage that is indexed against that treasury bill. Sometimes, there are major disconnects between short-term and long-term rates, which is what we have during widened credit spreads. When short-term rates are higher than long-term rates, an inverted yield curve takes place, which often is an indicator of an impending economic downturn. Long-term rates are determined by expectations of inflation and the demand and supply of long-term credit.

When the Federal Reserve lowers its rates, the value of the dollar declines. That presents a problem given that foreigners invest heavily in U.S. Treasuries. That means the value of their dollar holdings is in decline. What do we do to get them to buy more? We offer higher rates on the long-term U.S. Treasury bonds such as the 10-year bond. That means we have to pay more in interest abroad, and the dollar falls in turn, we get to buy less with each dollar here at home. Although the downward move of the 30-year fixed rate mortgage is likely, it is not guaranteed. So, it is almost always a wait-and-see as to how our best customers, Japan and China, react to buying U.S. treasury debt and mortgage-backed securities. Everything changed after the Panic of 2008.

The "going rate" that customers ask about is the prevailing 30-year fixed rate for conventional mortgages that Fannie Mae and Freddie Mac will purchase. That going rate is a function of both the bond market as well as the incremental differences among lenders that are the result of forward commitments for large blocks of money. As stated earlier, price shoppers looking for the "going rate" would do well to look for them published on Freddie Mac's home page under Primary Mortgage Market Survey.

Moving Treasury Average

The 12-month Moving Treasury Average Index, also referred to as the MTA Index, is an adjustable rate index. It was created to smooth out the sudden spikes in interest rate movements and to reduce the payment shocks to consumers. This smoothing of the interest rate is done by averaging the monthly yields on the U.S. Treasury bill over a 12 month period. The key benefit of this index is that the market volatility of the underlying index is reduced, which is reflected in the slower and more gradual change of the interest rate. The negative aspect of this index is that when the U.S. Treasury rates suddenly drops, the Moving Treasury Average Index will not since the interest rate is calculated based on an annualized average. Conversely, when the U.S. Treasury rates suddenly increases, the Moving Treasury Average Index will not due to the same formula.

The 6-Month LIBOR

The 6-month London Inter Bank Offered Rate, or LIBOR, is the index used most commonly used with subprime loans (see Figure 4.1). Consequently, borrowers with subprime adjustable rate mortgages need to pay closer attention to the movement of the LIBOR since it is not associated with any of the rates tied to the Federal Reserve or the 10-year treasury.

Figure 4.1 – 6-Month LIBOR Rate

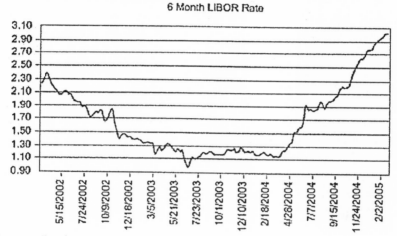

6 Month LIBOR Rate

Source: Bankrate, Inc.

Like other adjustable rate mortgages, the same key elements apply: the index, margin, and caps. The LIBOR rate is the index, and that index has remained low for the last several years, which accounts for its prevalent use. All LIBOR-indexed adjustable rate mortgages, however, are not the same, and, therefore, the margin and caps may be different. These mechanics are spelled out in the adjustable rate rider to the note.

Figure 4.1 shows the risk to borrowers of a LIBOR-indexed adjustable rate mortgage. The first obvious risk is that rates were erratic, but in an upward direction. The second less obvious risk is that the LIBOR index is tied to England's market place. This suggests that the bond holder of the mortgage may be tied to England. More importantly, it implies that the borrower should read *Times of London* or *The Wall Street Journal* in order to understand that city's economic pulse beat. Foreign market interest rates do not always follow what takes place within the United States economy. Given these points, a LIBOR index loan is not suitable for most consumers.

Popular Option ARM Indices

The Eleventh Federal Home Loan District Cost of Funds Index (COFI), Cost of Savings Index (COSI), and Cost of Deposit Index (CODI) are associated with the Option ARM (also referred to as the Pick-A-Payment® Mortgage). World Savings / Wachovia, Washington Mutual, and Countrywide were among the nation's leading originators of Option ARMs. Although there are other indexes for the Option ARM, the following is limited to reviewing only those from the eleventh district in the Federal Home Loan Bank System.

Cost of Funds Index: World Savings / Wachovia (a Wells Fargo company) defines the cost of funds index "as the monthly weighted average cost of funds for savings institutions that are members of the Federal Home Loan Bank System, Eleventh District (the 'Bank')."[134] The Federal Home Loan Bank of San Francisco states, "Only Arizona, California, and Nevada savings institutions that are members of the Federal Home Loan Bank of San Francisco are eligible to be considered for inclusion in the COFI."[135]

The cost of funds index consists of the monthly weighted average cost to members of savings, borrowings, and advances by the bank. The bank tabulates and announces COFI on or near the last working day of each month, reflecting the costs for the previous month. For example, the bank announces the February cost of funds index at the end of March.[136] Real estate writer M. Anthony Carr said of this index, "The COFI historically has been the slowest moving index in the U.S. and Europe."[137]

Cost of Savings Index: The cost of savings index is the weighted average of the interest rates paid on certificates of deposit held by World Savings / Wachovia. The index is calculated monthly and, along with the margin that is charged, serves as basis the interest rate on this particular mortgage.[138] When certificate of deposits are low or on the decline, the Option ARM indexed against the cost of savings index will be low as well. The converse, of course, is also true. As rates paid on certificates of deposit rise, the cost of savings index will rise as well resulting in higher mortgage payments.

Cost of Deposit Index: The cost of deposit index is based upon the 12 month average of the monthly average yields on the published three month rates on certificates of deposit. Since this index is based on averages, index movements tend to be smooth. Moreover, this index fluctuates slightly more than the cost of funds index, but closely tracks its movements.

Government Loans

Government loans are priced differently from agency and subprime loans. These loans are purchased through the Government National Mortgage Association (GNMA), which is a corporation inside of the U.S. Housing and Urban Development. Government loans that fall into GNMA I—spoken as Ginnie Mae one—have fixed-rate mortgages dispersed across the country. GNMA I loans have interest rates in half percent increments. In contrast, government loans that fall into GNMA II—spoken as Ginnie Mae two—include both adjustable rate mortgages and fixed rate loans and are similarly dispersed across the country but have rates that are slightly higher than GNMA I due to slightly higher risk. GNMA II loans are priced in one eighth percent increments.

Yield Spread Premiums

Mortgage loan interest rates are available at a premium, par, or discounted price. Simply put, a premium price is the result of a lender buying up the rate. This pricing mechanism is known as a yield spread premium, or YSP. Conversely, a discounted rate is the result of a lender buying down the rate. These pricing mechanisms are important for lenders since they permit needed flexibility for themselves and their customers. A discounted rate may be needed to force a borrower's income qualifying ratios to fall within underwriting standards in order to obtain a loan approval. Conversely, a premium rate may be needed to permit the borrower to access more cash after closing due to the lower cost to originate the loan. Consequently, these pricing mechanisms are important for both the lender and the borrower.

The topic of yield spread premiums has taken on controversy due to the suspicion of lenders abusing customers by price gouging, consumer groups not fully understanding the importance of this pricing dynamic, and due to inadequate disclosure on the Good Faith Estimate that fails to clearly and meaningfully communicate to the consumer the implications of what a given yield spread premium does to the interest rate or cash after closing. Direct and correspondent lenders have different pricing mechanism called an overage. The net impact is the same as a service release premium or yield spread premium. But, when it comes to overages, no disclosure is required on the Good Faith Estimate, which leaves customers in the dark and undermines the spirit, though not the letter, of Real Estate Settlement Procedures Act and the Truth in Lending Act.

Some investors wholesaling mortgage capital to mortgage brokers refer to this pricing mechanism as a service release premium, or SRP. Although the net impact to the borrower is essentially the same, there is a technical difference since the service release premium represents compensation to a lender to release servicing rights to another lender.

The years of 2003 and 2004 were characterized by incremental drops in mortgage rates. As rates dropped, borrowers repeatedly refinanced—often many times in just one year. This made sense if they took a premium rate so closing costs could be reduced or zeroed out by having the lender pay some or all of the closing costs through a yield spread premium, a service release premium, or an overage. First-time homebuyers typically took a par, or zero point, rate due to being tight on funds to close. Those moving up with experience and planning for the long-term often financed points, or a percentage of the loan amount, in order to discount the rate. A discounted rate for the borrower meant lower monthly payments. In a market that has bottomed out, on the other hand, borrowers tended to take a discounted rate due to the long-term benefits of the lower rate. A sideways market, in contrast, is like a hot day without a cool breeze. In these moments, loan officers more frequently monitor the Federal Reserve and bond market trading hoping for a movement in any of the benchmark rates.

The yield spread premiums, or service release premium, is at the heart of the price of all mortgage loans. Table 4.1 shows a hypothetical wholesale rate sheet. A bank's retail rate sheet is similar with the exception that the overage is built into rates that would be slightly higher than what is noted in Table 4.1. Starting from the top of the table, the 5.250 percent discounted rate on a 30-day commitment costs the originator 1.875 percent to secure. The 5.625 percent par rate on a 30-day commitment pays the originator nothing. And, the 6.250 percent premium rate on a 30-day commitment pays 1.875 percent to the originator. In a real estate purchase transaction, the transaction costs are more transparent. In a refinance transaction, they can be less given the fluid nature of the market and changes in loan terms between application and closing that sometimes result from a change in the borrower's credit profile or the borrower's desire to renegotiate terms like cash after closing.

Table 4.1 – Hypothetical Wholesale Rate Sheet
30-Year Fixed Rate

	Interest Rate	15-Day	30-Day	< Commitment Period
Discounted Rate>	5.250%	1.625	1.875	
	5.375%	0.875	1.125	[.875% & 1.125% is the cost]
	5.500%	0.250	0.5	Charged to borrower
Par Rate>	5.625%	0	0	< Par Rate
	5.750%	(0.625)	(0.375)	
	5.875%	(0.875)	(0.875)	
	6.000%	(1.375)	(1.125)	
	6.125%	(1.750)	(1.500)	[(1.750) & (1.500) is the YSP]
Premium Rate >	6.250%	(2.125)	(1.875)	Paid to Lender

Source: Peter Hébert

A rate at a premium price is available at an above-market interest rate. The premium may be reflected as a sell price. That sell price in turn is conveyed to the loan originator either in the form of a service release premium, a yield spread premium, or an overage. Although the yield spread premium and the service release premium will be disclosed on the HUD1 settlement statement at closing, the overage will not. In either case, this pricing mechanism permits either compensation to the lender or a lender credit to the borrower to occur. A rate at a par price has no yield spread premium or service release premium and costs the lender nothing. Since the lender provides services for a fee, either an origination or broker fee may be charged to the borrower. Par rates are lower than the available rate at a premium price. Finally, a discounted rate is priced lower than the par rate, and the borrower pays for the lower rate in the form of points, which translate into a percentage of the loan. The money has to come from somewhere to cover the lender's services, and if there are "no closing costs," the money has to cover those closing costs as well. From a consumer's perspective, the safest rule of thumb to remember is that there is no free lunch. "No closing cost" loans have the cost built into the rate or terms. Although the marketing of this may be less than ideal when it comes to full disclosure, this is an important means of pricing flexibility.

Interest Rate Constituents

The elements that go into an interest rate vary from loan to loan. But, at its simplest an interest rate paid by the consumer is comprised of the loan's underlying index, the margin, and the servicing fee. If it is an agency loan over 80 percent loan-to-value or a Federal Housing Administration loan, then there will be mortgage insurance. If it is a private labeled loan from an investment banker's subsidiary, the mortgage insurance may be blended into the interest rate, which would mean a higher margin. The composition of an interest rate, or "the stack," can be expressed in the manner shown in Table 4.2.

Table 4.2 – A Hypothetical Interest Rate Stack

Servicing	0.250% + / -
Mortgage Insurance	0.500% + / -
Margin	2.250% + / -
Index	3.000% + / -
Total Interest Rate	6.000%

Source: Peter Hébert

The interest rate constituents stack up to produce the rate the consumer pays for the loan. If the loan is an adjustable rate mortgage, then the rate would fluctuate given the movements of the underlying index. The half percent mortgage insurance covers the collateral risk in the event of foreclosure. The borrower pays this premium to insure the interests of the bond holder. In a conventional loan, the portion of the loan balance that is over 80 percent loan-to-value is insured. In Ginnie Mae securities from Federal Housing Administration loans, guaranteed pass-throughs apply. Even when a government loan borrower does not pay in a timely manner, that additional half or so percent built into the cost of all Federal Housing Administration loans enables holders of

Ginnie Mae securities to receive their fixed-income stream payments on time, all the time. As a result, government mortgage interest rates tend to be a little lower than prevailing Fannie Mae and Freddie Mac conforming rates. The above example is for illustrative purposes only and not necessarily an exact or actual breakdown since each scenario is slightly different.

Skipping a Payment

After closing, most borrowers elect to skip a payment since mortgage interest is calculated in arrears, the opposite of rent, which is charged in advance. But, borrowers who decide to make a payment at closing will find that the principal balance will immediately decline by the amount of the payment. The difference in thinking between one customer and another can be summed up as one is driven by cash flow and the other is driven by eliminating the debt as soon as possible. Those driven by cash flow will more than likely have mortgages longer than they need had they taken the time to count the cost.

Sometimes, lenders offer inducements that permit borrowers to skip one or even two months of payments. But that money has to come from somewhere. More often than not, it comes from a slightly higher rate that produces a larger yield spread premium, which, in turn, is credited back to the borrower in order to permit skipping a payment.

Deciding whether to skip a payment is important. It is simply a matter of calculating the difference in payments with a slightly higher rate compared with a lower rate over a period of several years. For example, if a 5.875 percent rate is at par and a 6.375 percent rate pays 1.750 percent in yield spread, then on a $100,000 loan at the higher rate, the rebate equals $1,750—enough to skip two payments. At the higher rate over 30 years, principal and interest payments are $633.23 per month. At the lower rate without the skip pay, payments are $600.41 per month. That $32.82 monthly payment difference may seem insignificant, but over ten years it adds up to $3,938.40—more than six times the monthly payment. In this case, the cost exceeds the savings. But, many borrowers will elect to skip a payment nevertheless. The important thing is to understand that there is a cost and that the money has to come from somewhere.

On a related note, if a loan officer tells an applicant to not make a scheduled mortgage payment, ask a few questions: What if the new loan does not close on time as promised? What if the loan is not approved or cannot close for other reasons? What will happen to the mortgage history rating and credit score? But, this is the question borrowers need to ask the loan officer that says not to make the mortgage payment on a current mortgage— "Wait, don't tell me. We're on *America's Funniest Home Video*, right?"[139]

Let's think about this issue for a moment. The media made sure that anyone half awake in the United States and also around the entire planet was aware that we were experiencing a financial crisis due to many American homeowners not paying their mortgages. The only person that should make the call to not pay the next payment is the closing agent or settlement attorney, provided they have the closing package in hand and closing is scheduled. Loan officers saying otherwise discredit their company and provide a genuine disservice to not only the consumer but the entire series of relationships in the financial chain as well. Why? Some loan officers over promise and under deliver. And, not all loans close on time. Misled consumers not only are harmed but so are investors who expect payments to be made on time. When payments are not made on time, the bond value declines, the premiums to insure the asset increases, and eventually an insurer cannot meet all claims. A seemingly assuring, though misguided word, can have significant consequences.

Concluding Thoughts

I again conclude with a series of brief discussions. These address the mechanics of mortgages interest rates. Some of the ideas may not sound right at first. So, please review this chapter again if necessary. Please use this as your check list.

Mortgage interest rates are tied to indexes. This holds true whether a fixed rate or an adjustable rate mortgage. It is important that consumers do their due diligence prior to application and closing since once the loan funds, the repayment obligation begins. The hurdles to overcome and then prevail in a dispute with a lender are significant. Therefore, it behooves all prospective borrowers to better understand how indexes impact an interest rate. Those borrowers with subprime adjustable rate mortgages are subject to interest rate changes based on what happens in England's economy and foreign financial markets since subprime loans are indexed against the LIBOR. There are additional informational sources on the Internet spanning a wide spectrum from the Federal Reserve to Mortgage-X, a mortgage information service.[140]

Points, SRP, and YSP have their place. They provide lenders with needed flexibility essential in pricing a borrower into a loan and also providing the lender with compensation. With this said, high cost loans are prohibited by law under the Home Ownership and Equity Protection Act. The key issue here is timely and adequate disclosure followed by consent. Unlike mortgage brokers, mortgage bankers and correspondent lenders can skirt the fee limits since overages are viewed differently in the eyes of the law than yield spread premiums and service release premiums. The consumer's counter to this is comparison shopping. This is where the Good Faith Estimate and the Truth in Lending disclosure come to play. Comparison shopping, it should be noted, should be restricted to a comparison of like kind products under identical terms and interest rate commitment periods. Borrowers, who feel they may have a high-cost loan as described by the Home Ownership and Equity Protection Act would need to file suit in civil court. More information is available online with the Federal Trade Commission.[141]

Stop and think twice. Some borrowers are looking for temporary relief from their mortgage obligations, and follow what can only appropriately be described as a penny wise and pound foolish logic that was promoted during the refinance boom. Savings $50 per month in exchange for $7,000 in closing costs, a higher loan balance, and a loan term rolled back from 25 to 30 years is not prudent. It is the height of fiscal mismanagement of the household's net worth and long-term well being. A more prudent approach is to look elsewhere in the household budget and cut there.

Pay it off. Those determined to be mortgage free can achieve this goal in one of at least two ways. Either prepay towards the principle balance on an existing mortgage, or refinance to a shorter term that is more aligned with the predetermined time horizon. Setting up a bi-weekly payment program is a popular means of curtailing the balance, and it works since 26 payments equals 13 full mortgage payment in one year. At the end of the day, the best mortgage is the one that is paid off.

Chapter 5
The Promotion

*"The very first law in advertising is to avoid the concrete promise
and cultivate the delightfully vague."*

—Bill Cosby

Promotion at its very heart is advertising in various shapes or forms. Good advertising is concerned with stimulating desire. Over marketing, however, while resulting in solid company or product branding, can result in the consumer confusing wants with needs. Promotion is like the contact sport of marketing. Marketing has to be frequent and vigorous in order to produce excitement in order to further pursue the game. When done properly, promotion produces not only sales, but repeat sales as well. When overdone, which is what happened during the boom, too much of a good thing can produce unintended consequences. These unintended consequences include not just fewer customers, but the devastation of communities and the broader economy as well.

In the 1980s, just a few years before facsimile machines caught on, one loan officer described his position as that of a "glorified delivery boy." The day's rates and programs were photocopied onto 8½" by 14" quality paper and then delivered by hand to local real estate offices and banks. Being on call 24/7 meant that loan officers had to be on the run to meet borrowers to collect documents, meet real estate agents and collect contracts, and then go back to the office to carefully review everything. If something was missing, he had to go back out to play fetch.

The successful traditional loan officer from the past had a conservative and traditional image: pin-striped banker grey business suit, starched oxford cotton white dress shirt, suspenders, silk tie, hand-made Italian shoes, and Mont Blanc pen. Mornings were spent providing new real estate agents with "Financing 101" training sessions. Some afternoons were spent in the office fielding phone calls driven by advertisements in the newspaper. Some evenings were spent using the expense account to take real estate agents out to performances in order to maintain a solid relationship. The temperament was always the same—think like a surfer prepared to ride the wave and do what it takes for as long as it takes while the market was good. Underwriting guidelines from all the different investors were packed into oversized three-ring binders and stacked on shelves that circled the office. This, of course, was prior to investors archiving everything online. After closing, either a bottle of wine from a nearby vineyard or a framed hand drawing of the borrower's home was presented as a gesture of thanks for doing business.

During the refinance boom, the successful loan officer's self-perception may have been a little different—think like a capitalist, talk like a hippie, and aspire to live like a rock star. The suit and tie were optional or limited to the face-to-face appointments depending on customer expectations. Today, of course, almost everything is online. But, customers are still pretty much the same—an eighth of a point difference in the rate can either make or break a deal.

Regardless of the image or customer expectations of what a loan officer should be like, professionalism, ongoing learning to improve product knowledge, and repeat business are the backbone of the business. The loan officer's role in promotion is to be honest with people, provide good customer service, and keep in touch with contacts and customers, because over time, business will grow based on customer satisfaction that leads to a growing referral base.

Outside Sales

Traditional loan officers in retail lending are outside sales representatives, and they push product to the customer. Loan officers often are the vehicles of promotion via speaking engagements and in-house visits to real estate brokers with an eye to purchase money loans. The traditional loan officer is focused on building and maintaining a book of business comprised of relatively loyal real estates agents and new home sales representatives.

Typically, the company provides a fairly generous expense account to the loan officer for automobile and entertainment-related expenses associated with cultivating business. One traditional loan officer described his role in promotion as being in a state that resembles "perpetual dating." He described that state as one coffee date after another in places like Starbucks where he would meet with preferably a highly productive real estate agent over a latté to review his company's programs and guidelines while bragging about how he had the best processors and underwriters in the industry. Another senior loan officer described one of the failings of this business model by noting that business dies off as the top-performing real estate agents retire or leave the area to pursue other ventures. Newly licensed real estate agents have enough training to get started, but not enough to endure. This is where a seasoned loan officer can make all the difference. But, for some traditional loan officers, that means perpetually training people new to the business with little to no assurance of loyalty, but certain assurance of much time invested in exchange for purchase money loan originations.

Some traditional loan officers with an established book of business take the opposite tack in directing how they acquire and maintain their business. If the real estate agent does not have at least three years experience, their approach is to simply state, "Please, call someone else." This latter type of traditional loan officer recognizes the 80/20/30 rule where 80 percent of the business is bread and butter, 20 percent is gravy, and 30 percent is scraps that should be thrown out. The numbers are not meant to add up to 100 percent. In this case, that 30 percent represents the high-maintenance transactions that result from alliances with inexperienced real estate agents, who prematurely structure deals without sufficient managerial oversight. They are liabilities.

Sometimes walking away from a potential loan is prudent if the real estate agent or borrower are difficult or if the borrower profile and loan file are marginal. In the end, the loan officer's reputation in a real estate office he services will be weighed against his last transaction. If the loan does not close, it can adversely impact 20 to 30 people if back-to-back transactions that connect move up buyers and sellers with movers, agents, lenders, appraisers, and title companies are involved. Given these considerations, competition can be viewed by more experienced loan officers as a welcomed relief of not a missed opportunity but of foregone aggravation including reduced liability. This practice of turning away business can rest on a fine line between possible violations of federal laws designed to protect consumers if a protected class is involved.

Many traditional loan officers do face to face visits with real estate agents, and can work with 20 to 30 real estate agents during the course of any given year. In the purchase money realm, lending is about constant deadlines tied to loan approvals and closing dates. The role also requires reading sales contracts, which is time consuming. In a short sale, purchase contracts can have close to 60 pages. They are not on the standardized REALTOR® association forms, but instead privately written.

Many loan applications go bad midstream in the hands of an inexperienced lender. Sometimes this is due to borrower procrastination. Sometimes, an Internet-based lender with no purchase-business experience can undermine the purchase. Experienced real estate agents, who are compensated by commissions, often exert customer control by insisting on a switch in lenders so that the purchase closes on time. Given that at least one of the agents to a sale is a fiduciary to the fee-paying client, this can be a prudent business practice.

Loan officers do not need to have a graduate degree in finance, but they do need to really understand the underwriting guidelines for the loan programs they originate. This is not an industry secret: But, a lot of loan officers in the mortgage lending business do not know what they are doing. In-house training, mentoring programs, and state-mandated continuing education requirements in order maintain a mortgage license help to address this shortcoming. Lending is more complicated today than 20 years ago, loan applicants need to understand that there will never be a substitute for experience.

Mortgage brokers have to take some loans to different investors because of the investor's internal rules that are at odds with Fannie Mae or Freddie Mac. This goes back to another loan officer adage: the golden rule. The one with the gold makes the rule. Even with an automated approval, an underwriter can over rule and deny a loan approved by an agency underwriting engine. Therein rests the competitive advantage of a mortgage broker over a direct lender—the freedom to broker to a wide assortment of lenders in order to deliver the customer's expectations of "common sense" underwriting.

At the end of the day, the traditional loan officer's goal is to produce more by working smarter, not harder—and certainly not longer hours. Nonetheless, the traditional loan officer in the outside sales role is ideally matched with the purchase-buyer psychology that often requires reassurances only possible through the face-to-face contact and "hand holding" often required with nervous homebuyers from application to closing. This "hand holding" oftentimes is the result of the buyer buying on emotion, buying more than he or she actually is financially comfortable with, and then rationalizing the purchase decision after the fact. That rationalization process often is reinforced by both the real estate agents and the loan officers involved in the transaction.

Inside Sales

The call center model turned the traditional business model on its head. This business model is built on inside sales representatives. This model pulls consumers in and matches them with the product. In some inside sales business models, loan officers are only order takers with low levels of skill and experience.

Once the call comes in, the processor pulls a credit report and gets the borrower's credit scores from the credit bureaus. The manager determines the loan program, and the loan officer presents a program to the customer at the direction of the processor or manager. In some of these business models, the title "loan officer" is not appropriate for the representative of the lending institution given that the only skill set required is the ability to sell.

Call centers may use television, radio, direct mail, and the Internet to generate refinance loans. In either case, promotion efforts are tailored to the specifics needs of both the business model, markets served, and anticipated buyer psychology. This model, typically, offers lower payments, debt consolidation, or cash to the consumer after closing. Lower payments are available through a host of different products or simply due to the product's interest rate. Debt consolidation loans are cash-out refinances, which more often than not results in better monthly cash flow and, more than likely, additional tax-deductible benefits as well. The caveat is that consumer debt is spread out over a longer period of time, which is why it is important that a careful cost-benefit analysis be made prior to agreeing to apply. Mortgage applications for cash typically go down one of two roads: a refinance with a new loan balance with a new term at the prevailing market interest rate or a second mortgage in the form of a closed ended mortgage or a home equity line of credit.

Some call centers retain the services of telemarketers to call lists of prospective borrowers who have expressed interest in a mortgage by virtue of a recent application and who are not on a Do Not Call list. The credit bureaus own the data they collect on consumers. On this point, the Federal Trade Commission states that:

> It's not that the company you applied to is selling or sharing your information. Rather it's that creditors—including mortgage companies—are taking advantage of a federal law that allows them

to identify potential customers for the products they offer, and market to them.[142]

If a consumer applies for a mortgage, his name is placed on a large list of other applicants in the market, and the lists are for sale. As commercial free speech, the reasoning behind this practice is to permit the consumer to competitively shop at the moment they are in the market for an extension of credit. Critics of this practice complain about the bombardment of unwelcomed phone calls.[143]

Examples of call centers include companies with ongoing direct mail, television advertisements, and radio commercials. Some included major lenders like Countrywide, which dominated the market on several levels. Others include brokers representing many lenders like Lending Tree and Ditech.[144] Companies like these have filled our mailboxes, made us laugh at silly but catchy attempts to get our attention on nightly television, and caused us to think.

Television

Televised mortgage ads during the refinance boom appealed by striking a chord of interest—lower monthly payments, cash to pay off high credit card balances, or cash for other pursuits like home improvement. Countrywide, the nation's leading lender during the boom, dominated the airwaves with low key and friendly messages that adapted to the changing market.

As rates started to again drop in 2008, Countrywide ran no cost refinance ads. It was near impossible to see if adequate disclosure was made to consumers that adequately described the mechanics of their "no cost" loans. Televised ads did not disclose either in the spokesperson's script or mouse print at the bottom of the screen that a zero-cost loan is a premium rate that is higher than prevailing rates. Moreover, the ads did not disclose that there were, in fact, many itemized costs that were paid through an overage to the bank. But, Countrywide's website did make the disclosure clear with the following:

*Affects pricing. Some fees may be charged and credited back at funding. Borrowers who choose to pay lender fees and closing costs up-front may qualify for a lower rate. **Borrower must still pay certain costs. Ex. Payoff demand fees; negative escrow account balance on old loan; prepaid interest on new loan; etc. Call for details.[145]

The goal of the ad was to sell the sizzle, not the steak. The message was clear: it focused on benefits, not features. Although puffery is not permitted in advertising financial services or products, this type of ad apparently is permitted by the Federal Trade Commission. The take away lesson here is that televised ads from mortgage companies should be viewed for what they are: a means to capture the audience's attention and to make the call center phones ring.

Perhaps the leader in mortgage *shtick* was the Ditech ads featuring the middle-aged, bald, and overweight buffoon who could not get his own mother to refinance with him. The actor's role was not dissimilar from *Seinfeld's* George Kastanza. Ditech has resorted to cartoon-like figures sawing people in half and its "People Are Smart" campaign—followed by disclosures in mouse print that is deliberately blurred. Funny, stupid, odd, over the top—they get our attention and make us remember them. Again, the take away here is more about corporate branding: Ditech is fun.

Ditech ran numerous $295 in closing cost ads for years during the boom that led consumers to believe that they were the low-cost provider of mortgage loans in the industry. As noted earlier, the money has to come from somewhere to pay the closing costs and there is never a free lunch. After the boom, however, Ditech shifted gears by running ads that showcased a modern mortgage operation with glass cubicles and floor-to-glass windows. As ads go, this was brilliant in that Ditech sought to convey transparency. Given that brief ads tend to be void of meaningful content, the feel good ethereal impact nonetheless was clear. With this point made, for most consumers, lending is cloaked in secrecy and is not transparent even if Ditech's ads suggest otherwise.

In many regards, television advertising functions to serve more as entertainment and less about information. Recall that the purpose of Real Estate Settlement Procedures Act and the Truth in Lending Act was for consumers to have more meaningful information in order to make better decisions. Consequently, televised ads should be seen as public relations, a high cost means by which financial corporations can shape public perception in order to manage the brand name. Let's now consider Ameriquest.

When Ameriquest was facing class action suits across the nation, the company responded through a public relations strategy employing theatrical rhetoric to counter the brutal facts that were staring the company in the face. Litigants had accused the company of predatory lending practices that included bait and switch tactics, high costs, and loans that could not be repaid. The class action story made the headlines. That was bad press for the nation's leading subprime lender.

One of the roles of public relations is to reshape an issue and plant a wedge of doubt in the public's mind concerning a controversy. The easiest way to do this is to create some ambiguity by swapping roles with the victim, the villain, and the vindicator. The media stories tied to the crisis and advertisements that come about in a public relations campaign will suggest who the public should like, believe, and distrust. The crisis fades when the defined roles of these three characters are sufficiently blurred as the roles are switched. In the arena of managing public perception, this is not difficult.

To do the job, Ameriquest retained DDB Worldwide out of Los Angeles to create two hilarious commercials under the campaign's theme "Don't Judge Too Quickly. We Won't." Each ad "cleverly used everyday every day events to demonstrate the consequences of jumping to conclusions."[146]

The Knife to the Cat ad featured a woman walking in on her husband holding a knife in one hand and a cat clutched in the other hand while standing over spilled tomato soup. He was seemingly caught by surprise. The tomato soup looked like a pool of the cat's blood. He was trying to get the cat out the kitchen while cooking, and the moment the wife walked in, it looked like the kitty cat just got knifed.

Another ad featured two doctors, one reviewing a chart over a sleeping patient in a hospital room. A fly buzzes the room, and the other doctor uses a heart defibulator to electrocute the fly, which falls onto the patient's stomach. He then leans to take a closer look at the motionless fly. He looks like he is listening for a patient's heartbeat. The patient's wife and daughter walk into the room while holding a balloon with the message "Get Well Daddy." The doctor then lifts his head and says to the other doctor, "That killed him." The ads then went nationwide since they were provocative and diversionary from the real issues facing Ameriquest.

These ads were successfully designed to counter adverse nationwide media coverage shining the light on Ameriquest, pending litigation, and predatory lending. The ads more than likely succeeded in planting the idea for both existing and prospective customers familiar with the charges that the company may be innocent. If Ameriquest was possibly innocent, then customers perhaps would not feel inclined to not do business with the company. On this level, television can be used to disarm the consumer. The reason for that is because television, and even some print media, is crafted to move people to *feel*, not to think. Nonetheless, Ameriquest was sued out of existence with the help of the nation's attorney generals representing customers who were victimized.

Radio

Radio is the technology wonder of the Roaring Twenties. Today, radio advertising reaches a broader and mobile audience more than television. People listen to it on their commutes, at home, and at work. Moreover, digital technology, the Internet, and satellites transformed radio's reach and cache. With satellite radio, for example, listeners can go from the premium radio broadcasts in the car to satellite television at home and not miss programming or advertising. Streaming audio and archived content on the Internet, moreover, keep radio relevant and competitive to television as a source for information or diversion. Advertisers compete across technology mediums for eyeballs and ears, including radio, to pull on the heart strings so that consumer wallets will yield under repeated coaxing and open to release its contents.

Jon Shibley of Lenox Financial is a wonderful example of the use of radio advertising. The essence of Shibley's ads are him saying, "We'll convert your adjustable rate mortgage to a fixed, and we won't charge you an arm and a leg. It's the biggest 'no brainer' in the history of earth!™."[147] At the height of the boom, Shibley was ahead of the curve in communicating a disdain for the lending associations, to which his company does not belong because, as he claims, "they do not represent the consumer—they represent the banks." His strategy with his customers appears to be delivering premium rates in order to minimize costs while preserving the borrower's equity, which he communicates. Moreover, he makes it clear that he has a team of managers that will manage the mortgage by watching the market and make lower rates available as rates drop, which suggests repeated refinances. "If you come in with a $200,000 balance, you'll walk out with a $200,000 balance."[148] Shibley's ads differ from those from the big companies in that he says that his company will pay the closing fees, which implies at least that he is selling a premium rate in order to secure a higher yield spread premium or overage as the case may be.

From an informational content standpoint, the Lenox Financial ads are far more direct, informative, and candid than Ditech's televised glass cubicles which attempt to communicate transparency in lending without getting into any meaningful detail.

Direct Mail

Unlike television and radio, direct mail is intrusive, more tangible, and has a longer shelf life. When a lender begins to communicate financial information, regulations apply since the information must be meaningful for the consumer. A quick closing is a clear consumer benefit of an efficiently managed company, but it can undermine a consumer's ability to carefully think, shop, and weigh alternatives, which take time. Consumers should save direct mail pieces in a folder, compare them with each other at a later date, and approach companies after having done the due diligence on them—that means consumers should do a background check on any company they are considering working with regardless of its size and reputation.

During the boom, households were inundated with direct mail from mortgage bankers and brokers. Also known as "junk mail," these pieces tend to include similar marketing-related features: a reservation number, enticing benefits, value propositions, a call to action, and an element of urgency with a stipulation that the offer is only valid up to a certain date.[149]

At the market's peak in 2005, Washington Mutual sent out offers to "reduce your mortgage payment by as much as 40 percent" with a "fixed payment based on 1.000 percent." The offer also offered "no payments for 60 days." The too-good-to-be-true offer was loaded with a call to action and a sense of urgency since, "Program Ending. Call within 72 hours or risk losing this rate." In the mouse print, there was disclosure of this being a generic Option ARM that could possibly be tied to several different underlying indexes, such as the LIBOR, moving treasury average, or the cost of funds index.

Citibank's vice president of marketing sent out preapproved offers for a home equity loan in September 2006. The offer focused on low monthly payments, saving more money by consolidating high-interest credit card debt, an option of a variable rate rather than a fixed rate. The "quick and hassle free" assurance included a ten-day closing.

A joint offer from Chase and United Airlines directed from the president of Chase's home equity division and the vice president of the airline's Mileage Plus program referenced no closing costs, a rate at 0.26 percent below prime, and a generous line of credit. Given that this offer arrived in April 2008, it was unlike offers in previous years from other companies. Chase took the time in an additional one-page document to disclose in a user-friendly question and answer format likely questions consumers may have regarding why Chase over others, whether the offer was promoting a "teaser rate," and if this was really a no closing cost loan.

The Online Business Model

Internet-driven business is big, and timing is everything. One may never think about an online stock brokerage firm getting into the consumer banking and mortgage lending businesses, but that is exactly what E*Trade® did. We examine this company here briefly to illustrate the rise and fall of an Internet-based mortgage subsidiary with no brick and mortar presence.

E*Trade Group Inc. acquired Arlington, Virginia-based TeleBanc Financial Corporation in January 2000 just as the refinance and purchase rush was to take the country by storm. Telebank was the largest online bank offering savings and checking, but it had no lending products at the time. E*Trade® ran online discount stock brokerage, and Telebank, FSB, ran retail banking. In February 2001, E*Trade acquired the Irvine, California-based Loans Direct. They were an early adopter of the Lending Tree Internet-based lead generation model. Loans Direct was a big buyer of mortgage leads from Lending Tree. E*Trade® had set up an online Call Center mortgage shop. It bought leads from online lead machines like Lending Tree and NexTag, and also ran advertisements on radio, television, and in newspapers. Direct mail campaigns promoted the company's home equity line of credit. E*Trade® went from $1 billion company to $10 billion between just 2000 and 2003, and by June 2006 had hit $45 billion. J.P. Morgan chase and Morgan Stanley financed the company's abilities with a revolving credit line. Over the course of that time, E*Trade bought huge amounts of home equity line of credit- and other mortgage-related securities. E*Trade®, however, got caught up in the lending crisis and lost billions. On September 22, 2007, E*Trade shut down its wholesale lending operations and on April 22, 2008 the company was no longer taking loan applications from the public.[150 and 151] E*Trade® successfully continues in its core businesses: online banking and online stock trading. The take away lesson here is that consumers should be mindful of the core business of a mortgage company's parent company.

Corporate Web Sites

A well-designed and structured corporate website from a company's perspective should function like a lead generation machine. In the best of all possible worlds, where business organizations are flattened, there are no loan officers. The web site functions as the loan officer. Costs are low, margins are high. Consumers are directed to the frequently asked question section for self-directed problem resolution. From the customer's perspective, a website should be easy to find, easy to navigate, and intuitive to browse. From an information technology perspective, a good website gets top search-engine placement due to carefully selected metatags.[152]

When it comes to websites, now defunct Countrywide knew what it was doing, and in fact, made the other major lenders look like first-rate amateurs insofar as leveraging the Internet is concerned. Browsing its website was easy and intuitive. That website was exactly what any website should be: a lead generating machine, which in part helps explain Countrywide's dominance during the boom.

Consumers need to understand something very fundamental when it comes to corporate websites: they function like mouse traps. That is it. A good website is baited with just enough cheese for consumers to get their noses snapped down: to drop contact information. With this point made, consumers should stick with the basic warning throughout this book: do the due diligence on the company prior to dropping personal information on a website and especially prior to applying.

Banner Ads: Numerous mortgage brokers do not have a strong Internet presence yet rely upon the web to generate business. Banner ads at strategically placed sites and portals permit mortgage lenders and brokers to attract prospective borrowers. To illustrate, at Bankrate.com, an

Internet site that claims to be "the Web's leading aggregator of financial rate information," banner ads appear on the main page. Lenders pay to be listed there. One ad clicks through to Lending Tree, which is a broker representing numerous banks. Lending Tree may be best known for its television ad, "When lenders compete, you win." The Bankrate.com site also has an easy to access section specifically for advertisers. Browsing the Internet is no different than driving the highway and being distracted by billboards that make promises. At the end of the day, consumers are better off taking control and self-directing their financial planning and debt management needs rather than reacting to an electronic billboard that redirects

Chat: Some lenders on the leading edge of technology have embraced instant messaging as an option for site visitors to make a loan inquiry. This chat feature demonstrates not only flexibility but willingness to not have 100 percent customer control. The result is that this becomes another means through which a lender can reach out and build trust on the customer's terms. In this marketing communication model, the customer may feel more comfortable communicating and in control should there be a desire to disengage.

Consumers need to be mindful that lenders have numerous ways to reach out to prospective customers in order to establish and build trust. With this said, consumers can and should use every opportunity to turn this point on its head while understanding that looking at a monthly payment within a chat dialogue undermines the ability to see the bigger picture. This point cannot be more strongly emphasized: comparative shopping needs to be limited to like kind products with similar commitment periods and disclosure needs to take place on those disclosure forms required by the federal government: the Good Faith Estimate and the Truth in Lending. There are no short cuts to making informed decisions that require careful thinking and analysis.

Concluding Thoughts

I again conclude with a series of brief discussions. These address how the industry uses different types of promotion to attract prospective customers. Some of the ideas should confirm some of your suspicions about how lenders advertise. Please consider this as your check list.

It's all about the promotion. Promotion is one of the elements of marketing, and each of the tactics briefly described here has its strengths and weaknesses. Consumers, mindful of these, would do well to stick with the basics and not to expect lenders to do their homework for them. The burden of due diligence, after all, falls on the consumer. This chapter closes with the adverse impact that direct mail can have on targeted consumers and the lending industry. Moreover, consumers cannot and should not wait for a federal or state regulator to act since history is the best indicator of future performance. It was not until the subprime meltdown and the foreclosure crisis took center stage in the summer of 2007 that the federal regulators announced that they would be more carefully monitoring mortgage lending advertisements. By this time, the damage to communities across the nation and the broader economy was well underway and irreversible.

Beware of scammers. In September 2008, during the near hysteria climate of the credit crunch, direct mail from some mortgage companies hit mail boxes that said "no credit check required" and "government program." These pieces were directed by companies desperate to secure some origination volume and specifically targeted veterans with fixed rate loans in order to offer them a slightly lower rate three year adjustable rate mortgage. There is no law that prohibits a veteran from refinancing a 30 year fixed rate loan into an adjustable rate mortgage. But, common sense and good judgment dictate that this type of marketing practice goes against sound reason and appears abusive rather than a bona fide financial service. In other words, corporate desperation led to what can only be labeled as predatory.

Credit checks are required. Those unsuspecting veterans who fell for this will be churned: repeatedly refinanced until they are "used up" as a manager once described those borrowers who no longer had equity as a result of being good, repeat customers. These veterans may save $50 to $75 per month and skip a payment after financing closing costs. The unethical and dishonest brokers, desperate to "build value" for the customer and originate more for themselves, may even verbally assure veterans that they were entitled to skip two or three payments after closing (when only one typically is permitted since all too often there is not enough money in the deal to offset the additional monthly payments). As a result, investors continued to take losses since a closed loan that had a 30- to 60-day-lates on the mortgage after settlement, or an early payment default, was worth 70 cents on the dollar and less. And, these unsuspecting veterans will see their credit scores drop as 90-day-lates on the mortgage hit their credit reports.

Do not believe all claims. The unexamined promotional claim is not worth pursuing. Instead, they should be investigated, and those responsible for issuing misleading promotional claims should be held accountable, which can only happen as consumers file complaints with the Federal Trade Commission, the media, and consumer advocacy groups; and post them online to social networking websites. The most common regulatory violation is when lenders advertise an interest rate without noting the annual percentage rate. Those ads are prohibited, because they are misleading. Consumers have the power to end rogue lender behavior when they are armed with information and act.

Chapter 6
The Placement

"We find that marketing works the way the grass grows.
You can never see it, but every week you have to mow the lawn."
—Andy Tarshis of the A.C. Nielsen Company[153]

Product placement is through wholesale, correspondent, or consumer direct retail channels. Banks and wholesalers representing Wall Street firms increasingly relied on brokers as outsourced origination for product placement. Well-capitalized large brokers use warehouse lines that enable them to function as correspondent lenders. This chapter will break down the role of placement in the mortgage lending industry.

The Wholesale Channel

Wholesale lending is the means through which large and small depository institutions, mortgage bankers, investment bankers, insurance companies, real estate investment trusts (sometimes referred to as REITS), private equity firms, and hedge funds outsource the availability of capital in order to increase their own origination volume, servicing portfolios, and fee income at a lower cost. Mortgage brokers, therefore, are credit intermediaries between consumers and many investors. Consequently, behind many retail lenders, there are numerous wholesale loan officers that provide guidance on the protocols for doing business with their company, underwriting guidelines, and even collateral marketing material.

Mortgage brokers do not use their own capital to fund a transaction. The key indication that a loan was brokered is that the loan will not fund in the name of the broker but will instead close in the investor's name as indicated on the settlement statement that itemizes closing costs. This fact will be evident as a line item on the Good Faith Estimate. Instead, mortgage brokers act as intermediaries between consumers and an array of strategic relationships with the previously mentioned financial institutions. As such, a mortgage broker is not owned by any other entity, but instead leverages relationships that enable a competitive advantage in the market place. This means the broker can play one price or program against another where all things are equal with the cost benefit accruing to the brokerage, the consumer, or both. Moreover, a mortgage broker will release servicing rights, or sell the loan through the yield spread premium or servicing release premium pricing mechanism, to the investor that funded the transaction. Finally, some mortgage industry analysts place a finer distinction on identifying and defining what constitutes a broker by placing the caveat that a large bank or financial organization does not use a warehouse line for over half of its origination volume, nor retain servicing rights. This is an important point for two reasons. First, the larger mortgage brokers have the capacity to function as a correspondent lender by using a warehouse line of credit from one or several strategic partners. Second, many financial institutions, not viewed as brokers by the public, in fact have the capacity to broker originations as well.[154]

Wholesale loan officers are know as account executives in the lending business. Account executives through their firm typically represent one or more investment banks, mortgage lenders, or depository institutions with a mortgage lending division. Account executives work with mortgage brokers, or loan officers at banks, to push loan products out to the public. A typical account executive may work with 40 mortgage broker offices and bank managers or more. As such, the account executive's role is to keep the accounts current with underwriting guidelines for the different product lines, provide wholesale rate sheets during the day, assist retail loan officers with prequalifying prospective borrowers, and provide problem resolution for loans in underwriting. Wholesalers service their accounts through periodic visits to brokers and banks, frequent e-mails, and occasional phone calls. Some wholesalers do not have any retail presence. As a result, they rely heavily on the broker channel for production. Others have up to four channels of production: mortgage brokers, correspondent lenders, retail lenders, and consumer direct lending.[155]

The systemic risk in the mortgage lending industry is tied to compensation alignment and the standard of due care, which means that account executives and loan officers are fiduciaries to the financial corporations for whom they work. They do not represent the borrower. In wholesale, the name of the game is volume and deal flow, not diligently training the network of loan officers or ensuring quality loans. It only takes one rogue accountant executive or one rogue loan officer to wreak havoc throughout the system. Moreover, it doe not take long for an insider to learn how to game the system, to work within the rules (typically an automated underwriting system or set of underwriting and price matrices) to get desired results even if a deal does not make financial sense to the customer.

According to a 2006 Wholesale Access study, there were approximately 53,000 mortgage brokerage companies that employed an estimated 270,000 loan officers in the United States.[156] The firm's founder David Olson noted that most mortgage offices employ only a handful of people and have a very limited market reach. Of the larger companies, only a few have a strong, continuous, and penetrating market presence in the major markets by virtue of aggressive televised advertising and direct mail campaigns. Countrywide, Ameriquest, Ditech, and Lending Tree, for example, were among the top names that come to mind due to how they saturated the televised advertising media. That said, borrowers tended to favor doing business with a mortgage company with a local presence. By Fall 2005, close to 65 percent of the nation's loan originations were coming through the wholesale channel.[157] This means mortgage brokers clearly dominated originations across the nation. By 2006, moreover, mortgage brokers grew their subprime market share to 63.3 percent, with the retail channel taking 19.4 percent, and correspondent lenders originating the remaining 17.4 percent of the subprime market.[158]

Olson said his firm conducted a study that indicated the reasons for the large broker share in the market as well as the lowered costs for lenders. Olson stated that:

> The wholesale-broker channel is the lower-cost production channel for lenders. The three main components of this lower cost are lower benefits, occupancy/office space, and overhead expenses. This explains brokers' growth and success in the past decade.[159]

Olson further observed that since there is little capital required to build a wholesale channel, there is little cost to eliminate it as well. "Using wholesale converts a fixed cost to a variable cost," said Olson.[160] From a cost management standpoint, lenders would be fiscally irresponsible not to wholesale and allow production to come in from nontraditional sources.

During the boom years, the A-paper side of the banker's house was more often than not kept separate from the subprime side of the house, which did the B-C-D paper loans. Since an increasing number of borrowers did not have strong ties to financial institutions and chose to work with brokers, brokers as a result originated more subprime loans than the banks, which tended to cater to those with an existing banking relationship. These factors help understand the strategic relationships and marketing efforts by the banks through the wholesale channel. This in turn explains why mortgage brokers had a large percentage of the overall origination volume during the boom.

The Correspondent Channel

The correspondent lending channel is what brokers seek from their strategic alliances with large lenders. A broker with large consistent volume that was within regulatory compliance can be delegated by the lender to underwrite and even fund closed loans more often than not using the lender's line of credit, which is referred to as a warehouse line. Jack Guttentag,[161] finance professor at the Wharton School of the University of Pennsylvania, said, "Under the law, the broker has morphed into a 'lender'—the type called 'correspondent lender.'"[162] A correspondent lender funds more than half of its mortgage originations using a warehouse line of credit that comes from one or numerous sources. Due to the high net worth requirement, smaller brokers cannot meet the requirements established by the big banks. As a correspondent, a lender retains more control over the transaction, enjoys better pricing, and closes the loan in its own name as indicated on the Good Faith Estimate. This is what larger mortgage brokers aspire to as their business develops since it results in more independence and control.

Due to the law, correspondents are not required to disclose yield spread premiums or service release premiums, but brokers are required to disclose. Instead, they are regarded as overages and there is no disclosure of such on the settlement statement. The large banks, however, limit overages through internal polices.[163] The capping on overages typically looks like this:

0.250% above market rate = 1 point in overage
0.500% above market rate = 2 points in overage
1.000% above market rate = 4 points in overage

If a lender is able to charge an additional one percent higher rate, either through a lack of customer shopping or through the competitive advantage it has due to having a unique loan product, then that translates into four points "on the back" in overages to the lender. On a $100,000 loan, four points "on the back" is $4,000 in compensation to the lender.

Regarding the seeming disparity on disclosure requirements in the law Guttentag said that:

> This has created a different set of disclosure rules for brokers and correspondent lenders, who are competitors, and much more alike than they are different. It has also created a wholly artificial incentive to pull brokers into larger entities, called "net branches," which are lenders and therefore don't have to disclose rebates.[164]

The problem here is not the amount of the overage, but the lack of transparency to the consumer since there is an increasing sense among regulators that the consumer has a right to know and decide.

The Retail Channel

The typical retail channel is the depository financial institution—mostly banks, thrifts, and credit unions, with a mortgage department. Some retail channels are strictly retail mortgage branch offices, sometimes adjacent to a real estate broker's office. Others are depository institutions as well. Retail lenders are those institutions consumers deal with directly. They can be either direct lenders, which tend to have limited product offerings, or brokers, which tend to aggregate the offerings of many direct lenders through the wholesale channel in order to offer consumers a fuller menu of products.

The typical mortgage broker operation across the United States during the boom was made up of an average of just seven people.[165] Other operations have either a regional or national presence. Small or large, they rely on the major lenders and investment banks wholesaling product as a means of outsourcing their own production volume.

Mortgage brokers have competitive rates by virtue of rate shopping all of their wholesalers' rates. Brokers can have a bad connotation if they do not know what they are doing. But, once an experienced mortgage broker demonstrates that he can close a loan that a bank cannot or will not do, the occasional negative stigma of brokers disappears because brokers have a lot more types of loans to offer than a bank and typically can offer a lower rate because their costs are cheaper. Moreover, as noted earlier, an insider can game the system while also staying compliant with the law. This simply means that an insider over time will uncover holes in an underwriting matrix or set of guidelines that can be exploited as a competitive advantage since, after all, the one eyed man is the king of the jungle, and customers demand "common sense" underwriting that takes their unique circumstances into account.

Politicians, working with talking points from the major lenders and banking associations, have placed the mortgage broker on the chopping block. In his October 15, 2007 article "Dead Man Walking—Wholesale Lending is Marching Towards Extinction,"[166] Morgan Brown pointed to several facts that suggest the writing is on the wall for the retail mortgage broker. Brown pointed to several wholesalers that have confided that their employers are anxious to end wholesale; strategic shifts, downsizing wholesale staff, increasing retail staff; wholesale production volumes are dropping at faster rates than drops in retail originations; and forward-looking statements by the big banks clearly state increasing direct-to-consumer channels.[167] Brown pointed to two compelling reasons for the likely seismic shift changes. First, there is a perception that investors may be willing to pay for the protection from retail originations provided that they can assure the underlying asset of the securities. This would suggest that an originated loan would be more rigorously quality controlled prior to funding and then becoming part of a security. The borrower's credit profile and income and assets would be verified. Moreover, an arms-length transaction in ordering an appraisal would not only ensure an objective reflection of the property's true market value, but the underwriter might even corroborate the appraised value by either ordering a field review or referring to an automated valuation model. Second, the public expects accountability. Mortgage brokers are the most vulnerable link in the financial chain to undergo more rigorous legislative and regulatory action.[168]

Olson countered some of Brown's points by noting that mortgage loans identically perform regardless of the origination channel when analyzed based on the FICO score, loan-to-value ratio, the property location, and the documentation type.[169] To illustrate, savvy mortgage brokers who follow different underwriting guidelines across the lending industry know how to work the system. Underwriters representing direct lenders and investment banks that are willing to accept unlimited 30-day lates on new Federal Housing Administration loans, for example, invite adverse selection from brokers since they will be flooded with applications that other lenders may shun. The broker will be in compliance of regulations and the law and earn his origination fees, but the lender will be stuck with the "sold with recourse" provision on the Federal Housing Administration loans that become Ginnie Mae securities. In this case, an increased incidence of early payment defaults would not be the result of the mortgage broker, but the result of the borrower, whose credit profile clearly indicated an inability or unwillingness to repay as agreed. Moreover, any mortgage broker can push the risk envelope by monitoring one's own as well as competitor default and foreclosure rates on originated government loans by following the U.S. Department of Housing and Urban Development's Neighborhood Watch database.[170] The nongovernment lenders and the general public can look on as well.[171]

Users of Neighborhood Watch can browse the website to find different metropolitan statistical areas and loan performances of different lenders, including the number of nonperforming loans, as well as the lenders that push that risk envelope as far as the U.S. Department of Housing and Urban Development permits. Going too far can result in U.S. Department of Housing and Urban Development cutting off a lender's ability to originate government loans for two years.

Should the death of the wholesale channel take place, it will kill the small retail mortgage broker operations—the result of the major lenders blame shifting their own poor underwriting decisions that resulted from an over reliance on technology, loosened standards, and inadequate due diligence on their part. No doubt, many mortgage brokers grew, produced significant volume, and contributed to the higher incidences of nonperforming loans. But, this was as much a result of some brokers working the system to the breaking point as much as it was due to the negligence of the bankers that worked with them as strategic partners.

To illustrate, Wachovia had a relationship with a broker-partner under investigation in both Georgia and Maryland for not having a license. It was not until media coverage came to play that the bank's liaison with the broker was terminated.[172] Without the media shining the light and grinding the axe of journalism, the money will decide how business is conducted.

In some cases, start-up capital and a desire to get into the business was all that was required for anyone to become a mortgage broker. Counterintuitive hiring practices that included bar room recruiting and blind ads placed in the employment section of papers that read: "Top commission paid, must be aggressive, no experience required, leads provided" provided a staff and a testosterone-driven work culture that featured 20-something-year-olds sporting tattoos. When we take that, along with inadequate in-house training from the broker-owner and a negligent wholesale account representative from the bank failing to do the hands-on training, we have the essential elements for widespread and first-rate incompetence. Couple this with incentive structure and compensation alignment, and we have the elements that make up the systemic risk of the lending industry.

In early 1990s, loan officers studied corporate tax financial analysis in order to originate loans for self-employed borrowers. Today, that skill level is virtually nonexistent at the retail origination level in the lending industry. Stated income, or Alt-A, and bank statement programs have instead taken the place of the due diligence that was once required. The benchmark used by many underwriters to check on the applicant for stated income loans instead is the 75th income percentile at Salary.com. This percentile represents the higher end, not the middle range, for compensation paid within a geographical area for a given position.[173]

One of the major lenders in a May 2008 credit risk seminar noted that they found that four times the credit losses came from the wholesale channel, or loans originated by mortgage brokers. In comparison, two times the credit losses came from the correspondent channel. How do we account for brokers doing more high-risk loans? Was it due to the originate-to-distribute model? Or fraud? Or a host of factors that embedded systemic risk and that dovetailed together?

These findings make sense when we consider that some brokers focused their marketing outreach efforts towards low-credit score borrowers, who had higher credit risk profiles. Many of these borrowers were minorities with weak or non-existent relationships with traditional depository institutions. Moreover, mortgage brokers were much more aggressive and/or innovative in getting loans approved for their borrowers than their counter parts at the big banks. Brokers accessed the loan programs of multiple lenders, they know how to game the system, and many were in legal compliance. Some bank loan officers may not feel an obligation to help the borrower out due to compensation alignment. Brokers, on the other hand, work for the borrower and know that if they can not get the loan closed, they will not get paid. [174] Not every broker, however, focused on borrowers with just low credit scores. Wholesale mortgage firms concentrating on subprime and Alt-A loans usually had no retail network but relied totally on brokers. The difference in financial losses across the industry derives from the fact that brokers tended to do more high-risk loans than did the other channels.[175]

Concluding Thoughts

I again conclude with a series of brief discussions. These are focused on how the big banks use different lending channels to reach as many customers as possible. These ideas may be new. Please consider these as reminders.

There are three lending channels. The three channels—wholesale, correspondent, and retail—together account for the means by which mortgage loan products are placed in the marketplace. While there are clear definitions that distinguish one type of lender from another, overlaps are common in the industry. Mortgage brokers, however, had a competitive market place advantage over their retail bank counterparts by virtue of having access to a wide array of loan products. Moreover, they reached out to underserved populations, which tended to not have strong relationships with depository institutions. Since the system in place across the industry was designed to incentivize profit in the form of the yield spread premium, adverse selection should be understood as business opportunity that was driven by the loan officer acting as a fiduciary to the corporation. Consequently some brokers applied adverse selection in program and pricing and thereby placed both borrowers and their investors at greater risk of loss. Any systemic risk built into this loan selection process among brokers was rooted in the originate-to-distribute model, whereby the broker assumed little to no risk since risk was passed on to investors.

Brokers are headed towards extinction. The significant diminishment of the wholesale channel after the boom was as much due to retail lenders shifting blame onto mortgage brokers as it was due to retail lenders failing as a result of underestimating and mismanaging risk. Had the major retail banks and strictly wholesale operations exercised greater control over training mortgage brokers and engaging in more rigorous quality control of brokered loans, risk of loss could have been mitigated. The risk mitigation solution that many banks exercised after the boom was to close down their wholesale operations and make up for the volume that otherwise would have been driven by brokers through the Internet.

In the fog of war, there is an acute sense of ambiguity and confusion. There is a significant difference between seeking accountability for contractual and regulatory compliance and creating a fall guy—a bogeyman—to appease an angered public and policy makers after the boom. As we will later see, a lot of blame shifted away from the retail banks and Wall Street's investment banks and it was instead placed onto mortgage brokers, the Community Reinvestment Act, and minority borrowers. We will see that the problems that started in Wall Street with predatory securitization ended on Wall Street with a global credit crunch.

Chapter 7
Key Market Players

> *"Lead, follow, or get out of the way."*
> —Chrysler's 1992 Ad Campaign, Lee Iacocca

Year after year, the same key players have almost always controlled the message, set the tone, and thereby controlled the mortgage market. This chapter will briefly survey the key market players in the mortgage lending business. Here, we will break everything down by overall originator volumes, size of the markets, and the product types that fly off of the shelves. A word to the reader on these points: just because a lender ranks number one in production, it does not necessarily mean that they are number one in customer service or in delivering the most suitable problem free loan products to customers.

Top Originators

The problem with the lending industry is that it is like a pack of huskies pulling the rest of the industry along with consumers sitting in the sled. Unless you are the lead dog, the view is always the same. Each year during the boom, the same four mortgage lenders vied for market dominance: Calabasas, California-based Countrywide Financial Corporation, Des Moines, Iowa-based Wells Fargo Home Mortgage, Seattle, Washington-based Washington Mutual, and Iselin, New Jersey-based Chase Home Finance. Together, these companies originated and funded more than 42 percent of the home loans in the United States in 2005. Large financial institutions like Charlotte, North Carolina-based Bank of America and O'Fallon, Missouri-based CitiMortgage Inc., while jointly controlling about nine percent of market in 2005, were lesser players in the greater scheme of things. With two of the largest financial institutions controlling so little market share, we can to some extent infer that not only were they really not in the mortgage business during the boom, but they had other revenue streams as part of the their core business model.

Table 7.1 shows the top ten originators and ranks the country's leading mortgage lenders for 2005 and 2004, posts the origination volume for each, lists each company's market share, and notes the change in origination volume from one year to the next. Countrywide's staggering 35 percent growth from 2004 to 2005 was more than likely due to its relentless campaign of nonstop televised advertising coupled with programs and interest rates that more prudent lenders would not bother to compete against. For the same period, Chase lost seven percent of its origination volume, which more than likely was due to holding to sound underwriting practices rather than ineffective marketing.

Table 7.1 – Top Ten Originators

Lender	2005 12 Months	Share	2004 12 Months	% Change
No. 1 Countrywide	$490.95	15.70%	$363.01	35.20%
No. 2 Wells Fargo	$392.33	12.60%	$298.46	31.50%
No. 3 Washington Mutual	$248.83	8.00%	$255.35	-2.60%
No. 4 Chase	$183.49	5.90%	$197.35	-7.00%
No. 5 Bank of America	$158.82	5.10%	$146.63	8.30%
No. 6 CitiMortgage	$124.29	4.00%	$103.21	20.40%
No. 7 GMAC	$91.54	2.90%	$87.45	4.70%
No. 8 Ameriquest	$79.68	2.60%	$82.70	-3.70%
No. 9 GMAC-RFC	$64.27	2.10%	$44.13	45.60%
No. 10 IndyMac	$60.77	1.90%	$37.90	60.4%
Top Ten Volume	$1,834.20		$1,578.29	
Total Market Volume	**$3,120.00**		**$2,920.00**	

(For 12 months; dollars in billions)
Data Source: Inside Mortgage Finance Publications, Inc.

During the boom, mortgage brokers with a nationwide presence included companies like Houston, Texas-based Allied Home Mortgage Capital Corporation, San Rafael, California-based Residential Mortgage Capital, Anaheim Hills, California-based Windsor Capital Mortgage, Charlotte, North Carolina-based 1st Metropolitan Mortgage, and Centerville, Virginia-based Carteret Mortgage Corporation. While there were many more, it is sufficient for the purpose of this discussion to recognize how companies like these fit into the overall scheme of things within the mortgage lending industry. These types of companies tend to have numerous offices across the country. While smaller brokers are local and sell all servicing rights on the loans that they originate, these larger players in the aggregate funnel massive production volumes into both the broker and correspondent channels to the major lenders and investment banks. Some retain servicing rights due to their ability to operate as a correspondent.

At the market's peak in 2005, Allied Home Mortgage originated $15 billion in mortgages, which was up from $12 billion in 2004 making it the nation's largest mortgage broker.[176] 1st Metropolitan grew by acquiring Olympia Funding, and for 2004 the merged company had just over $6 billion in production.[177] Residential Mortgage Capital funded $5.5 billion in 2005. Windsor Capital Mortgage funded $4.7 billion in 2005. Carteret funded $3.4 billion in 2005.[178] With mortgage brokers, not all companies report data since many of the companies are privately held.

Carteret filed for Chapter 7 on October 1, 2008. Though it had grown to $4 billion in originations by 2006, the threat of at least seven lawsuits alleging breach of contract, predatory lending, and fraud forced the company to close.[179] These lawsuits also named the broker's wholesalers, or mortgage bankers, as defendants since they allegedly enabled Carteret to conduct business.

Production Channels

The three mortgage lending production channels—wholesale, correspondent, and retail—make up the mortgage lending sector. Table 7.2 shows that volume peaked in 2005 with $3.12 trillion in originations. Direct lenders originated more than 39 percent, brokers originated 31.3 percent, and correspondent lenders originated the remaining 29.5 percent of the industry's lending volume. The country's large regional and national brokers contributed to the broker and correspondent share of originations.

Table 7.2 – Originations by Channel

Year	Retail	Broker	Correspondent	Total
2001	$850	$645	$720	$2,215
2002	$1,185	$845	$588	$2,618
2003	$1,622	$1,104	$1,219	$3,945
2004	$1,205	$903	$812	$2,920
2005	$1,224	$976	$920	$3,120
2006	$1,120	$880	$980	$2,980
2007	$1,047	$686	$696	$2,429

(Dollars in billions)
Data Source: Inside Mortgage Finance Publications, Inc.

Market Share

There is a different market share in the mortgage lending production channels during the boom years. Table 7.3 shows the mortgage industry's market share by retail, broker, and correspondent lending channels. Wholesale lending is a combination of both the broker and correspondent channels.

As noted in Table 7.3, the wholesale channel produced between 58.7 percent of the loans originated in 2004 and 60.8 percent in 2005. By 2006, when underwriting standards had dropped at the big retail and investment banks, the wholesale channel churned out 62.4 percent of all loans originated in the United States.

Table 7.3 – Market Share

Year	Retail	Broker	Correspondent	Wholesale
2001	38.4%	29.1%	32.5%	61.6%
2002	41.1%	29.3%	29.6%	58.9%
2003	41.1%	28.0%	30.9%	58.9%
2004	41.3%	30.9%	27.8%	58.7%
2005	39.2%	31.3%	29.5%	60.8%
2006	37.6%	29.5%	32.9%	62.4%
2007	43.1%	28.2%	28.6%	56.8%

Data Source: Inside Mortgage Finance Publications, Inc.

In hindsight, several inferences can be drawn from this. As lending volume declined to $2.98 trillion for 2006, more direct lenders made a greater push for volume through the wholesale channel using brokers since that is a lower cost channel for the banks. Brokers, in turn, welcomed the opportunity for the banks, as well as other sources, to provide them with a broader array of products to offer to their customers. At this key juncture, mortgage brokers in 2006 dominated the mortgage lending business given several competitive advantages. Lower overhead cost was certainly a key advantage. Marketing to populations with weak relationships with depository institutions was another. Whether there was a cultural lag of a distrust of banks lingering from the Great Depression from the dinnertime stories or the preemptive conclusion from some consumers that banks would deny their loan applications, consumers increasingly turned to mortgage brokers as these numbers clearly suggest. Moreover, a rich product mix was a contributing factor for brokers gaining a competitive advantage over retail banks and mortgage lenders.

Purchase and Refinance Volume

The mortgage market during the boom was split between purchases and refinances, as shown in Table 7.4. The breakout of the overall origination volume is a function of a combination of factors that include interest rates, product availability, underwriting standards, and marketing.

Table 7.4 – Refinances and Mortgages

Year	Refinances	Purchases	Total
2001	$1,298	$917	$2,215
2002	$1,821	$1,064	$2,885
2003	$2,839	$1,106	$3,945
2004	$1,510	$1,410	$2,920
2005	$1,572	$1,548	$3,120
2006	$1,460	$1,520	$2,980
2007	$1,262	$1,168	$2,430

(Dollars in billions)
Data Source: Inside Mortgage Finance Publications, Inc.

As noted earlier, traditional loan officers at both the banks and brokers tend to focus on purchase business. Call centers tend to focus on refinance business. In 2003, 72 percent of the origination volume was refinance activity. Due to staff shortages and high call volumes, callers stayed on hold for considerable periods if they wanted their loan applications taken. Table 7.4 suggests that the mortgage lending industry succeeded in getting homeowners to refinance in record volumes, which rolled mortgages back to a new starting point, increased loan balances, and did all of this for the benefit of the financial sector.

Product Origination Volume

In 2003, agency loans had peaked with $2.46 trillion in originations and government loans made up $220 billion in originations. Together they dominated 76 percent of the entire mortgage market with the remaining 24 percent going to the private labeled market made up of firms on Wall Street.[180] As noted earlier, these are loans that tend to have escrows included as part of the total monthly payments. They come in all shapes and varieties and statistically they tend to have low default rates. After 2003, it was downhill for Fannie Mae, Freddie Mac, and government loans since subprime, Alt-A, and home equity line of credit loans eroded their share of the market with the help of Wall Street's wholesalers, broker promotion, and customer demand in part driven by a general lack of financial disciple as reflected by household savings. Subprime securitizations peaked at about $800 billion per year. In 2004 alone, Wall Street's investment banking firms paid out $8.4 billion in bonuses. By 2006, agency and government loans had dropped to 43 percent of total originations with the balance of 57 percent going to the private labeled market.[181] As of mid-2008, Fannie Mae and Freddie Mac owned or guaranteed $5 trillion in American mortgages, which was almost half of the nation's outstanding mortgage debt, as shown in Table 7.5.[182]

Table 7.5 – Mortgage Origination by Product

Year	Gov't	Agency	Jumbo	Subprime	Alt-A	HELOC	Total
2001	$175	$1,265	$445	$160	$55	$115	$2,215
2002	$176	$1,706	$571	$200	$67	$165	$2,885
2003	$220	$2,460	$650	$310	$85	$220	$3,945
2004	$130	$1,210	$510	$530	$185	$355	$2,920
2005	$90	$1,090	$570	$625	$380	$365	$3,120
2006	$80	$990	$480	$600	$400	$430	$2,980
2007	$101	$1,162	$347	$191	$275	$355	$2,431

(Dollars in billions)
Data Source: Inside Mortgage Finance Publications, Inc.

Subprime originations, reached 20 percent of the total origination volume by 2005, as shown in Figure 7.1. That is one out of every five borrowers. Many borrowers elected to take an adjustable rate mortgage since the rate was about one percent lower than the 30-year fixed rate. Since there was a cost to buy out the prepayment penalty if that was available from the lender, many borrowers reluctantly accepted what has become regarded as one of the most onerous and predatory of loan terms. By 2005, Wall Street's appetite for high-yielding subprime-backed securities peaked resulting in 81 percent of subprime loans that were originated that year were securitized and sold to private-labeled investors in the secondary market. While some policy makers mistakenly believed that this significant growth in subprime market share by mortgage brokers was due to the weak regulations governing them, it in fact was due to Wall Street's network of wholesalers and its appetite for risky debt with the promise of high yield.[183] The significant growth and concentration of subprime mortgage loans were concentrated in the corridor between the Boston to Washington, D.C. metropolitan statistical areas, the Florida panhandle, Las Vegas, and much of California.[184]

Jumbo loans made up the following 18 percent of the market. In mid-May 2002, there was $424 billion in outstanding jumbo loans in the United States.[185] These are non-agency loans more than $417,001 that ended up in the private labeled market. Close to half are in California due to that state's high cost of housing. The other high-cost states include Maryland, Virginia, New Jersey, Montana, Washington, New York, Connecticut, Massachusetts, and Maine. In June-July 2005, between 9.7 percent and 22.2 percent of all mortgages in these states were jumbo loans.[186]

These figures, however, underestimate the concentration of large mortgage balances in these states. When possible, borrowers often combined a conforming first mortgage balance with a second mortgage, which when combined approached $521,250. This means that with 100 percent financing, second mortgage balances behind the maximum conforming loan limit of $417,000 would be $104,250. The California and Florida markets alone accounted for 44.5 percent of the nation's piggy-backed lending[187] where simultaneous closings on first and second mortgages enabled cash-strapped borrowers, who overleveraged, to finance their mortgage debt in these high-cost states.

Alt-A, or stated income loans as well as no documentation loans, accounted for 12 percent of the overall market. Many of these loans went to self-employed borrowers, because of the difficulty for them to qualify under traditional underwriting guidelines. Since these borrowers may have seen themselves at a competitive disadvantage in the purchase market, or due to their own perceived need to borrower more, many overstated their incomes. This income overstatement placed them and their lenders at greater risk.

Home equity line of credit loans came in at 12 percent of the overall originations. These were stand alone first mortgages, second mortgages in a refinance, and also combined to be part of an 80/20 or 80/15 purchase or refinance where both a first and second mortgage were combined to become known as piggy back financing. These loans, as noted earlier, were fine when originated given the lower payments coming from relatively low rates. But, because home equity line of credit loans are adjustable rate mortgages, these loans pose risks to both lenders and borrowers given that as rates upwardly adjust, so do the payments. That, in turn, invariably causes an increase in loan nonperformance. As the market changed and home prices started dropping, most lenders froze the home equity line of credit loans, leaving their borrowers in a lurch. That meant homeowners could no longer tap the account to draw cash. That posed a significant problem to self-employed homeowners, who need these credit facilities—just like any other business—to fund their day-to-day operations.

Finally, Federal Housing Administration and Veterans Administration government loans made up a mere 3 percent of the market. The Federal Housing Administration was the horse that dragged the United States out of the Great Depression. This was the loan that helped countless first-time homebuyers buy their first homes. And, it was the number one loan of choice for marginal borrowers looking to refinance since they could get A-paper rates even if they were an A-minus, B- or C-rated borrower given their overall credit profile. Similarly, Veterans Administration loans grew prohibitive in cost and only made sense if the credit profile dictated that there were no other better options, or if the veteran was disabled, because the funding fee was waived in that instance. In a seller's market, which is what the United States experienced at the peak of the boom, there was no good business reason—other than patriotism—for a seller to be willing to sell their home under a Veterans Administration loan where the seller picked up closing costs. In the hot markets, ten to 20 people lined up and had their agents in some cases write offers sight unseen and were willing to buy the property in "as is" condition. In that type of market, government loans were less likely to be considered due to added requirements imposed by the U.S. Department of Housing and Urban Development and the Veterans Administration. So, 2005 ended with the government loan virtually on its deathbed. Those real estate agents acting as a buyer's agent—a fiduciary for the buyer who counseled them to buy a home sight unseen or in "as is" condition—more than likely found themselves in difficult to defend legal complaints after the bubble burst.

Another way to visualize the distribution of mortgage loan size distribution across the United States for 2006. The majority of the loans in the country cluster in the low $100,000 range. The small peak at $417,000 is the result of agency policy that limits the conforming loan size. Though the number of loans tapper off at $600,000, there are plenty of super jumbo loans outstanding in excess of $1 million.

Fixed Rate and ARM Volume

Table 7.6 may not exactly tell how the neighbors handled their mortgage financing during the boom, but it does break the market down into fixed rate and adjustable loans. In 2004, the split was close to 50-50, which indicates either a neutral predisposition toward loan type or a consumer perception held by half of the market that a short-term adjustable rate mortgage was safe given the belief that rates would hold steady, home prices would continue upward, and that they could again refinance. In other words, the market place's 19 percent acceptance of adjustable rate mortgages in 2001 grew in part due to consumers' perception of this particular mortgage loan as just another commodity that could be traded in again and again with the transaction costs associated with each refinance offset by the increased appreciation of real estate prices. This was the conventional wisdom that was reinforced into the public psyche by the Federal Reserve and loan officers across the United States.

Table 7.6 – Fixed Rate and ARMs

Year	Fixed	ARMs	Total
2001	$1,860	$355	$2,215
2002	$2,206	$679	$2,885
2003	$2,911	$1,034	$3,945
2004	$1,456	$1,464	$2,920
2005	$1,630	$1,490	$3,120
2006	$1,640	$1,340	$2,980
2007	$1,706	$724	$2,430

(Dollars in billions)
Data Source: Inside Mortgage Finance Publications, Inc.

A Deutsche Bank in New York study suggested that in 2005, about $80 billion, or one percent of the entire market, of mortgage debt would migrate to adjustable rate mortgages due to lower interest rates. By, 2006, however, some $300 billion of mortgage debt was projected to be adjustable rate mortgages.[188] The same study suggested that by 2007, $1 trillion in United States mortgage debt would be in adjustable rate mortgages, thus making up 12 percent of the market. In response to the trend observed by the global bank, Freddie Mac's deputy chief economist Amy Crews Cutts said, "I'm not sure that people are being counseled on really how big of a risk they are taking."[189] It did not help any given that in a 2004 speech, former Federal Reserve chairman Greenspan suggested that borrowers would benefit from adjustable rate mortgages, especially given that mortgage rates were then at a forty-year historical low point.[190] In other words, the general public would have been better off had borrowers in droves had stuck with their earlier hunches and had said: "The experts are idiots. I'll stick with a fully amortized fixed rate loan, thank you very much." With fewer adjustable rate mortgage adjustments in the pipeline, there would have been fewer foreclosures devastating every community.

The Stampede of the Marketplace

The loans sold to Freddie Mac indicate an alarming trend across the United States between 2001 and 2007. This agency's analysis[191] as noted in Table 7.7 of cash out transactions during the boom indicate that a progressively increasing number of homeowners—86 percent—took 5 percent or more in cash when they refinanced in 2006. That same year, only 5 percent of homeowners were paying their mortgages down when they refinanced by putting cash into the deal at closing. Moreover, in 2006, home appreciation rates across the United States averaged a record 31 percent per year, which gave borrowers the false sense that they could keep withdrawing increasing amounts of cash from their home's equity.

Table 7.7 – Cash-Out Refinances During the Boom
Percentage of Refinances Resulting in: Descriptive Statistics on Loan Terms and Property Valuation

Year	5% Higher Loan Amount[1]	Lower Loan Amount	Median Age of Refinanced Loan (years)	Median Appreciation of Refinanced Property
2001	53%	14%	2.6	15%
2002	47%	18%	3.0	13%
2003	36%	16%	1.8	5%
2004	47%	15%	2.1	10%
2005	72%	9%	2.6	23%
2006	86%	5%	3.2	31%
2007	82%	6%	3.5	24%

Source: Freddie Mac

[1]Higher loan amount refers to loan amounts that were at least 5 percent greater than the amortized unpaid principal balance of the original loan. "Lower loan amount" refers to loan amounts that were less than the amortized unpaid principal balance of the original loan.

When Winners Are Losers

Almost every player in the financial sector financially suffered and damaged their reputations as a result of underestimating and mispricing risk, taking on too much risk, and then mismanaging those risks. Most academic text books on financial management would describe it in those banal terms. Most onlookers, however, would prefer to say, that the industry's key players suffered from unfettered greed enabled by those on Capitol Hill who received ample campaign contributions and were then controlled by lobbyists, who dictated one-sided bills that became laws that placed American households and the economy in peril.

Illustration by David Dees

The last man standing phenomenon in the mortgage lending industry resulted in two distinct problems. The first problem was continued fraud that was cloaked as excessive risk taking at the expense of the industry. The second problem was greater consolidation in the mortgage lending industry, which resulted in less competition for consumers and a concentration of risk to the economy among the surviving too big to fail banks.

First, the market dramatically shifted towards Federal Housing Administration financing. Some of those lenders that carved out a niche for themselves by doing the tough to do deals eventually went under. Ocala, Florida-based Taylor Bean & Whitaker Mortgage Corporation secured a competitive edge during and after the boom due to Federal Housing Administration manual underwriting. By approving Federal Housing Administration loans that most lenders would not underwrite, Taylor Bean & Whitaker was able to continue operations until August 4, 2009 when the U.S. Department of Housing and Urban Development terminated its ability to originate and underwrite Federal Housing Administration loans. In the aftermath, Ginnie Mae took control of Taylor Bean & Whitaker's $25 billion Ginnie Mae portfolio. The U.S. Department of Housing and Urban Development posted on its website:

> Taylor, Bean & Whitaker failed to submit a required annual financial report and misrepresented that there were no unresolved issues with its independent auditor even though the auditor ceased its financial examination after discovering certain irregular transactions that raised concerns of fraud. The Federal Housing Administration's suspension is also based on Taylor, Bean & Whitaker's failure to disclose, and its false certifications concealing, that it was the subject of two examinations into its business practices in the past year.[192]

While manual underwriting does not imply fraud, this lender's business conduct apparently suggested to the U.S. Department of Housing and Urban Development that Taylor, Bean & Whitaker was engaged in the type of conduct that defined the majority of the lending industry between 2001 and 2007. Since Taylor, Bean & Whitaker's business model was tied to Federal Housing Administration, it shut down, and everyone lost their jobs. Mortgage industry recruiters came to the rescue, and some, no doubt ended up at the many loan modification call centers across the country to fix the loans they should not have approved.

Second, by the first quarter of 2009, the mortgage broker share of origination volume dropped to 14.9 percent. This was the direct result of Wall Street blame shifting and Capitol Hill accepting its version of the marketplace. Mergers among different firms reshaped the landscape in residential mortgage lending with stronger companies acquiring failed companies. Consider the following summarized partial highlights given Table 7:1:

Citi took over Ameriquest's $45 billion loan portfolio of mostly fraudulently originated loans in September 2007, which proved to be financially catastrophic. Ameriquest paid out $325 million in a class action settlement for predatory lending. Citi looked to sovereign wealth funds that doled out $12.5 billion to recapitalize its failing firm until tax payer-funded government assistance ended the sale of this American-based corporation to the Middle East. Investor lawsuits followed that alleged Citi had hidden risks and misled investors. Citi accessed $45 billion through the Troubled Asset Relief Program, $25 billion in October 28, 2008 and $20 billion on November 23, 2008. In an act of largess, the federal government—not the Federal Reserve, which is supposed to be the back stop to member banks—agreed to absorb losses on some of the $301 billion in fraudulent, predatory, and non-performing loans that Citi had originated, purchased, and serviced. On January 16, 2009, an additional $5 billion was committed as an asset backstop. Taken together, Citi was the biggest looser of the bunch taking 28.8 percent of federal government assistance. That does not take into account $10 billion committed by the Federal Deposit Insurance Corporation and $220 billion committed by the Federal Reserve. The firm contributed to the national unemployment problem between 2008 and 2009 by terminating 75,000 positions. J.D. Power and Associates rated Citi (CitiFinancial / CitiMortgage / Citibank) as being among the worst mortgage loan servicers in the lending industry for 2008.[193] At its heights, Citi was a global phenomenon. In the aftermath of its crash, Citi planned to scale back to a 1,001 branches in six major United States cities making it the least significant player among the big banks in the United States banking arena. Given the financial factors alone—a $280 billion hole, Citi became a zombie bank like those that defined the Japanese real estate and economic crisis that started in 1997. After the firm fired so much of its staff in an attempt to cut its operating costs, Citi resorted to paying for round trip airfares for prospective new hires in a desperate attempt to rehire staff after it had acquired funds from the federal government to remain solvent.[194]

Bank of America took over Countrywide Financial Corporation in July 2008 for $4.1 billion, acquired $25.4 billion in Option ARMs and $32.3 billion in home equity line of credit loans (mostly in California), and assumed all of its legal liabilities, which proved to be financially catastrophic and damaging to its otherwise solid brand name. Bank of America then acquired Merrill Lynch & Company for $50 billion on September 15, 2008, and again damaged its reputation in connection with the alleged use of tax payer money to pay $3.6 billion in bonuses when Merrill Lynch had lost money. Countrywide was hit with an $8.6 billion class action complaint for predatory lending. Bank of America attempted to settle with the Securities and Exchange Commission for $33 million in connection with harm to shareholders, but its offer was considered unfair and therefore rejected. On October 28, 2008 Bank of America sold $15 billion in stock to the government. On January 9, 2009 Bank of America took another $10 billion from the government in stock sales tied to Merrill Lynch. On January 16, 2009 Bank of America sold the federal government more of its stock for $20 billion. Bank of America received 25.9 percent of the federal bailout money. In addition, the federal government also guaranteed to limit Bank of America's losses on its $118 billion worth of mortgages. The U.S. Treasury committed an additional $7.5 billion, the Federal Deposit Insurance Corporation committed $2.5 billion, and the Federal Reserve pledged up to $87.2 billion. In January of 2008, Countrywide had cut 10,900 jobs. By December of 2008, Bank of America planned to cut up to 35,000 jobs. J.D. Power and Associates rated the Countrywide segment as being among the worst mortgage loan servicers in the lending industry for 2008.[195] So, the bank dropped the Countrywide brand name. Bank of America denied its shareholders criticial material facts during the Merrill Lynch acquisition, which resulted in shareholder-driven litigation.[196] Among the many issues was the fact that there was no disclosure to investors that in 2008 Bank of America paid $5.8 billion in bonuses while losing $27.6 billion the same year. On August 10, 2009, U.S. District

Court for the Southern District of New York Judge Jed S. Rakoff struck down a $33 million agreement negotiated between Bank of America and the Securities and Exchange Commission. On February 22, 2010, Rakoff revised the settlement to a $150 million fine, which at the time made it the largest on record for the Securities and Exchange Commission. The proceeds from the fine will be distributed to defrauded shareholders.

J.P. Morgan Chase acquired Bear Stearns, an investor in subprime mortgage-backed securities, in March 2008 for $240 million with the Federal Reserve Bank of New York assuming $30 billion in liability from the bad securities. J.P. Morgan Chase then took over Washington Mutual in September 2008 for $1.8 billion and acquired $52.9 billion in Option ARMs. With the Washington Mutual acquisition came all of the fraudulent appraisals, which supported the fraudulently originated loans that caused the New York Attorney General to accuse Washington Mutual of dictating home values of 260,000 of eAppraiseIT's appraisals between April 2006 and September 2007 in order to fund loans. On October 28, 2008 J.P. Morgan Chase took $25 billion from the Troubled Asset Relief Program. On April 13 and July 31, 2009 the government committed $3.4 billion to J.P. Morgan Chase for loan modifications.

Wells Fargo took over Wachovia in December 2008 for $15.4 billion, and acquired a massive portfolio of $122 billion in Option ARMs—448,000 loans with an average balance of $271,000. Wells Fargo agreed to absorb up to $42 billion in losses with the government absorbing the rest. Then the minority borrowers in Los Angeles, the City of Baltimore, the State of Illinois, Memphis, and Tennessee's Shelby County sued Wells Fargo on charges of reverse redlining, a violation of the Fair Housing Act. On October 28, 2008 Wells Fargo took $25 billion from the Troubled Asset Relief Program. On April 13, 2009, the federal government committed $2.5 billion for Wells Fargo to do loan modifications. On July 1 and 29, 2009 the federal government committed $1.45 billion to Wachovia for loan modifications.

GMAC is unlike the other leading mortgage lenders, because it is a financial sector subsidiary of General Motors—the Detroit, Michigan-based car maker. On November 30, 2006, General Motors sold off a 51 percent interest in GMAC to Cerberus Capital Management, L.P. On December 24, 2008, the Federal Reserve Board approved GMAC as a bank holding company under the Bank Holding Company Act. On December 29, 2008, GMAC sold the federal government stock in exchange for $5 billion. On May 21, 2009, GMAC sold the federal government stock in exchange for $7.5 billion. Both transactions were associated with auto financing. On April 13, 2009 the federal government committed $3.6 billion to GMAC for loan modifications.

The best analysis and commentary came not from the mainstream or financial media, but from stock brokers and industry analysts, who ripped into bank chief executive officers and the government-driven intervention in the free market due to the obvious consequences for employees, shareholders, customers, the industry, and the broader economy. Chief executive officers had promised shareholders that solid, well performing Option ARMs would propel stock prices to dizzying heights. They lied. And, the opposite happened. Securities-related lawsuits followed. Industry analysts forecasted that the entire financial sector would have a negative capital base—it would be entirely bankrupt—by 2010, but the industry was about a year ahead of schedule. The end result was more lawsuits, damaged reputations, and financial challenges that would require liberalized changes in accounting rules so that earnings and assets could be presented in a manner favorable to nervous investors. Moreover, the landscape of the financial sector was reshaped to resemble that of the 1920s when the depository function and the investment banking function of a financial institution were under one roof. In the creative destruction of the subprime meltdown of 2007 and Panic of 2008, the financial sector came full circle to a place it had never wanted to leave—those conditions that had led to the Great Depression.

Concluding Thoughts

I again conclude with a series of discussions. These address the largest lenders by volume and how they influence the marketplace and consumer behavior. Please consider this as your food for thought check list.

Marketplace dominance cuts both ways. In any business sector, being king of the hill like Countrywide Home Loans means that a firm can exert what economists and the Security and Exchange Commission refer to as market power. This is the chilling ability to control the market through prices and products at the expense of competitors and consumers.

Originate by any means necessary. Mortgage lending made up of 60 percent of consumer lending and 76 percent of outstanding mortgage debt at the end of 2007. The implications of the American household's need for credit was met with aggressive marketing by lenders fighting for more market share. The big banks originated about one-third of the mortgages with the balance going to their outsourced production channels—correspondent lenders and mortgage brokers.

Borrower behavior is telling. Purchase and refinance activity during the boom years indicates household behavior. In 2003, especially, refinances drove the mortgage lending industry, which suggests that heavy marketing, low interest rates, and the opportunity to convert equity into cash enticed American households to roll the mortgage clock back to a 30 year or longer term.

Customer-driven choice in mortgage lending is a myth. Subprime, Alt-A, and home equity line of credit products incrementally dominated the marketplace year after year. Given the choice, if a better mortgage product was made available, informed borrowers would not have made these poor choices in such record-breaking numbers. These choices provided to households were industry-driven for the industry's benefit at the household's expense.

Risks are taken when rewards are perceived. Households increasingly resorted to adjustable rate mortgages knowing that interest rate adjustments posed a potential financial risk. That risk was offset by the belief that home prices would continue to rise, and that either another refinance or the sale of the home could take place to avert the risk.

Cash out refinances are telling. The dramatic increase in cash out refinances after 2004 suggests households in record number were desperate for more credit, because they did not have the cash needed for their living expenses. Advertising and marketing played a role in shaping consumer perception towards equity and avoided any reference to the benefits of having no mortgage at all, which results in far more disposable income. Changing economic conditions, however, served to support the arguments that banks made with households.

Competition is essential. More companies in the marketplace breed innovation and better service provided that there is no industry-wide collusion or conspiracy against the consumer to stifle competition. When market conditions changed, consolidations followed, which resulted in fewer lenders to compete. The trend by the big banks is to shut down the broker and correspondent lending channels. That change in the marketplace will completely stifle consumer choice.

Too big to fail. Industry-wide consolidations created fewer, but larger, "too big to fail" banks. This chilling phenomenon means that when the next round of bank failures takes place, the impact on the broader economy will be worse. The obvious answer for customers and investors is to take preemptive action and terminate the relationships with the too big to fail zombie banks.

In the financial sector losers are winners. The big banks that originated and securitized all of the subprime loan with predatory features undermined the American household and the economy. According to the Center for Public Integrity, at least 21 of the top 25 of the big banks that received federal funds to offer the Home Affordable Modification Program to their struggling customer were leading subprime lenders.[197] The federal government, in other words, paid these lenders to modify and the government subsidized the mortgages of the borrowers that these banks had taken advantage of and defrauded.

Fannie Mae still securitizes subprime. Federal Reserve Bank of New York filled the gap after the collapse of the secondary market in July 2007, and purchased between 80 to 100 percent of all Fannie Mae and Ginnie Mae-issued securities with debt-to-income ratios of 50 percent. Subprime loans were perceived to be the problem in the mortgage lending industry, but that never meant that subprime lending ended.

Chapter 8

Real Estate Niches

> *"It's tangible, it's solid, it's beautiful.*
> *It's artistic, from my standpoint, and I just love real estate."*
> —Donald Trump

Warren Buffett's approach to investing is to stay within a defined circle of confidence. This means to only invest in what can be understood. Even when working with a tangible asset like real estate, this may not always be easy. The clarity of thinking can be clouded when mixed signals pour in from the media suggesting the market is headed south, from the business media saying that investors are doing well, or from local experts speaking to specifics of their areas of expertise.

A lack of clarity of thought also can come from homeowners overindulging themselves, as wonderfully described by Daniel McGinn in his book *House Lust*. McGinn said that:

> Everywhere we turned [during the boom], people were talking about, scheming over, envying, shopping for, refinancing, or just plain ogling houses—and in the process, we've transformed shelter from a basic necessity into an all-consuming passion.[198]

For anyone wondering about home purchasing, investment, and timing strategies—the right time to buy or what to buy as a home or an investment property—there are a few factors to consider. Let us first consider the size of the purchase market. There are an estimated 6.3 million homebuyers in the United States, with 85 percent of the market, or 5.36 million, in resale homes and the remaining 15 percent of the market, or 0.94 million, as new home sales. There are 2.5 million first-time homebuyers who make up 40 percent of the purchase market. For the most part, they were priced out of the market, barred from homeownership, as a result of inflated home prices during the bubble years. The remaining 60 percent of the market needs to trade up or down; are investors, speculators, and landlords; and second home buyers. They make up approximately 3.8 million households based on 2008 estimates.[199]

Some of the following factors provide reference points, others provide signals. How these are interpreted will be based upon the information gathered about the unique conditions of each local marketplace while keeping in mind the broader context of the national economy. We will also look at several key concepts tied to taking some of the mystery out of the drivers and supports of real estate values. Moreover, would be buyers should not lose sight of the fact that buying and selling a home is for many at the top of the list for the most stressful things done in life, following the death of a loved one and divorce. With this in mind, this chapter will address home-buying cycles, landlords, new home sales, and speculators.

Home-Buying Cycles

Homebuyers, at their simplest motivational level, are reduced to just a few purchaser profile categories: first-time homebuyer, move-up buyer, luxury buyer, and move-down buyer. These represent the various stages of life and reflect different needs and concerns in the next move. Borrower needs will vary based on each niche. The resale home market makes up on average about 80 percent of the real estate market, and the remaining on average of about 20 percent is new home sales. But, in each home buying stage, the same general rule applies: if homebuyers can get seven or eight items on the list of the top 10 "must have" items for the next house, they should be happy. Some homeowners play leap frog and trade up on average about six times in their lifetimes. And, some buy and hold as they move along in order to build up their holdings. Let us briefly examine these life stages.

The First-Time Homebuyer: The first-time homebuyer population as of 2007 was 2.51 million people, or 40 percent of the overall market.[200] The first-time homebuyer primarily is concerned with cost. With this niche making up about half of the purchase market, it is important to understand the dynamics unique to this market segment. This person or, often, young couple, wants to know how much cash is required to get into the home and what will it cost each month for the mortgage payments since payments on a first home may be more than rental payments. With the wonders of the mortgage tax deduction, an adjustment in payroll withholdings typically eases the transition from paying a lower monthly rental figure to a higher monthly mortgage payment. Seasoned real estate agents understand how to communicate this while also assuring this anxious segment.

As with any other big purchase, it is critical that homebuyers read and understand the entire purchase agreement. With regard to financing, it is crucial that purchasers understand that everything is negotiable. Though the process is shepherded by agents and lenders, the parties to the contract are the buyer and the seller. It is imperative, therefore, that if there is a provision in the agreement that states that the purchaser agrees to accept an alternative lending product at the lender's discretion and if the purchaser does not agree with this clause that the parties agree to strike a line through that phrasing, place hash marks near the section, and initial it. Otherwise, if, for instance, a buyer applies for a 30-year fixed rate loan and he does not fit into the lender's underwriting guidelines, he could close with an adjustable rate mortgage at a lower interest rate in order for the ratios to work. With a provision of that nature, failure to close due to refusing the alternative loan could result in a civil lawsuit by the seller against the purchase for specific performance.

An alternate to agreeing to accept an alternative loan is to secure a preapproval letter from the lender. Technically, this is an approved loan subject to an acceptable appraisal. A prequalification letter, in contrast, is not a firm commitment to lend. This type of letter states that the purchaser *appears* to be approvable based upon a preliminary review of the borrower's documents that could be as little as the credit report during a phone conversation. Consequently, the prequalification letter is of little value to either buyer or seller. In either case, a lender may issue a prequalification or an approval letter without committing to an interest rate, but rather agreeing to fund the loan at the prevailing "market rate." A customer agreeing to this type of lender letter is essentially stating that price is no object. A lender issuing this type of approval letters is essentially not able to commit to a rate due to numerous legitimate reasons, of which the primary reason is a lack of control over the broader market.

A Federal Housing Administration mortgage loan with 3 percent down, a permitted 3 percent seller concession, a two-month payment reserve requirement, verified source of funds, and rates slightly lower than Fannie Mae and Freddie Mac rates is the ideal loan for the first-time buyer.[201] Purchasers putting cash into the investment better vests the borrower with the property. Homebuyers looking for short cuts like down-payment assistance programs, as valid as they may be, have a significantly higher likelihood of going into default. This may be due to simply not mastering the self-discipline that is required with making and staying within a budget.

During the boom, Fannie Mae and Freddie Mac had 100 percent financing available at prevailing rates with some price adjustments based on numerous factors like credit score and cash in reserves. Moreover, 100 percent financing also was readily available with an array of choices in loan and amortization type from just about every private-labeled investor in the subprime niche. Typically, the preferred 100 percent financing option would be a 5/1 interest only LIBOR-index adjustable rate mortgage, which permitted a 6 percent seller concession, no verification of funds to close, and no required payments in reserve at closing. A 580 score required full income verification. A 620 score, on the other hand, permitted stated income documentation for 100 percent financing. After the boom, however, underwriting standards tightened. The take-away lesson from this is that product availability and guidelines are fluid and reflect the dynamic relationship between risk and reward. Everything is relative and guidelines change with market conditions.

According to a mid-2008 member survey by the National Association of REALTORS®, 23 percent of all potential buyers were on the sidelines waiting for home prices to drop and for better financing. The national median price home as of July 2008 was $214,000, which represented a decline of 7.1 percent from 2007 when the median price was $228,600. When the market reaches equilibrium, which is defined as a six-month inventory of homes, the forces of pent-up demand in the market should take over to help define the market's bottom.

The Move-Up Buyer: The move-up buyer primarily is concerned with square footage. A young or growing family may be the driving force to trade up. This customer profile, especially in the first move-up, more than likely will make some trade-offs by accepting a longer commute and less quality in exchange for a lot of space. This type of home may feature a larger kitchen with low end cabinets and granite tops, a family room with a fireplace, and a larger yard as the magnets to pull this buyer profile. But, compromises in architectural details and quality materials may appear in exterior trim work wrapped in vinyl, fireplaces without the traditional chimney, vinyl clad windows that could just as easily be put into a double-wide, and many other low-end details that builders use to drive costs down.

Cost and value are tricky. The traditional box-shaped colonial often has been reported to be a cost-effective model to build when coupled with an in-ground basement. For the builder, this means good margins. For the homebuyer, this means a familiar appearance coupled with being a good value for the money. But, for homebuyers, who have moved, many have found to their surprise that getting 50 percent more living space came with 100 percent more in real estate taxes, 100 percent more in utility bills and upkeep costs, and even more for the cost to replace items given the quality grade and size differences on items. These cost factors can be especially painful for homeowners trying to live on a budget.

Since the first move-up buyer wants more house, he more than likely is financially stretching while not taking into account the many hidden costs of homeownership. This borrower oftentimes is parlaying home equity from one home into another. In order to keep expenses down, the 5/1, 7/1, or 10/1 adjustable rate mortgage is often used since these loans offer predictable payments over a moderately long initial term, which typically correlates with a family's growth stage.

There are many signs that a move-up buyer has imprudently over stretched. The first one is the inability to furnish the home since it has more rooms. Typically, the new living room and dining room may remain unfurnished while furnishings from the older home find their way into the family room. In this case, bed sheets may be used to cover the windows of the unfurnished rooms. The second sign is furnishings that are not commensurate with the home's style, floor plan, or value. Moving all of the low end furnishings from a 2,000 square foot home into a 4,000 square foot home makes as much sense as putting the hub caps from a Volkswagen onto a high performance 12-cylinder Jaguar. Yet, many move up buyers do this without sensing any disconnect. This, of course, presents challenging opportunities for make over and staging specialists when the home comes up for resale. The third sign is deferred maintenance. This is evident in the lack of exterior and yard up keep, and on the inside, the lack of periodic painting and caulking of trim work. All of these factors require money from disposable income or savings, which many move-up buyers lack.

Some first-time buyers will do anything and everything they can to price themselves into their vinyl clad dream on a cul-de-sac that is hours from work. Even against the counsel of a certified public accountant advising not to apply for a stated income loan, but rather to fully document all income and assets and stay within their budgets, many first-time buyers will take on far more risk for themselves and families than they should. Due to high credit scores and misplaced confidence, however, some overstate their income and assets. The motive during the boom, oftentimes, was driven by fear of being frozen out of the market due to escalating prices. Even in a normal market, move-up buyers can be frozen out if they are looking to move into a nicer, better, or newer area. But, in a flat or declining market, those who want to move-up should always take into account what many fail to consider: what happens if the partner loses the job?

Stretching, or over leveraging, can permit getting a bigger house. But, if circumstances change, it can also mean a financial challenge that can place significant stresses on a relationship that can place all prior aspirations in peril.

The Luxury Buyer: The luxury buyer is keenly concerned with high-quality finishes inside and outside. Status as well as an artistic temperament tend to drive this affluent niche with higher levels of disposable income and assets. Sometimes, high-income buyers have quite a different sense of the dollar's worth. It is not unheard of for a purchaser to forfeit $50,000 or more in earnest money after going to contract, provided he finds a home that is better suited to his needs. As noted earlier, the relationship between cost and value are subject to perception. In the case of a forfeiture of deposit, the loss is offset by the perceived reward in the opportunity of the alternative choice.

In a society where conspicuous consumption is a given, and luxurious amenities have trickled down into the middle class segment of homebuyers, the luxury homebuyer is going to demand status in the way of exclusivity and perhaps a high-profile, designer-built custom home far beyond the reaches of everyone else. At the most easily observable level, luxurious homes are two- to four-times larger than average sized homes, cost five- to ten-times as much, and can be a hundred times nicer. It is usually about a thousand fine details that when combined into one home makes for a distinctive home. This may mean oversized hand-made bricks done on site in a modern interpretation of the historic *Carter's Grove* or *Wilton* on the James on the East Coast. Homes of this caliber often will employ reproduction interior woodwork equaling one fourth the cost of the home. On the coasts or on waterfront, internationally acclaimed architects may be tapped to produce nothing short of a contemporary masterpiece. In the worst of scenarios, however, the end result is blatant vulgarity evidenced by disproportionate scale and exaggerated architectural detail that displays poor taste—evidence of too much money and not enough good judgment. At the lower end, the McMansion phenomenon during the boom is an example. This is an oversized home that is the result of either a major makeover or a new home built on the lot of a knock down. It is disproportional in size to its community and the street scape given its size—a testament to poor community oversight adding to suburban blight. At the upper end, it is the multi-million dollar home where the designer-owner-builder did not retain the services of an architect, and therefore built a home destined to become a knock down. In the worst of these cases, an architect was in fact used, but due to the fusion of several distinct architectural styles, the end result is modern baroque—architectural vulgarity. In the best of scenarios, the end result is a home featured in architectural magazines that focus on how an acclaimed architect and a team of designers met the challenges demanded by the artistic vision of the home owner, who at this stage of the game is truly a trend setter and patron of the arts. Here, money is but a means to drive art and dreams into space, beauty, and function to create a tangible asset that will outlive its creators and indeed stand the test of time.

One of the better examples is Frank Lloyd Wright's *Fallingwater*. Even during the Great Depression, those who were successful in business did well during hard times. Department store owner Edgar J. Kaufmann retained the services of Wright and built *Fallingwater* on his family campground in the laurel highlands in the southern Alleghenies not far from Pittsburgh. Construction of the main house began in 1936 and ended in 1937 at a cost of $155,000, the equivalent of $4 million. The main house has 5,330 square feet, and the terraces have 2,445 square feet. *Fallingwater* became famous since it was built over a waterfall. The masterpiece is a National Historic Landmark. There was tension between the patron Kaufman and the architect Wright given that Wright had asked Kaufman if he wanted the balcony to be gold plated. Wright's sarcasm was made during a milieu of popular perception that the nation's commercial and industrial centers were corrupt and had bankrupted the United States leaving the general population in financial ruin.

The typical luxury buyer needing to borrow is typically more astute, brings a higher credit score, and is putting 30 percent down. It is likely that the luxury buyer has several sources of income that include a trust fund, gain on stocks, rents from real estate holdings, personal business or partnership income. Consequently, this jumbo borrower type may make financing decisions that are counterintuitive to a household living in a planned subdivision where everyone aspires to drive the same type of vehicle parked in the same type of driveway for the same type of odd display of conformity. If stretching to get into that trophy house, the luxury buyer may lean towards one of several interest only type mortgages to keep costs low while banking on the home to appreciate. One such financing option may be the 10-year interest only loan that fully amortizes after year eleven for the remaining 20 years. Regardless of financing option, what distinguishes this borrower type from others is that they do their homework and also tend to seek outside counsel prior to doing the deal, which makes them truly savvy borrowers.

The Second Home Buyer: Vacation homes at the beach, the mountains, a ski resort, or abroad are owned by those in the lower strata of affluence and above. A true second home is the compound for use by the immediate and extended family. If the home is not for vacation but for work, then it may be a luxury condominium in a full-service building close to work. If mortgage financing is required, Fannie Mae and Freddie Mac require that the second home be more than 50 miles from the primary residence.

Among some of the popular second home locations for the affluent within the United States are Florida's "gold coast" along the intercoastal waterways; Colorado's mile-high ski resorts in Breckenridge, Aspen, and Vail; Wyoming's majestic Teton mountains and Snake River valley in Jackson Hole; and any water front property along a river or bay with protected waters that can accommodate a deep water slip for a 40 foot-plus sailboat. In those small population segments of true affluence, homes were demolished and rebuilt; two condominium units were joined, gutted, and remodeled; and oftentimes more than one lot was purchased and joined to create an estate worthy of ascribing it a place name in Hebrew, Spanish, Italian, or Gaelic in order to evoke another era or place with mythical resonance. These are the spare-no-expense type of properties that Robin Leach showcased between 1984 and 1995 in *Lifestyles of the Rich and Famous*.

According to a 2007 survey by the American Affluence Research Center, those with incomes of $200,000-plus and a net worth of $1.5

million-plus tend to have second homes. A strong 64 percent of those with a net worth of $6 million-plus and 34 percent of those with a net worth between $1.5 million and $6 million have second homes. As an average, the second home was valued at two-thirds the value of the primary residence. Nationwide, the average price of a second home in 2007 was valued at $781,000 while the primary home of second home owners was worth $1.2 million.[202] Moreover, these second homes encompassed large sail boats, house boats, luxury motor yachts, and high-end recreational vehicles (RVs) since they all have the same thing in common—live onboard accommodations with a kitchen, enclosed bathrooms, and the ability to secure mortgage financing.

At the lower end of the second home segment is the fractional ownership property, or the time share, which for as much as $40,000 for a one week slice of time, hucksters abused the naïve for a one week slice of time to be near the roulette wheels in Las Vegas. Cash out refinances and home equity line of credit products were used to finance many of these purchases, which after the boom was over came back onto the resale market at steep discounts. The more savvy buyers eyed premier properties in premier ocean-front locations.

The Move-Down Buyer: There is never a one size fits all reason to explain why people move down and the expectations they have when they plan the move. The move-down buyer is often driven by amenities that may include a social club, a private shuttle service, or maintenance-free living perhaps in a 55-or-better community. This means a first floor master bedroom suite along with perhaps wider doorways to accommodate a wheel chair. It may mean a condominium not far from a boat club, social activities such as theater, or a collection of nearby restaurants and coffee shops. The driving motivations, moreover, may be a desire for community as opposed to neighborhood, which is typical in a remote suburb where long commutes invariably produce time-starved families that are too exhausted to socialize.

If the mortgagor has verifiable sources of fixed retirement income, all options are on the table. Like the first-time home-buyer, however, some move-down buyers will be concerned about low monthly payments. If there is no equity to parlay from one transaction to another, then either an interest only loan, or a 30-year fixed rate loan are the two primary options. If, on the other hand, there is plenty of equity from the sale of another house along with verifiable sources of fixed retirement income, then a 30-year fixed-rate loan is more than likely the ideal loan. If this homebuyer is 62 years or older and has enough equity, then the reverse mortgage might be the ideal choice.

The flip side, however, is quite different. It is unlikely that the lower end of the affluent in the $1 million to $2 million price range will consider a reverse mortgage for a few key reasons. First, there is no need. And second, diminishing the value of the estate would rob future generations of assets. That would be simply stupid. Those assets serve as the foundation for building the family's future for generations. The true luxury move down condominium purchaser is typically looking for a building that was designed by a renowned architect and finished to perfection by the best interior space planners and designers. A cue buyers should look for is a *residential architect* Design Awards bestowed on the project since this designation recognizes the best of kind, best of breed. In the $1 million to $2 million-plus price range are condos that are often ten times nicer than their single family counterparts. The reasons for this are due to the superiority of location, high end quality finishes, and a no maintenance lifestyle that when taken together translates into more meaningful free time. The challenges for the buyer in this real estate niche is careful comparison shopping.

There are three fairly easy to identify features to consider in a luxury condominium. First, some buildings are hotel complexes or time share units in a mixed use building. The result of this could mean lack of community and higher maintenance costs per unit given the fewer number of owner-occupied units for the operation costs to be spread amongst the other owners. Second, stunning and breathtaking views are priceless, and it is not always easy to quantify the value of something that is intangible. For example, a $1 million dollar condominium with no view may fetch an extra $1 million and more if there is a water view, a view of a spectacular city skyline, or a lake and a majestic mountain. Third, not all million dollar-plus condominiums are in projects that are built alike or close to comparable. Understanding this critical distinction comes from comparison shopping and asking a lot of questions. In some cases, what may have been intended as rentals were put on the market for sale during the boom. Though superbly located, the caliber of design and finish of these lesser projects speak volumes as to the initially intended use of the building's units. The genuine high caliber condominium projects are stunning and have the wow factor. They have floor to ceiling windows throughout and are designer ready, which means the customer's own design team is responsible for the choice of flooring, closets, and other details that personalize a home. The counterfeits were built by established single family home developers that ventured into the luxury condominium niche and failed to take into account something significantly important—not all architects or customer niches are alike.

Within the move-down buyer niche are those who return to their home country and those who expatriate. At the height of the boom, some borrowers cashed out the equity in their homes and made plans to retire abroad. Many foreigners returned to their home countries due to the language barrier, the lack of freedom as defined by excessive rules and regulations in America, and the desire for family and community. For some, the experience of life in America was no different than what is captured in the award winning 2008 Colombian film *Paraiso Travel* that depicts the harsh realities and illusions of seeking fortune in New York City. Real estate as an asset was at peak values during the boom and the value of the dollar was strong, which together provided an ideal moment to move. Some Americans, as hard as it may be for many to understand, gladly turned their back on the United States. Some motivating factors included knowing that the real estate market had to collapse and concern about the blow back from America's foreign policy. Some of the motivating factors were also failure of one form or another and resentment.[203] By purchasing abroad with cash, those who so timed their refinances and purchases may have been among the winners in the housing and refinance boom. Those who left embraced a willingness to adapt to a new culture, possessed a sense of adventure, and looked forward to the prospects of significantly lower living costs.

Non-Occupying Owners

The investor class of property owners, or the non-occupying owner, drove 40 percent of the real estate purchase market during the boom. After the high-tech bubble burst in 1999, many investors moved their money into real estate as an investment. These were landlords and second-homebuyers. Baby Boomers, those born between 1945 and 1960, fueled much of the demand for second homes.[204] The second-homeowner comes in two distinct types. At the lower end of the socioeconomic spectrum is the individual seeking a lifestyle beyond his actual reach. In the broader scheme of things, he is upper middle class based on income distributions and asset holdings. This type purchases what he thinks is a second home, the vacation property, but that in fact functions as a rental property that he uses only during accidental or planned vacancies. Beach and lake properties make prime vacation rentals. Since he is dependent on the cash flow from the seasonal rental income, he is either actively or passively managing the investment(s) through a property manager, leasing agents, and the cleaning help in between guests.

At the upper end of the socioeconomic spectrum is the individual seeking another home that functions as a personal retreat or family compound. Waterfront, water access, and scenic mountain view properties tend to appeal to this type. This second-homebuyer type is in the upper economic stratum and has no intention of leasing his second (or third or fourth) home, which more than likely was custom built by an award-winning team of architects, designers, and landscapers. This type of second-homeowner may have his accomplishments tied to his home's design, cost, and location make the cover of a lifestyle oriented magazine. In this instance, the publication will showcase the patron of the architectural arts, his professional background, and his aesthetic vision, which coalesced with the architect's, and will leave room for the professional bragging rights of his team.

Among both types, the landlord and the second-homeowner, each was able to snap up more than one additional home. Consequently, the upper-middle and upper class placed the increased demand pressures on housing, and home prices responded by going up as inventories diminished. The broad middle and lower-middle class benefited from this through unprecedented appreciation if they were homeowners, but suffered as a result of significantly higher prices that were paid if purchasing. Too many people in the upper 20 percent of the United States economy entered the real estate market, which made the inevitable collapse of housing prices even worse.

Landlords: Some investors accumulated real estate holdings simply by "intending" to occupy a Federal Housing Administration financed property. With a mere 3 percent down, and a suitcase near the front door, the intention to move in could change after closing. That is the way it was back in the 1980s. The U.S. Department of Housing and Urban

Development, however, has since wised up and now requires additional disclosures in the loan application that seeks to uncover the prospective borrower's real estate holdings financed with government loans.

The agencies limit real estate holdings, and these rules change from time to time with market conditions. Fannie Mae permits up to four investment properties that are one- to four-unit rentals.[205] During the boom, Freddie Mac, on the other hand, permitted a landlord to have up to ten of these properties. Each also has myriad nuanced differences in underwriting that, for example, touch on qualifying ratios and cash flow analysis. For the landlord seeking financing, that means a seasoned mortgage broker would have been a better financing alternative since lenders tend to be either Fannie Mae or Freddie Mac lenders. Real estate investors with a significant number of properties do not conform to agency guidelines and therefore by default would become subprime borrowers.

Mortgage holders suing for foreclosure and landlords suing for eviction are not too different. Each has similar interests: timely payments and recovery of the income producing asset in the event of default. The role that aspiring investors played in permitting tenants to have relatively affordable housing, sometimes below the carrying costs, is important in understanding the housing boom. While landlords should not be viewed as public minded servants by providing housing, they in fact do just that with the motive of gleaning income and building wealth through the real estate.

The Property Manager: A property manager at a large real estate brokerage may collect rents on more than 100 homes on behalf of absentee landlords. Many of the landlords took employment out of state and chose to hang onto their home in the event of a possible return. Some, on the other hand, were landlords by choice. They bought the homes as investments to be professionally managed. The property manager's role is that of a credit analyst, leasing agent, general contractor, plaintiff, and evictor.

As a credit analyst, property managers screen out prospective tenants based on credit, income, employment, and the results of a reference check. The credit report shows the prospective tenant's readiness and willingness to repay obligations and says a lot about the applicant. If the tenant looks low-risk on paper, then the property is leased.

Acting as a general contractor may be an overstatement, but many property managers have unlimited discretion on property repairs and maintenance-related issues up to a nominal dollar amount. Over a certain amount, then written authorization from the landlord is required. Either way, the landlord is required to maintain a maintenance escrow account with the property manager who, in turn, dispatches plumbers and air conditioner technicians when service is required.

Suing and evicting tenants is another matter. One ongoing issue for landlords is the need to consistently file lawsuits against tenants for the failure to pay rent—even when they are just five days late. This is an essential duty since the law, which varies from state to state, permits a tenant to be in arrears several months. Acting as a fiduciary for the landlord, the property manager is bound to proactively represent the financial interests of the client who pays a fee for his services. In order to mitigate future loss, the landlord or his property manager must file lawsuits in order to ensure a prompt eviction should it become necessary in order to mitigate financial losses. This necessitates that the landlord or the property manager fill out the court papers, evidence the right to evict with a copy of the lease, and include a check for the filing fee. The eviction rate on homes under property management should be about 3 percent and higher based on how much risk the landlord was willing to take as he lowered the criteria on accepting new tenants. Each eviction is an awful event for the tenant, but redemption of the property for the landlord is a relief. Unlike a foreclosure, rental homes are more quickly prepped and reoccupied without the burdens to the communities posed by the ill-equipped big banks that failed to take into account the adverse impact that foreclosures can have.

After the court finally grants the right to evict, and the dreaded date comes, a bail bondsman doing side work in evictions shows up in front of the rental house. The scenario may look like this: He comes in a suburban van with three beefy body builders complete with tattoos, piercings, and an attitude that replies to, "Good morning," with, "That's your opinion." Baseball bats stay on the floor of the vehicle. The sheriff shows up, and the property manager's role is to observe, to be the landlord's eyes and ears on the ground. If all goes well, everything ends up unbroken and on the sidewalk. If there is a less than pleasant verbal exchange, then the dining table might be placed on a mirror resting flat in the front yard so that the yard would not be disfigured by the table's leg. The mirror, of course, would break. The hardened nature and street smarts of the bail bondsman, and the dynamics of humiliation at play in this eviction scenario is right out of Andy Kane's 1981 book *Care and Feeding of Tenants*.[206] So, why would someone want to be a landlord?

Lord of the Estate: Landlords are an interesting breed. Landlords have taken upon themselves the role of providing subsidized housing, either through default or choice, to a transient and sometimes underpaid work force. This assumption of risk to themselves is done with the hope that over the long term, their tenants will build their net worth. For some, this is indeed the case. The success of the landlord is, more often than not, tied to having significant income and cash reserves to cover vacancies for extended periods of time, should that become necessary. With that said, landlords must understand that the Pope in Rome will never canonize them as saints for providing housing to lower income households or professional transients of society. Moreover, no city in the world will ever erect a statue in the honor of a landlord for providing subsidized housing.

The marginal landlord operates on luck, not solid income or deep pockets, and not an adequate understanding of the rental market and how to actually be a landlord. And, in these cases, they are despised by their tenants for providing what they believe is substandard housing and acting as on-call amateur plumbers on holiday weekends when Sponge Bob Square Pants again gets stuck head-first in the toilet. These landlords get the predictable phone call, "If you don't fix the damn toilet, I'm not paying the rent!" Rather than enforce the terms of the rental contract, or play by the rules distilled by Kane, these amateurs inwardly behave like cowards and their tenants exploit this weakness to their financial detriment. The result is tenants take the upper hand, they violate the lease provisions that prohibit deductions or demands, and landlords end up capitulating based on fear.

Real estate investors made up about 25 percent of the purchase market during the housing bubble. Typically, they are upper-middle income—a broad range of household income between $50,000 per year to $150,000 per year and more for any of the major metropolitan statistical areas. Financial news reporters on *CNBC*, on the other hand, may define the nation's middle class as earning between $20,000 and $100,000 per year. The break down would look like this: 20 percent in the United States make over $100,000 per year, 60 percent in the United States make between 20,000 and $100,000 per year, and 20 percent in the United States make under $20,000 per year. As points of reference, the U.S. Census Bureau reported that real median household income remained unchanged between 2003 and 2004 at $44,389.[207] The nation's median household income in 2006, however, bumped up to $48,851.[208] In contrast, the wealthiest 1 percent of the nation's population reported 22 percent of the nation's total adjusted gross income in 2006.[209]

During the boom, as underwriting guidelines dropped, the lower segments of the middle class sought entry into investing in real estate with the hope of becoming landlords. What were they thinking? To a great extent, they wanted to earn rent, make a profit, and enjoy a tax shelter. As a result, the increased number of buyers in the market helped pushed prices higher by virtue of the added demand placed upon the housing inventory—all in order to get rich in real estate. But, this lower segment had no cash reserves. Lenders did not require them, which set them up for failure by encouraging them to take on excessive risk.

Those who buy for tax shelter tend to sweep up new homes near public transportation and shopping. The *nouveau riche* typically make the same mistake: They think that tenants are willing to pay on a monthly basis what homeowners pay. The evidence of this misguided overshooting is row upon row of new homes with "For Rent" signs that stay planted month after month. Sometimes, the name of the real estate broker would change, but the homes remained vacant evidencing too much money and not enough common sense backed up by due diligence that could have been provided by a seasoned real estate agent. Asking prices, for example, might be $2,400 per month while the average rents for a zip code are $1,600 per month. The $800 difference is for the granite countertop in the kitchen and the new-home smell that these landlords believe will fetch a higher income tenant. Property managers typically handle the leasing, move in, move out, and the many details that follow. Incidental service calls are overseen by the property manager: the landlord has no worries even if he takes a loss. And, of course, he never gets his hands dirty. In these cases, only the accountant and property manager get the unpleasant workplace hazards: paper cuts.

Newcomers to the landlord business typically do not know what lies before them. Solid employment and enough cash to purchase a rental home often are not enough to qualify someone as a good renter. Landlords should have six months worth of payments in the bank set aside just in case unforeseen events happen, because they more than likely will happen when least expected. But, even that is not enough cash in reserves since when an economy heads south, it can wipe out the landlord and a foreclosure can result.

The romantic notion of wearing $1,500 Armani suits and $300 hand made silk ties while collecting rents from the holdings spread across Baltic Avenue to Boardwalk Avenue is also misguided. Marginal landlords—those without the financial wherewithal or experience—will more than likely find themselves learning how to become do-it-yourselves plumbers unclogging the tenant's toilet, electricians, drywall repairmen, painters, landscapers, and seasoned trash removal experts with newly acquired skills in filing and petitioning for eviction. Some will adapt to reality and learn to pack a piece as they make the collection rounds based on what they own and where it is located, especially if it is a Baltic or Mediterranean Avenue-type property in any one of the hundreds of affordable yet less than desirable parts of town across this great nation.

Kane's 1981 landlord guidebook, *Care and Feeding of Tenants*[210] is really a guide on how to be a slumlord. Kane's book is an over-the-top, tongue-in cheek primer written by a professional landlord with a knack for both building an empire of holdings as well as making sure that the rent comes in like clockwork. Kane was probably what we today would call a calloused and hardened slumlord with absolutely no compassion toward those less fortunate than himself. Nonetheless, Kane's concepts were taught as continuing education credit for maintaining a real estate license in the 1980s. The take-away lesson was the importance of suing for eviction—all the time no matter what. On evictions, Kane said, "Ninety-nine percent of the times an eviction is necessary, it is due to unpaid rent."[211] In his book, failure to pay rent is tantamount to robbery since the amount the tenant owes is double the cost the landlord will bear as the shortage will have to come out of personal funds. Kane's advice is, "Don't be nice."[212] His philosophy can be summed up with: get them evicted and make sure all neighbors—other tenants and even property owners—know that if you don't pay, you don't stay. The mortgage lending industry understands this mentality as evidenced by the foreclosure crisis.

A lease is a private contract between the landlord and the tenant, and the failure to pay rent demands that the landlord file for eviction. Each jurisdiction has different rules, and evidence of sufficient filings may be required prior to an eviction that complies with a state's laws. This means if the rent is due on the first of the month and is not considered late until after the fifth, a failure to pay rent complaint should be filed on the sixth of each month like clockwork. For the novice, filing for eviction can be an intimidating process simply because America's legal system holds the public in disdain and contempt and expects landlords to pay hundreds of dollars for routine administrative services that can be done for about $20. The absurdity of filing documents with phrases in Latin, a dead language, whose only purpose is to disempower the public of its rights to act on its own, is evidence of not cultural lag in some of the nation's courts, but the arrogance of the legal profession to ensure that justice for all comes at a hefty price. Landlords, once they have filed for an eviction, should report the tenant's payment history with the three credit bureaus as part of a disclosed term in a lease. Third-party information providers like the former Washington, D.C.-based Failure to Pay Rent Registry, Inc. use to gather court filings from landlords and made them available for a fee as a screening service. An eviction should be viewed like a foreclosure by those extending credit or lease terms.

The brutal nature of being a landlord for many is rooted in the quest for riches without doing the homework. One retired veteran, for example, complete with pension and free time on his hands, spends his early retirement years managing a half a dozen properties scattered across a 50 mile radius from home. He is a cross between a proactive rent collector and maintenance man hauling garbage to the dump after tenants pack up and leave without notice. All of his financial anxieties, however, are self-inflicted. One part stems from the less than ideal choice he made in financing his investments, and the other part stems from not fully understanding the rent collection and eviction roles of being the landlord.

Eviction rates with tenants and foreclosure rates with homeowners in default are similar. The landlord trap can be nothing more than a part-time maintenance man's job behind the desk of the complaint department with frequent trips to the court house filing papers for eviction for failure to pay rent. In the losing proposition scenario, the landlord serves as the automated teller machine, forever doling out cash for property repairs and mortgage payments between tenants. One former landlord described his negative cash flow experience being like having an eight-cylinder car where only four or five cylinders were hitting at any given time. Eviction has to follow in order to ensure the viability of the private sector's ability to provide rental housing. Typically, landlords who experience financial challenges between tenants will always pay the mortgage on their primary residence, but may be forced to not pay the mortgage on the rental property due to inability. This typically results in a lower credit score and a higher interest for that landlord if he seeks to refinance or purchase another property within 12 to 24 months.

While Kane's arguments about suing are spot on, evicting is not a necessity given the right once granted by the court. The counter to the calloused approach is the financial hardships that arise from mindlessly acting per the lease contract's terms. Vacancies between tenants are givens, especially when rental inventories increase. A prolonged vacancy not only can produce a financial devastation, but can also wipe out the rate of return. Moreover, increased competition serves to lower rents, which in turn lowers the return on investment. Finally, in a tough market evicted tenants can behave similarly as foreclosed homeowners by totally trashing and even burning the property as they leave. Given these considerations outside of contractual agreements and the rights of landlords and tenants, prudent landlords may better serve their long-term interests by exploring alternatives to eviction that produce win-win relationships.

When Lenders and Agents Enable

During the boom, Guadalupe (Lupe) Barrera[213] ran her own business as a nail technician doing pedicures and manicures. Lupe, who was 57-years-old when the market crashed, came to the United States from Ecuador in 1987 in order to enjoy a better quality of life. Ten years after coming here, she got her United States citizenship.[214]

Lupe bought a small single-family home in Rockville, Maryland, in 2000. She sold it in 2004 and made $98,000 in profit. She then paid $140,500 for a condo in Rockville, and borrowed $40,000. Her problems began when she was enticed by real estate agents to become a real estate investor and landlord. With equity in her condo, $25,000 in annual income, and the availability of stated income loans, she was able to buy two additional properties. But, that is when her problems started.

Since Lupe had excellent credit, a real estate agent helped her find a lender who did not verify her income. Lupe then overstated her income at the direction of the real estate agent—not the lender—in order for Countrywide to approve her loan application. Everything was in English.

She understood some of the documents, but as she said, "I could not read all 200 pages."

Lupe's primary residence went up in value to $250,000, but by June 2008 had a mortgage balance of $157,000 due to cash-out refinances during the boom to make the two real estate purchases at the urging of the same real estate agent. One purchase was a $195,000 condo in Rockville that she picked up in 2005. The second was a $190,000 condo in Palm Beach, Florida, which she nabbed in 2006. On paper, Lupe held $635,000 in real estate holdings due to excellent credit and stated income loan programs, which her real estate agent helped locate.

From a cash-flow perspective, Lupe said that it was all a mistake. She said she was too trusting with the real estate agent, who by law was supposed to act as her fiduciary. As a result, she suffered from severe negative cash flow. The total negative monthly cost to carry her two condos was $1,167, which came out of her own pocket each month. The Rockville property cost her $300 per month, but the Palm Beach condo cost her $600 per month. Since taxes were not escrowed for Palm Beach, an additional $3,200 was due every twelve months.

From an investment standpoint, she said that this, too, was a mistake. Lupe lost about $90,000 in equity between the two condos. The Rockville condo dropped in value to $125,000 but her mortgage balance had held steady at $165,000. She financed the purchase with an interest only loan, but afterward refinanced into a fully amortized 30-year fixed-rate mortgage. The West Palm Beach condo dropped to $140,000, but her loan balance had remained at $167,000. Fortunately, the purchase money loan for West Palm Beach was a fully amortized 30-year fixed-rate mortgage.

When the mania that drove the boom was over, she said she wanted to sell her investment condos. She said that she was more cautious and less trusting of real estate agents. Lupe worked seven days a week, sometimes 16 hours per day in order to earn the extra money she needed to feed the two extra mortgages. She said that she was afraid of bankruptcy. She knew that she made a mistake. As misfortune has a way of latching on and not letting go, Lupe also became the victim of a debt consolidation fraud in the Washington, D.C. area, which was reported on the local news.

Landlords and Refinancing: Landlords have to refinance, too. Many landlords seeking to refinance at the tail end of the boom faced serious set backs. Lenders typically carefully interview the applicant to make sure that everything is in order. They review the credit and tie each mortgage entry against each rental property. Rental income figures are noted as are the real estate taxes and homeowner's insurance premiums. Everything should be in order. But, what happens when there is no valid lease with one of the tenants?

If there is no beginning and ending date on a lease, which is one of the elements that make for a valid agreement, there is a problem. Moreover, a lease cannot have different font types printed over sections that have been covered with Wite-Out® —a signal of suspected fraud. Moreover, the alleged rental incomes for all of the properties need to be reported to the Internal Revenue Service—otherwise, it is another instance of suspected fraud. Rental incomes need to be evidenced in the federal tax returns.

Given these factors, the borrower's debt-to-income ratio can be too high, because of the lack of real evidence of rental income to offset the carrying costs of the mortgages tied to each property. This type of applicant, which is not uncommon, becomes an objective denial. Suggestions to the applicant to amend the tax returns, claim the rental income, and then reapply typically will go unheeded due to the tax liability. This type of landlord will apply everywhere in hope of finding a loan officer not careful with details or not caring due to compensation alignment rather than integrity in underwriting. In other words, landlords tend to drive routine mortgage fraud in the industry.

In another landlord scenario, a first-time homebuyer decided to get into the market at the peak of the housing bubble. He used 100 percent financing to invest in a four-unit building in 2006. The plan was simple. He would live in one, place tenants in the other three, and over time be set for retirement. But, by 2007 he wanted to refinance out of his private-labeled subprime loan at 8 percent, which had all the onerous features consumer advocates complain about. He was told that the Federal Housing Administration did not permit 100 percent financing and that he owed more than the property was worth given a decline in value. Loan-to-value aside, the borrower had no assets, because he used them in property repairs in order to attract tenants to the vacant units. But, more telling was the debt-to-income analysis: even at a lower rate, it came in at 65 percent.

He had done a stated income loan on the purchase, and obviously over stated the income in order to get the income ratios to work to satisfy the lender and to qualify for the needed loan amount to satisfy his goals.

This type of fraud requires the aid of the lender. Moreover, that real estate sales adage, "Buyers Are Liars,"[215] certainly applies here. His income had been grossly overstated when he took out the purchase money loan. An FHA's 203(k) rehab loan program, while staying within his true price range, would have been a far more prudent means of acquiring a multi-family home. These points made, this is a classic case of self-inflicted suffering due to borrower and lender directed fraud. Had this investor done his homework about his financing options, he could have had the best combination of circumstances with the Federal Housing Administration loan. With a low fixed rate, his cash flow would have been better. And, declining property values would have more than likely been a non-issue since rent from tenants is not pegged to property values, but rather median incomes from the renting class in given market along with supply of rental housing.

Landlords acting as their own property manager would do well to take a cue from professionals. Lenders require that a landlord have cash in reserves for a reason. Vacancies, leasing fees to brokers, and the cost to clean, maintain, and repair between tenants add up. Of course, attorney and filing fees in the event there are frequent trips to the courthouse need to be taken into account as well. And, in the event of an eviction, it is a good idea to have the process overseen by a professional—typically the bail bondsman-type doing side work with a muscle-bound crew to ensure the tenant's smooth transition from the house and onto the sidewalk. As a result of these factors, having three to six months of mortgage payments tied to each rental property is playing it conservative and safe. Anything short of that can amount to gambling, and Lady Luck never smiles always. She is fickle.

Moreover, landlords need to understand that mortgage lenders will only give about 75 percent credit for proven rental income. The conservative assumption is based on the premise that for every dollar the landlord brings in from his property, 25 cents will go out in overhead-related expenses. The reason for this is because that is what actually ends up happening. In this regards, the lending industry has it spot on.

Average rental rates vary based on markets and rents tend to target the bottom third to the middle of the socio-economic spectrum in many of the real estate markets. Unless targeting a clearly defined niche, like short-term executive housing that is furnished and close to major employers, would-be landlords should stick with the basics since it is much safer.

If a landlord is managing the property on his own, this means that a good rental house should be less than an hour commute from where he lives. It is always a good idea to check on the real estate since it is an asset, and to visit with the tenants since they provide the income.

New Home Sales

Builders and their trade group the National Association of Home Builders claim that the high cost of new homes is due to an assortment of fees imposed upon builders by jurisdictions for inspections, permits, and the like. Some point to land prices, raw construction costs, and consumer preferences as leading reasons for the high cost of new homes. Many fail to consider that the average size of a new home in 1957 was 1,000 square feet, by 1970 it was 1,500 square feet, but by 2007, the average size of a new home increased to 2,400 square feet—a 60 percent move upwards from the dated 1970s and a staggering 240 percent larger from the grossly outdated one bath homes with tiny kitchens from the 1950s. The significant growth in size certainly has driven home costs higher. Moreover, there has been a tendency towards better design and materials, which have served to drive new home prices upwards as well. To the angst of homebuyers, there has been a move away by builders in using the cost per square foot as a comparative benchmark since it does not take into account significant differences that can exist in building materials and finishes. Either way, new homes do fetch a premium since buyers get the latest in home design with all new materials. But, if the builder is still building, builders will control the resale market in a new home community, and from a home seller's perspective, that may serve to keep prices down until the builder closes out. Finally, unlike new cars that depreciate in value the moment the front tires roll off the lot, in normal market conditions new homes tend to experience better appreciation rates than older resale homes. The exception to this general rule, however, is location. In many major areas, older homes that are functionally obsolete and smaller yet much closer to major employment areas tend to fetch significant premiums due to location. The charm of the older home designs is an added bonus as is the major remodeling opportunity, which is welcomed by those with creative impulses and a budget. The converse to this point on location is that an older home can present a knock down opportunity—for a new home.

Some who purchase new homes move every few years for another new home for a few reasons. First, there is nothing like a new home, even if a stiff premium is paid. But, there is no repair and maintenance for upkeep that can run up credit card debt, which can occur in older homes that have not been well cared for by previous owners. This is an important consideration given that too many would be homeowners never take into account the many and significant costs of homeownership over time—maintenance, repair, and replacement. When an appraisal says a new home has a functional and economic life of 20 years, it means that almost everything needs to be replaced over this time frame. Moreover, the appreciation rates on new homes tend to be the strongest in the first several years from construction. Given these factors, for those who are happy to stay on the move, new homes offer many benefits in addition to the latest designs and incorporated technologies that make for better living.

New home sales are an important barometer of the nation's economic health. For every house that is built, about 40,000 people secure work, and this produces a positive ripple across the economy. Brisk sales demonstrate consumer confidence. But, when unsold inventory across the nation reaches a ten-month supply as happened in 2008, price cutting and greater buyer incentives are inevitable.[216]

Year after year, builders across the United States tend to make the same mistake of listing their new homes in a multiple listing service at ground breaking with the hope of attracting buyers with open checkbooks. But, with the adage "if you can't see it, you can't sell it" ever so true in real estate, builders would be better off listing their new homes after everything has been installed, tested and actually working, and the house and grounds are ready to show. This counter intuitive approach will actually serve to shorten the days on the market. Otherwise, a listing of 180 days and more on the market can raise eyebrows while also skewing the absorptions rate numbers, which buyers and appraisers notice.

The same eleven builders dominated the national new home building scene year after year, and historically grossed over $1 billion in revenue according to *Builder*, an industry magazine. These market makers were Centex Corporation, Hovnanian Enterprises, Jim Walter Homes, KB Home, Lennar Corporation, M.D.C. Holdings (or Richmond American Homes), NVR, Pulte Homes, The Ryland Group, Standard Pacific Corporation, and Weyerhaeuser Real Estate Company.

Like Toll Brothers, D.R. Horton, and Beazer Homes were on the *Builder* list, but not at the top year after year. All have controlled business arrangements, or affiliated business arrangements, with either a mortgage division and/or a title company, which made them cash cows for their shareholders during the boom. By having their own mortgage brokerages, access to the private labeled market took place, which meant 100 percent subprime financing enabled more buyers to qualify and purchase.

During the boom, the nation's publicly held builders controlled about 30 percent of the new home sales market and took between 22 percent and 25 percent in profit margins. These builders bought up massive land parcels, which drove land prices up. Those costs, of course, were passed onto consumers. At the market's peak in 2005, just 12 publicly held new home builders controlled 2.16 million building lots. By 2008, that grip dropped to 1.08 million.[217]

Mara Der Hovanesian's article "Bonfire of the Builders" in the August 2007 issue of *Business Week* described in painful detail the challenges that faced the nation's largest builders as the subprime market collapsed. G. Hunter Haas IV, head of mortgage research and trading for Paramus, New Jersey-based Opteum Financial Services, said that, "Homebuilders really started to push these more aggressive mortgages down the throats of potential buyers to boost sales."[218] Some of the new homes used as collateral for the mortgages were worth less than the builders had claimed, and their borrowers did not have the incomes to support their actual debt obligations. "Homebuilders were getting sloppy, and Wall Street was giving more scrutiny," Haas said.[219] By June 2007, Opteum exited its role in providing financing to real estate developers and then reselling the loans to investment banks, which in turn packaged them as securities to be sold to hedge funds and insurance companies. In short, some of the major builders pushed the risk envelope too far and exposed themselves to too much risk—not too different from the behavior of many reckless lenders.

As of November 2008, seven of the nation's largest banks—Bank of America, Wachovia, SunTrust, BB&T, National City, Wells Fargo, and Regions—had over $4.37 billion in single family construction loans on their books. These loans made up between 1 percent and 4 percent of these bank's total assets. But, these same banks had $137.7 billion in all construction loans making up between 2 percent and 15 percent of these bank's total assets. The delinquency rates on all construction loans were between 4 percent and 13 percent. The picture is not as bright for the nation's top ten smaller regional banks with construction loans on their books since between 24 percent and 57 percent of the loans make up the entire asset base of these banks.[220]

These facts suggest the obvious: smaller banks heavily vested in construction loans are likely to fail. Builders that are in delinquency and facing bankruptcy are likely not to complete and deliver a new home to buyers. The take away here is that new home shoppers need to engage in due diligence on the builders in the new home communities of interest.

Speculators

Real estate speculation is a cross between investing and gambling that comes in many forms: opportunists, entrepreneurs, and arbitrageurs seeking to profit from a perceived mispricing in the market either due to value or currency exchanges. Some speculators buy and hold. And, some buy and sell. For the risk they take, they justly earn a profit. But, when the market goes against them, their losses are commensurate with the degree of leverage as well as the misperception of the opportunity they sought to exploit.

In many standardized real estate contracts, there is a provision that permits the buyer to assign the contract to a third party. In an appreciating market with high customer demand, it is not outside of convention to place a deposit on a home, line up financing as a back-up plan, sell the contract to another for a profit, and have that new buyer go to closing on that purchase. These lucrative opportunities during the boom were plentiful for those who identified the right properties, risked some capital, and then sold their contract rights to others.

Provided that there is no price escalation clause, assigning a new home contract of sale is oftentimes fairly easy provided that purchasers actually qualify to consummate the purchase in the event of an inability to secure an assignee. Given that a new home delivery could be upward of one year in a hot housing market, it is not uncommon for a new home purchase to be a superb profit-making opportunity—given the right market conditions. This is the real estate equivalent of taking a long position or placing a call on a stock that is believed will rise in price in order to make a profit. But, if speculators bet wrong, as some learned when the market turned, they need to consummate the deal—and move in to the property or risk loss.

Hector Vega[221] of Bogotá, Colombia, was among the cadre of foreign investors who dabbled in the Florida real estate market during the boom. Between 2006 and 2007, Vega went to contract on four new construction condominiums in Florida. One was in Aventura, two were in Daytona Beach, and the fourth was in Sonesta in Orlando. The price range for each unit was between $550,000 and $610,000. His plans were to either rent out the units or resell them at a profit. Vega closed on one, waited for delivery on two due to delays in construction tied to the changes in the market, and renegotiated with the developer on another unit due to an appraisal below the contract price.[222] Moreover, Vega exploited the currency arbitrage opportunity and profited. To his advantage, the Colombian peso exchanged at more favorable rates in 2008 than in 2006 due to the United States dollar's devaluation that took place in the wake of the subprime crisis.

Consider Keith Thai of northern Virginia. Kendra Marr's account in "Luxury Foreclosures" that appeared in *The Washington Post* described Thai as a former WorldCom systems engineer, who started his career anew by looking to none other than Donald Trump. During the boom that Thai helped fuel, he nabbed about ten luxury properties in the $1 million price range. He would buy from builders and then sell the contract prior to the home's completion for a hefty profit. Over time, he had enough play money to buy other homes financed with 1 percent negatively amortized Option ARM loans so that the rents came close to covering the $3,200 to $3,700 in carrying costs per property—but not quite close enough. In a rising market, he was rightfully confident. When interest rates on his adjustable rate mortgage loans used to finance his investments significantly adjusted upward as the market turned, Thai had no other choice but to seek lender permission for short sales. But, with only six months of savings set aside, he was soon wiped out. After the boom, Thai was left homeless and on the edge of bankruptcy.[223] Leverage cuts both ways. It is euphoric on the way up, but frightening on the way down.

Speculating also has another dimension that is focused on rehabilitation and reselling. On the resale market, an aging housing inventory presents numerous opportunities. Numerous television shows dominate the airwaves on how to transform a dump into a head-turning show place. It may have started with *This Old House*, but it looks like *Flip This House* and *Mobile Home Disaster* dominated a niche in the reality-based remodeling and house speculation shows.

The general rule of thumb is that for every dollar of work needed, the house is worth two dollars less than the fair market value. So, if a prospective house needs a $5,000 new roof, a $10,000 new kitchen, and a $3,500 new bath all totaling $18,500, then the offer should be at a minimum of $37,000 less than fair market value. Once the purchase loan closes, typically either hard cash or a line of credit attached elsewhere will be used to bring the home up to snuff for a quick turn around. But, if the owner-occupied speculator knows financing, he will use the FHA 203(k) loan since it was designed just for this purpose.

Some house flippers just churned through properties in a rising market in order to make a quick buck. In their article "Tales from Inside: Borrowers Discuss Housing Crunch," *Bradenton Herald* reporters Duane Marsteller and Jennifer Rich described how one enterprising agent made serious money during the boom:

> Real estate agent Joseph Kandel made lots of money buying and re-selling residential properties in Southwest and Central Florida before and during the 2004-06 housing boom. During one 18-month period, he said, he made $440,000 flipping five properties.[224]

When the market turned, Kandel attempted to unload by trying to sell his properties at a loss.

Regardless of motives, we as a people have at a minimum a two-fold love affair with real estate: making money off it and transforming the homestead. Many should recall that one of our founding fathers, Thomas Jefferson, lived above his means and was in a perpetual state of remodeling *Monticello*, which is perched 900 feet above sea level. His 5,000 acre spread was actually a private village with a population of 200 people. Of those, 150 were slaves. When he returned from Paris after having served as the United States ambassador to France, Jefferson expanded the size of *Monticello*. This was understandable, because he loved his home and it, along with the grounds, served as a refuge from "the splendid misery of politics." While serving two terms as America's third President, Jefferson spent 10 percent of his salary as President on imported wines for festive parties while at the White House.

Jefferson, like some today, was a man of contradictions. He was an idealist, kept imported wines in *Monticello's* cellar, and had a secret lover. That love was not a consensual relationship, but rather a master-slave relationship. He had sworn on the altar of God hostility against anything that would impede free thought, yet was part of the colonial Virginia legislature that forbade slaves from learning how to read and write. He viewed slavery as a moral and political depravity, but only freed 5 slaves in his will. His book collection was sold for $25,000 to buy time from impending bankruptcy, and served as the beginnings of the Library of Congress in Washington, D.C. Jefferson's finances, however, were over-leveraged. He died bankrupt with $107,000 of debt with the collapse of Virginia's tobacco-based economy. In current dollars, that debt might approach $2 million-plus. *Monticello* was left to his daughter, who had financial difficulties, and his Palladian-styled dream villa eventually fell into disrepair. Today, in its restored and properly cared for state, *Monticello* represents the aspirations of many, who are part of the American Dream—the ability to personally design and build the dream home that will endure through generations and stand as evidence of architectural genius. *Monticello* also serves as a reminder to Americans that sometimes it is not possible to make money off of real estate, especially if property is repeatedly pledged as collateral for more and more debt.

Concluding Thoughts

Real estate at its most fundamental level is shelter. It is the place we call home, where families are raised and memories are made and shared. Whether in a small town, a large city, the suburbs, or along a country road, the place we call home symbolizes the American Dream. It is the tangible expression of being part of the ownership-based society. In its more rarified forms, real estate is a tangible asset transformed into art.

Values and perceptions change over time. A significant change in perception towards housing took place between the 1970s and the early twenty first century. Homes increasingly became viewed as investments that could grow in value over time, and as a result, become a significant means to trade up to another home, and also become the means for retirement given a zero mortgage balance. During the boom, however, homes were viewed as sources for cash—a radical change from earlier years given the seemingly universal change in values regarding savings and planning for the future.

Beware of the market psychology. The psychology of the market during the refinance boom and housing bubble was driven by the "greed is good" adage much like the theme in the movie *Wall Street* along with a healthy rush of adrenaline—the true animal spirits that Adam Smith wrote about in *The Wealth of Nations*. These spirits drove both Wall Street and Main Street. Refinances dominated 2001 to 2003, but purchase loans seemed to be equal to the refinance volume between 2004 and 2006. Many home purchasers and homeowners who refinanced lost money and equity due to making a series of bad decisions while also not paying closer attention to changes in the market as well as warnings issued by the media.

Manias are periods of collective delusion. Both homeowners and investors were caught up in the mania that exists in bubbles that warp perception. Significant changes in the markets followed, and as result, have forced many to reconsider their plans. At the end of the Reagan Era, for example, those on the verge of retiring had to readjust their plans since home prices dropped. When the dot com bubble burst, high tech stocks plummeted in value, and that forced some investors to postpone retirement. The market signaled fear and uncertainty towards United States government intervention in the nation's financial sector, and in October 2008 the stock market lost significant value causing an unsettling among those ready to retire. Those who were counting on real estate values to keep climbing did not realize that they were speculating and helping to inflate the bubble—oblivious to the fact that incomes must be able to support home prices.

The upper crust is flaky. In the purchase realm, real estate speculators and investors—two completely different demographic profiles—drove a considerable share of the market during the boom. Short-term thinking speculators who lost money in real estate were caught up in the intoxicating mania that is common in any bubble. They were taken in by the seductive lure of quick profits. Many bought properties financed with highly leveraged debt with interest only or negatively amortized terms with the expectation of a quick sale. This strategy worked on the upside of the appreciation rate curve. In a real estate bubble, however, mania and euphoria drive the market. It is the downward slope that is painful since adrenaline-driven euphoria gives way to fear and panic. Long-term investors, on the other hand, know that it is not a good idea to be irrationally exuberant when making a business decision since the best way to get rich in real estate, typically, is slowly—unless, of course, there are steeply discounted opportunities. Investing in real estate is safer over the long term. Overleveraged borrowers who borrowed at the peak, or at the market's downward turn, invariably lost when the market abruptly plummeted. For many, what remains is not wealth in the form of income and assets, but memories of what was and what could have been.

The nation was drunk on home equity. In the refinance realm, some homeowners squandered their equity by regarding the home as a private automated teller machine. Some thought that equity was a bottomless pit given the breakneck speed of appreciation rates, tapping into the growing value of their homes for low-rate equity loans—while throwing the thought of retirement years out the window—without carefully considering the long-term consequences of repeated transaction costs with each refinance and exotic loans that do not retire the debt. They continued to cash out at higher loan-to-value ratios as the market peaked and then began to decline. Why did they do this? First of all, they ignored one of the rules of attending any wild and crazy party: leave while sober. Everyone knows that. Leave early. When is it time to leave? The answer to that question will vary based on the metropolitan statistical area. Timing an entry into and an exit from a strong market like the Washington, D.C. area may be quite different from a devastated market like Miami, Florida. It pays to have a subscription to at least *Business Week* since it is the best investment that will deliver an executive summary on the market. Moreover, follow the real estate absorption rates, which can be obtained by a seasoned real estate agent knowledgeable in the local market.

Profit is good, but gluttonous greed is stupid. Some short-term thinking speculators and refinancing homeowners who repeatedly refinanced and overleveraged, however, were overindulgent and reckless and did not know when to stop. They ignored all of the warning signs that made headlines in the newspapers and led the nightly news across the country. That brings us to this painful lesson for consumers, lenders, and investors: Pigs get fat, but hogs get slaughtered. That is how the market works.

Beware of asset seizure laws. In the United States, the federal government has repeatedly voted itself more and more authorization to seize private property—real estate, cars, boats, planes, art, jewelry, cash, bonds, stocks, and other assets—based not on fact but the belief that there was unlawful use of property. In 1984, the Omnibus Crime Bill passed and opened the flood gates for the organized theft by government of private property. Congressman Henry Hyde (R-Illinois), the author of the 1995 book *Forfeiting Our Property Rights: Is Your Property Safe From Seizure?*, said regarding these laws:

> Civil asset forfeiture has allowed police to view all of America as some giant national K-Mart, where prices are not just lower, but non-existent—a sort of law enforcement 'pick-and-don't-pay.'[225]

The Patriot Act further expanded these asset seizure powers.[226] More than 200 federal forfeiture statutes exist to target private assets, which makes this a $1 billion-plus annual windfall industry for federal and state agencies. Even cash has been criminalized. Failing to report to the Internal Revenue Service the purchase of more than $3,000 in money orders within 24 hours or a cash sale that is over $10,000 may result in asset forfeiture. All of this rests on the presumption of illegal activity, not *actual* illegal activity.

Federal forfeiture laws rest on a bizarre legal doctrine of *in rem* that tainted property is guilty, not the person, and that therefore the property must be punished. This is the same legal theory employed prior to the collapse of classical civilization in our Western heritage. In the classical world, the knives of murderers were put on trial, found guilty, confiscated, and then destroyed. The killers were let go under the theory that the knives were at fault.

In the view of government asset seizures do not constitute punishment, which is the rationale used to circumvent freedoms and rights. The presumption of innocence does not exist in these cases. Instead, the standard used by judges is hearsay and probable cause. Informants get the equivalent of a finder's fee for notifying federal agents. Moreover, attorney fees may be confiscated, which denies the injured public access to legal counsel. For citizens across the country who understand this issue or have been victimized by the government, there is no proportionality, the punishment does not fit the alleged crime, and it is nothing but organized theft under the guise of the rule of law. The series of laws have placed insurmountable administrative, legal and judicial hurdles that abolish not just the Bill of Rights but a legal tradition established in 1215 in the Magna Carta.

The legal theory that justifies asset seizures is evidence that elected officials hold tax payers, voters, and property owners in disdain and complete contempt. There is a defensive approach—secure legal counsel, because a tenant in a cash business or with drug habits could result in a lost asset and with no recourse. And, there is an offensive approach—fight back for forfeiture reform laws and denounce law enforcement lobbyists, who claim that reform amounts to a "soft on crime" policy. Remove from office the elected officials, who enacted the laws that clearly violate private property rights. More information on asset seizure laws and what property owners can do to protect their rights can be obtained through the Mill Valley, California-based Forfeiture Endangers American Rights Foundation, which can be visited online at www.fear.org.

Chapter 9
Needed Change

Just because everything is different doesn't mean anything has changed.
—Irene Peter

During the boom many conducted themselves as if on automatic pilot and within their comfort zones of familiarity. That continued until the foreseeable changes in the marketplace that were ignored occurred. Even with foresight and advanced warning, painful events forced change onto households and onto pockets of the financial sector. Those changes in the marketplace happened against the will of many and forced an uncomfortable series of behaviors to occur.

Home prices were pushed so high at the peak of the housing bubble in 2005 that only 11 to 15 percent of households could afford to purchase a home in any of America's major metropolitan areas.[227] In other words, housing in America remained affordable only for the top 15 percent of the nation. There was no stunning growth in population that placed added pressure on home prices. There was no real inflation as a result of scarcity or excessive demand. Building costs did not skyrocket. Labor costs associated with new home construction and remodeling did not rise. Incomes remained constant while household savings dropped. There is, however, an explanation for home price appreciation that is based on the true nature of the American economy.

The United States is not a cash-based economy. It is a credit-based economy and therefore synthetic. Home prices are synthetic, or elastic. As a result, home values have never been based on the real economy, because most households are cash poor.

Home values are not based on the fundamental economic laws of supply and demand and the absorption rate, which are the key benchmarks that real estate agents tend to address. Home prices, in contrast, are more closely tied to flexible underwriting standards, interest rates, and the receptiveness of the secondary market to invest in mortgage bonds. When these factors are coupled with low unemployment and high consumer confidence, America's real estate market is not normal as most would argue—it is inflationary.

The secondary market for residential mortgages collapsed July 2007. It became clear to policy makers that if mortgage credit vanished, home values could plummet to a small fraction of the cost to actually build. The importance in understanding this point is that incomes did not support unsustainable home values. The market for mortgages that the financial sector created propped up these values.

The Federal Reserve filled the void created by the flight of global investors away from America's securitized mortgage bonds. Mortgage underwriting standards, as a result, reverted to the standards from 20 years prior, when many lenders were far more prudent in their decision-making process. That set into motion a linked series of events across the economy.

Since jumbo financing disappeared, Congress passed the Housing and Economic Recovery Act of 2008, which did several things. It authorized the Federal Housing Administration to permit jumbo financing up to $625,000 for a single family home in a high cost area. The intention was to enable home sales that required loans in excess of $417,000 and to permit refinances for borrowers, who had taken 80/20 loans where the first mortgage was $417,000 and the second mortgage was $104,250. If refinancers had equity, they could get out from under their 5/1 interest only first mortgages and home equity line of credit second mortgages.

The foreclosure crisis followed, and that contributed to the financial and economic challenges across the United States. From the financial sector's perspective, foreclosures are about bad mortgages. Those non paying customers forced the banks to issue 3.9 million foreclosure filings against 2.8 million properties across America in 2009.[228] The foreclosure trends have increased since the crisis started and should slow by 2012. From the real estate industry's perspective, foreclosures are about more unsold inventory. From a municipality's perspective, foreclosures are about a decimated tax base, homeless shelters with a wait list, and new tent cities. From a household's perspective, foreclosures are personal and meant the end of the American Dream.

Foreclosures shocked households and communities in waves based on the types of loans originated. First, there were roughly $1 trillion in subprime loans many of which were adjustable rate mortgages and made up the first wave of foreclosures between 2007 and 2009. Second, there were roughly another $1 trillion in Alt-A mortgages. Many of these stated income mortgages were extended to high credit score homeowners, speculators, and investors and they experienced challenges when it came to refinance. Some experienced foreclosure. These Alt-A loans were forecasted to default in larger numbers between 2010 and 2012. Third, there was roughly $500 to $600 billion in outstanding Option ARMs.[229] This loan type in the pipeline is different from the others, because many borrowers took these loans in order to lower their housing costs by making the minimum payment so that they could afford to live in high cost areas. That fact suggests that mortgage balances that have increased by between 115 to 125 percent within five years of origination were secured against homes that have dropped by between 20 to 40 percent in value over that same period. That spells disasters for lenders and communities.

Widespread foreclosures and deliberately trashed homes by angered homeowners at the edge of foreclosure or eviction hurt the value of homes in the surrounding areas. That dampened resale activity and depressed home values further due to the unintended consequence of placing more homes on the market. The end result was a fiscal crisis at the state level with 41 states in the nation facing serious budget shortfalls with California and Florida in the lead. Economic recovery rests on getting the unemployment rate far below 10 percent, and not permitting that high unemployment rate to become the new normal. This is critical since consumers drive 70 percent of the American economy.

For any family that has gone through foreclosure, this is the opposite side of the coin of the American Dream. On the surface, the foreclosure crisis was due to mortgage lenders on a wide scale aggressively over marketing and originating an array of mortgage products that were not designed to sustain homeownership. Many household were victims of not having adequate financial literacy and over relying on a series of verbal assurances that came from everyone with a vested interest in closing the deal. When examined more closely, however, borrowers took on far more risk than was prudent due to their faith in the system and belief that the economy was vibrant and healthy.

The collapse of home values undermined the banks, communities, and the incentive for many homeowners to keep paying when it made more sense to mail in the keys and rent instead. For homeowners, a loss of value meant a loss of equity, wealth, and retirement plans. By 2010, approximately 21 million homes had negative equity. This made up 29 percent of homeowners with mortgages. Some of these white elephant real estate investments were among the pool of distressed home sales that come on the market as short sales and bank-owned properties. For first time buyers and speculators on the sidelines, a drop in home values meant welcomed relief and an opportunity to again enter the market. It also meant dealing with financial institution incompetence and inordinate delays due to the many short sales on the market that required third party approvals.

Households. The decision-making and loan process should not be rushed. No household should permit others regardless of their experience to manage a process with words like, "We need to get those papers in by Monday or you will lose the loan." These are artificially manufactured threats that needlessly create panic when just the opposite should be taking place—calm, carefully reasoned, and informed decision-making. Customers need to 100 percent turn the loan process on its head and take and retain complete control from beginning to end. The fact is loan commitments on an interest rate come and go. No decision should be hurried over one eighth or one fourth of a percentage of an interest rate. Households should contact the attorney general's office, file complaints with the appropriate regulatory agencies, and sue lenders for damages stemming from misrepresentation when interest rate assurances are based on 15 day pricing, but mortgage loans are closed in 45 to 60 days. These fairly common customer abuses are due to poor management and staffing shortages.[230]

Regardless if they are government-sponsored and subsidized, loan modifications serve the interests of the lender and can reduce struggling homeowners into prolonged financial servitude under one-sided and misleading terms that permit lenders to modify the terms at their discretion and without borrower recourse. While loan modifications can help struggling homeowners with more affordable terms, they come at the price of a longer term on what could be an investment not worth holding. A trusted attorney and a financial planner should be consulted prior to entering into any lender's contract to modify a mortgage's terms.

When attempts to modify the terms of a mortgage fail, a solution may be to sue the lender according to New York City attorney Carl E. Person. In states with judicial foreclosures, Person stated that there are many defenses borrowers can make that can result in saving the home and securing a lower rate. He stated that instead of throwing every penny at the bank, borrowers in the foreclosure process should instead stop paying, use those funds to retain legal counsel, and fight back. The key is to act early. He stated that the overwhelming majority of homeowners in foreclosure do not know their rights and, as a result, permit the lending community to have their way without a challenge.

There are a several reasons for those looking for a biblical explanation rooted in the Judeo-Christian tradition as to why the American dream became a global nightmare. First, there is no angry God in heaven that sent foreclosures and an economic crisis as punishment for mankind's sins. People created the problems in society. Second, the root of all evil does *not* rest in money, contrary to what the lyrics of Pink Floyd's 1973 song *Money* claims. Money is a good and an essential tool. It is the *love* of money that is the root of all evil.[231] Many consumers confused debt with money and many lenders driven by the desire for fee income believed that they were helping consumers by encouraging them to take on unsustainable debt under onerous terms. The *love* of money was beneath much of the misguided thinking by both lenders and homeowners. Third, the financial sector's ability to control credit that enables money to flow and stop in the economy is the ability to control government and wreak social chaos. Fourth, some homeowners did exactly what a desperate Esau did when faced with the choice presented by his brother Jacob that is described in *Genesis*.[232] They sold their birth right of security, stability, homeownership, and the prospects of no mortgage debt over time in exchange for the immediate gratification of a lot of cash made readily available through a home equity line of credit or a cash out refinance. The driving force for some was the temptations of increased consumer consumption that resulted from advertisements to buy now and pay later. Clearly, many confused their imagined wants to be real and pressing needs. That confusion led to financial misfortune. As a result, many Americans believed it to be morally wrong for the government to intervene and rescue households from the consequences of their misguided financial decisions.

Minorities. "Borrowing while black" meant black Americans were given the short end of the stick by the financial sector.[233] The descriptive statistics indicate that blacks as well as Latinos paid more for their loans, were given higher interest rates, were offered less favorable loan programs, and were more likely to suffer the indignities of foreclosure, the ruination of credit, and a greater diminishment of wealth than non minorities. Consequently, the nation's racial minorities should file an Equal Credit

Opportunity Act complaint with each mortgage loan application as a part of doing business. This preemptive action will put both the regulators and corporations on notice that they understand how they have been treated over the years. They have this right under the law, and they should exercise that right.

Blaming blacks and Latinos for the subprime meltdown and the foreclosure crisis was the moral equivalent of blaming Jews for the economic crisis. Neither was logical. Both were bigoted. Yet, both ideas persist. Black and Latino advocacy groups strangely enough were largely silent, which was remarkable. Pushing for increased homeownership through Fannie Mae and Freddie Mac and Community Reinvestment Act lending was initially presented by the media to pin the blame on misguided policy that set up minorities for failure. The homeownership rate of 64 percent in 1994 increased to 69 percent at the market's peak. Many blamed government for policies that pushed homeownership on minorities, who would have been better left alone and renting. The earlier estimates in 2007 were 6.5 million cumulative foreclosures by 2012, but were increased to 8 million at a projected cost of $702 billion to the economy. In 2008, Credit Suisse forecasted that 13 percent of American homeowners with mortgages could lose their homes to foreclosure. In other words, by 2012 the homeownership rate could be far below what it was in 2007. This suggests that the modest 5 percent gain in homeownership was not the source of the nation's problems, but instead a veiled form of bigotry aimed at blaming minorities given that 13 percent of homeowners will be on the streets. Simply put, that was due to predatory and fraudulently originated loans that were aimed at Americans that were too trusting. Mortgage lenders transformed their own customers into victims for the federal and local governments to handle the clean up.

Blaming minorities and government programs that encouraged broadened homeownership were rabbit holes that the media used to take the public into the dark. The source of the nation's Wall Street-driven problems was rooted in lopsided legislation. That resulted from the financial influence of corporations over elected officials. These facts, blame shifting, and deceptions were propagated by the financial firms, disseminated through the mainstream media, and then became the object for jokes on late night talk shows in the United States and in other countries.

America has been and will always be a nation of immigrants. Mastery of the English language is not easy even for many native born Americans.

Given these facts, those where English is a second language need to understand that assent is an element to a valid and binding contract. This means that there may be legal recourse available if a contract was signed without comprehension. Contracts, regardless of the language, should not be extended by lenders and signed by borrowers unless there is a reasonable degree of certainty that the borrower has understood the terms and its ramifications.

Investors. The upper end of the socio economic strata of society has significant assets, much more disposable income than other income strata in America, and has the ability to purchase many properties. This affluent segment took advantage of 90 to 95 percent investor financing programs that were available. Since Fannie Mae and Freddie Mac had lifted restrictions on the number of properties investors could own, these agencies enabled many to purchase up to eight properties. In the non-traditional, private sector lending niche, there were no restrictions and some investors purchased in excess of 20 properties. This factor coupled with the ability to secure no income and no asset verification loans with interest only features were the primary reasons home prices escalated to absurdly unsustainable levels. The end result was that would be owner occupants chose to rent, because they were priced out of housing in many of the nation's real estate markets.

Investors have their place in an economy. Many, without fully realizing the end result of their business decisions, serve society by providing subsidized housing for renters who do not have to pay real estate taxes, maintenance costs, and the costs for capital improvements as properties age and render homes functionally obsolete. The amateurs managing their holdings hope to become wealthy, which is not possible if the mortgage is not paid off and if properties are not appreciating in value. They also believe that they will enjoy income streams, which for many was not possible since they took out large mortgages under terms that required refinances. The primary beneficiaries in this skewed scheme are tenants, who need hassle free interim or short term housing. The secondary beneficiaries are real estate agents, property managers, loan officers, contractors, and handymen. Investors, who act as landlords, are last on the list provided that they have the tax benefits, positive cash flow, and equity over time. Struggling landlords, who for whatever reason have their rental properties go into foreclosure have other risks that are greater. Many who do not live in a homestead exemption state or have their personal residence paid off and shielded behind a trust, lose their personal homes to foreclosure as well as lenders seek to satisfy deficit judgments that arise when rental properties go into foreclosure. Given the benefits and risks, prospective investors should better understand the financial and legal ramifications of becoming a speculator or landlord and have the financial ability to absorb the costs of several unexpected turn of events.

Corporations. Mortgage bankers and brokers have lost the right of respect in the marketplace and need to face this as an indisputable fact. Trust was earned. Reputations were made. Brand images and loyalty grew over time. Customer loyalty came with these. Employees were happy to build the company with an eye to the future. Investors bought shares based on reasonable expectations of company growth. All of these were squandered in pursuit of more originations and securitizations. The corporate failures that followed ended with the manipulation of the federal government and the abuse of the American tax payer.

The clearest example comes from the power of one individual. Roy De Young posted a video on You Tube on April 21, 2009 and articulated what millions across the nation felt, the inherent injustice of credit card issuers financially hobbling households by virtue of a credit card rate hike by the too big to fail banks that had destroyed the economy, took federal bailout money, and then claimed a change in market conditions necessitated higher rates. De Young, a vice president of a marketing firm, took to You Tube, ripped up his Bank of America check book, and told the American public that he was not going to take it any more. De Young urged viewers to do the same, but in large numbers.[234] He then rebranded Bank of America as Bend over America due to the institution's conduct. He used the letters F and U as part of the red and blue logo. De Young then promoted the corporate rebranding through T-shirts, baseball caps, mouse pads, coffee cups, bumper stickers, and even cute teddy bears available through CafePress.com.

De Young was not alone in his anger towards the big banks and their destructive credit card terms. His message is simple—"Customers, not institutions, own the brand."[235] When the "Countrywide Sucks" message went viral across the Internet, Bank of America had no choice but to pull that destroyed brand name and replace it with the Bank of America brand label. That changed none of the less obvious facts: Countrywide employees with Countrywide's training and business practices were within Bank of America.

Management. Hiring standards during the boom were rock bottom. Forget the state's low licensing standards. Hiring managers need to set the bar higher and prevent those with criminal backgrounds from entry into the lending business. The same applies to the urine test. These should be used not to demonstrate who is in charge, but to protect the public from the "victimless crime" of "recreational" drug use by employees that results in impaired judgment within the financial sector.

Management pressured loan officers to get more prospective borrowers qualified rather than making sure each prospective borrower had an ability to repay. They used in-house training and seminars that emphasized sales techniques, customer control, increased production, and new "affordability" loan programs rather than focusing on sustainable homeownership programs. That pressure on loan officers was the result of management's desire for more closings each month and the larger paychecks that served as the evidence of another good month of production. The compensation alignment in almost all lending institutions was such that quantity of production, not quality of production, became the guiding force. As Carroll Quigley noted in his 1966 book *Tragedy and Hope*:

> Each individual, just because he is so powerfully motivate by self-interest, easily loses sight of the role which his own activities play in the economic system as a whole, and tends to act as if his activities *were* the whole, with inevitable injury to that whole.[236]

That guiding force of how compensation was aligned within the mortgage lending industry was misguided, and needs to be reformed. Capping fees helps, but will not prevent customer abuse.

Target marketing was one of the wonders of actionable data, good technology, and reliable outsourced services. Niche marketing into specific minority groups, however, needlessly exposed many companies to charges of reverse redlining. The benefits of "working smart" were costly in legal defenses, and more costly due to damaged reputations. Even when cases of this nature are dismissed or a verdict of innocence comes forward, the public will remember the accusations that lenders targeted and exploited minorities and devastated their communities. As a result of these factors, management should become more cautious in how they determine where and to whom to target their marketing communications. That managerial caution should take place by reviewing case studies on reverse redlining, understanding the impact of racial discrimination in housing and lending, counting the cost of defending lawsuits, and understanding the damage from lost professional reputations and how that results in fewer customers and qualified personnel not willing to be associated with firms perceived to be irresponsible.

Loan originators. Loan officers are the liaison between a corporation and its customers. There is no worse representative in a knowledge intensive business than an employee, who does not read a newspaper or a magazine. Moreover, there is no worse representative in the lending business than those who do not understand the basis for fair housing and fair lending legislation. Yet, approximately one third of loan originators based on a survey of those in attendance in continuing education credit courses fall into this category.[237] The public sees them as economists and financial advisors, yet that is the furthest thing from what originators are. Many loan originators do not bother to stay informed by taking the time to read a magazine or a newspaper let alone books on economics or finance. That needs to change.

Training and continuing education. Ethics is the foundation and the next layer is an understanding of history. Failure to understand the connection between the assassination of Martin Luther King, Jr., the civil rights movement, and the housing and lending laws that followed demonstrates a rote memorization as an approach to training as opposed to understanding the reasons consumer protections laws came about. That training approach may be the reason so many reverse red lining lawsuits occurred.

The Secure and Fair Enforcement for Mortgage Licensing Act of 2008 is a catch, tag, and release program for mortgage brokers and loan officers in federally and state chartered banks. The theory is that licensing and continuing education requirements will standardize and raise the bar higher within the lending industry. A national data base of licenses will permit regulators and perhaps watch groups to monitor lenders for rogue behavior, and thereby have a basis to take action. The Act was met with widespread resentment in the lending industry due to self-interested thinking. The Act, however, was an overdo step in the right direction, but will not be a cure all for preventing either incompetence or rogue behavior that characterized the industry during the boom.

Compliance departments and personnel need to be independent of sales departments and not subordinate to them. Legal departments fear legal action from consumers, municipalities, and the attorneys general due to complaints that arise due to a lack of compliance. Yet, litigation is factored in by corporations as the cost of doing business. Pushing the risk envelope invited mortal risk for many corporations. That risk included lost reputations, loss of financial standing, and seasoned talent that more than likely will never return.

The big banks have incompetent personnel on staff. Those borrowers seeking loan modifications perfectly understand this point. Low level employees, who have little to no industry experience, are poorly trained and do not even understand the documents that they ask their borrowers to sign. The treatment customers receive when they ask questions is no different than the frustrating and time consuming experience of being in a car dealership where the salesman has to go back and forth between the customer and either a credit manager or a sales manager to clarify every point of concern. That problem will be solved when the big banks again fail or are dismantled through preemptive regulation into more manageable sized businesses. This will permit subject matter expertise and customer service to be recognized as valued employee skills rather than as added overhead costs associated with an employee's experience.

Trade associations. They are up there on America's "most hated" list and for good reason. With industry experts warring against the nation's many communities and setting up households for failure, the associations demonstrated that they had no shortage of misguided captains at the helm of leadership.

The Mortgage Bankers Association fought against the nation's municipalities and consumer groups as they implemented legislation to curb predatory lending practices. Its spokesman John Mechem said, "These lawsuits can scare lenders out of the market."[238] The lending establishment, through its association and industry lobbyists, had essentially told local governments and the general public: it's going to be our way or the highway. The best thing that could have happened for the United States would have been if many lenders had been forced out of the market. The doctrine of preemption in *Watters v Wachovia* provided lenders with federal support to wage war and overcome. The after math was a fore-closure crisis, a fiscal crisis across most states, and a political crisis with citizens and states that fought to contain the federal government.

The chief economist for the National Association of REALTORS® David Lereah at the peak of the bubble in February 2005 published his book *Are You Missing the Real Estate Boom?: Why Home Values and Other Real Estate Investments Will Climb Through the End of the Decade - And How You Can Profit from It.* Lereah argued that the boom would last another decade due to a next generation of homebuyers, who would fill the void left by the baby boom generation.[239] Nothing could have been further from the truth, because the collapse of housing prices will in the best of scenarios result in at least a decade of stagnation provided that no monetary crisis follows the fiscal crisis due to the nation's heavy fiscal spending in 2009.

These two associations, culprits in faulty thinking and bad counsel to the media as well as their respective memberships, need to publicly admit to their wrong-headed approach as representatives of their industries while committing to serving the best interests of not just their dues paying members, but the American public. The American people are more astute about the public relations craft in the 21st century than in prior decades, so it will take far more than the clever advertisements used by companies like Ameriquest that had planted a wedge of doubt in the public's mind regarding its culpability tied to institutionalized predatory lending. Putting the customer first within a code of ethics, free of self-interested motives, is the place to start.

Consumer groups. Most of the consumer oriented groups that have spoken out against bad corporate conduct and predatory lending practices have been vilified by the right wing media. This happened, because the news media no longer functions as a vehicle for journalistic news, but instead serves as unbridled propaganda to unleash smear campaigns against political opponents of the financial sector. These groups have their place and are essential in balancing a lopsided playing field where corporations and their lobbyists have unparalleled resources and access to political power to shape one-sided legislation at the expense of the American household.

Real estate agents. For many people, the first contact that is made for a home purchase or even a mortgage loan is with a real estate agent.

Marketplace knowledge and experience means a competitive edge. Like loan officers, however, approximately one third of residential real estate agents based on a survey of those in attendance in continuing education credit courses do not read a major newspaper or magazine and do not understand the mechanics of why the economy collapsed. More troubling, too many do not understand that credit means debt and that a mortgaged property could adversely impact retirement. That short coming needs to change through more rigorous continuing education courses as a condition for having a license.

Set the bar higher. Chris Sorenson of the Temecula, California-based Homeownership Education Learning Program (USA HELP) has stepped in to fill a void in the real estate and lending industry. Sorenson's non-profit organization has a two-pronged approach. One is with industry professionals, and the other is with consumers. USA Help raised the bar higher than state and federal mandates, and put in place a system for consumer recourse. Sorenson said:

> First, USA HELP requires industry professionals secure more education in order for them to be listed on our website as holding to the highest ethical and knowledge standards. Second, educating the struggling homeowners as well as those who are doing fine and then offering them a list of real estate, lending, and loan modification professionals that the public may hold accountable has been a long time coming. Our consumer education is designed to set the proper expectations to avoid this on going challenge. Third, if a consumer has been wronged, a simple one page form will be all that is required to address the issue. If the professional is found to have been at fault by a review panel, they may be suspended from the list our removed all together. If the offense is egregious, USA HELP will file the complaint to the proper authority on behalf of the client.[240]

The underlying idea is a carrot and stick approach, which suggests that the existing carrot and stick approach with state and federal regulators were inadequate. As important, USA Help is national in scope.

Closing attorneys and title agents. They have a specifically defined and limited role. They are licensed by the state to close loans by following lender instructions. They do not represent borrowers or purchasers in the transaction. Their role is not to read and interpret a contract. These people are not financial experts. They are not financial planners or economists. Given these facts, purchasers and borrowers would do well to secure an independent third party that is a subject matter expert to review promissory notes, mortgage modification agreements, and other closing documents. Since mortgage fraud is almost always an inside job with the closing being one of the most vulnerable links in the chain of third party contacts that customers pay, it behooves everyone to pay far greater attention to the closing process rather than to the nice mahogany table in the conference room.

Regulators. Contrary to their allegedly designated roles, banking regulators protect banks, not consumers. The nation's leading banking regulator the Federal Reserve took just three actions against subprime lenders between 2002 and 2007. Two were tied to accounting-related issues in Puerto Rico.[241] Only one, however, was specifically tied to mortgage lending. After the financial and economic crisis made global headlines, the Federal Reserve's regulatory investigations spiked. But, its actions were irrelevant and too late since irreparable harm to households, member banks, and the economy had already occurred.

Regulators were aware of the fact that short-term hybrid adjustable rate mortgages were often mismatched with the subprime borrowers' ability to sustain their obligations. Regulators, however, did not act on their own to protect consumers. After waiting several years from their initial investigations on predatory lending practices, they acted under public and congressional pressure to protect consumers. Federal banking agencies and state regulators adopted the "Interagency Guidance on Nontraditional Mortgage Product Risks" of October 2006[242] and the "Statement on Subprime Mortgage Lending" of June 29, 2007.[243] As a result, the 2/28 and 3/27 subprime hybrid adjustable rate mortgage products were pulled off the shelf. This was not a true product safety recall since borrowers with these products would still suffer the consequences of these poorly engineered products that produced financial devastation to more than just the borrowers. The irony of the "Interagency Guidance on Nontraditional Mortgage Product Risks" is that the free market preempted the regulators since investors stopped investing in subprime securities. In other words, the secondary market place drove the regulation as the market collapsed. The regulation simply reflected what the marketplace was indicating. That abysmal failure to regulate was rooted in a lack of accountability in America's fourth branch of government—the administrative agencies.

Congress rescues Wall Street. When the subprime and foreclosure crises started, U.S. Treasury Secretary Henry Paulson blamed housing for the nation's unfolding economic problems. He chose not to blame bad debt rooted in mortgage fraud and predatory lending that he and others in government labeled "toxic assets." Paulson's misleading pronouncements that deflected blame from the financial sector became the dominant and accepted narrative in the media and on Capitol Hill.

The secrecy of the nation's manager of monetary policy concerning its nontransparent role in the $700 billion Wall Street bailout served as the nation's wake up call to bring the institution under more careful scrutiny and greater accountability. The bill passed into law in an environment of panic, hysteria, and under collective emotional distress. An extra $84 billion was added for other needs. The money for the Wall Street bailout, however, was not applied for purposes as sold to Congress by Henry Paulson, Timothy Geithner, and Ben Bernanke. Approximately 83 percent of the too big to fail banks used Troubled Asset Relief Program funds to encourage more consumer debt by issuing new credit cards with higher limits at higher rates. About 43 percent of those banks used government money to add to their capital cushion. About 31 percent of the firms went shopping, bought other firms, and made other investments.[244] The true cost of the Wall Street bailout, depending on the sources, ranges between a low of $2 trillion and a high of $23.7 trillion.[245] A third source said that the true cost of the bailout would be 20 times higher than the $700 billion that was sold to the U.S. Congress—or $14.4 trillion.[246] The United States Congress has no idea where the bail out money went, because the Federal Reserve refused to completely disclose where the money went.

The special inspector general for the U.S. Treasury's Troubled Asset Relief Program Neil Barofsky said that there were 35 criminal and civil investigations against firms and individuals. These investigations included mortgage fraud, securities fraud, accounting fraud, tax fraud, insider trading, and public corruption. Barofsky singled out Timothy Geithner when he was head of the Federal Reserve Bank of New York for being the single culprit responsible for overpaying Wall Street firms that enabled the bonuses to executives that had bankrupted the firms.[247] Those bonuses outraged the nation. In spite of the widespread opposition by the American people, the Senate confirmed Geithner to serve as the secretary to the U.S. Treasury.

The Congressional response to the regulatory negligence of the Federal Reserve was H.R. 1207 – Audit the Federal Reserve introduced by Congressman Ron Paul (R-Texas). The grassroots response was a call to abolish the Federal Reserve as evidenced by a nationwide grassroots group called End the Fed! At the core of the concerns was the fact that the Federal Reserve is a privately held, member bank owned institution that invariably has a conflict of interest to serve as a government agency while at the same time having an obligation to its shareholders to maximize returns.

End The Fed! organizer Anthony Lombard of New York City said that Aaron Russo's 2006 film *America: Freedom to Fascism* was the inspiration for his entry into political activism. Lombard said he would like to see the American dollar backed by a stable commodity and the U.S. Treasury and the Government Accountability Office in charge of the nation's currency. Lombard's basis for this is because these agencies are accountable to and transparent before the Congress, which represents the American people. In contrast, the Federal Reserve is not transparent, but instead represents the interests of its private shareholders and members banks.

The Federal Reserve has marketplace power to expand and contract credit across the banking system. That is the power to facilitate and also undermine consumer confidence. As the nation's regulator of the money supply contracted credit in conjunction with the marketplace's rejection of securitized bonds that had subprime mortgages, Alt-A loans, and Option ARMs, staggering job losses put a chill on the broader economy.

Consumers cut back on spending. As a result, businesses across the nation dependant on consumers engaged in discretionary spending shut down, and more people started loosing their jobs. As the nation's 30th President Calvin Coolidge (1923 – 1929) once observed, when many people lose their jobs, unemployment tends to rise. A corollary to that astute observation was echoed by the nation's 43rd President George W. Bush (2001 – 2009) who once said, "It's very important for folks to understand that when there's more trade, there's more commerce."

Of course, due to the lack of "trade," or consumer purchases, the unemployment numbers rose each month. The official unemployment figure by the end of 2008 hit 10.6 million. The unemployment rate was unevenly dispersed across the population with 6.3 percent of whites, 11.5 percent of blacks, and 8.9 percent of Latinos looking for work or underemployed.[248]

By March 2010, the economy still had not improved. The Obama Administration said that the economic stimulus programs had made a positive impact. In fact, the economy got much worse. The fact is, unemployment impacted 15 million Americans—a 50 percent increase from 2008.

The misleading nature of the official unemployment statistics published by the Bureau of Labor Statistics should have been apparent to the public since the official unemployment rate was 9.7 percent—a number that only represented recently unemployed, not those who could not secure full-time employment or those who were unemployed for more than 6 months. A comprehensive unemployment statistic takes into account the official unemployment "plus all persons marginally attached to the labor force, plus total employed part time for economic reasons, as a percent of the civilian labor force plus all persons marginally attached to the labor force the discouraged worker and loosely attached," which leads to 16.9 percent of Americans as of March 2010.[249]

The under reported news in the United States is that the suicide rate approaches the murder rate. Crisis hot lines field more calls during a recession and suicide rates increase during a bad economy. In Los Angeles, for example, crisis hotline centers fielded 60 percent more calls during 2008 while mental health experts claimed that what would normally be considered a seasonal case of the blues became a serious crisis with fear as the leading reason that led everyday people to place 2,400 calls per month to the suicide hotline operated by the Community Mental Health Center in greater Los Angeles and over 50,000 calls per month at National Suicide Prevention Lifeline—1-800-273-TALK (8255).[250] While 90 percent of suicides are linked to a mental illness like depression or anxiety disorders,[251] one study "consistently found economically disadvantaged people at higher risk for suicide."[252] However, those who have the highest risk of suicide, according to another study, are those who had high social and economic status and then lost employment, income, social standing, and a marriage.[253] Suicide, as an escape, therefore can bee seen as an escape from humiliation.

Once the mainstream media got the message from the experts to tone it down, the subject quickly changed to 24/7 coverage of the H1N1 virus labeled "swine flu"—the hyped pandemic that never happened. That took place at the financial expense of America's hog farmers. Then, health care reform, anarchy in the Town Hall meetings, and cash for clunkers served as sensational diversions from the underlying national story—the role of the financial sector acting as hit man on the American economy.

Academics and students. Academic writers, educational trade associations, educators and trainers, and students need to reassess every financial and business model that supported the paradigm of Western finance. Capitalism and finance are not the same. Finance is the handmaiden of capitalism.

Classic explanations for price levels based on the equilibrium point of the supply and demand curve are simplistic and misleading when it comes to an asset like stocks and real estate since prices tied to these are a function of the synthetic economy, not the real economy. In the real economy of cash based transactions, it is easy to understand the relationship between supply and demand. The synthetic economy in the developed nations, however, is radically different. Price levels are determined by interest rates and credit terms that can be relaxed or tightened. Moreover, price levels are also impacted by government intervention through tax credits, tax deductions, fiscal stimulus, changes in accounting rules, and direct government intervention that distorts the free market.

The stock market is a reflection of confidence among speculators, not investors. An uptick in the stock market has little to do with the real economy. Only in the initial public offerings are companies better capitalized by investors in order to grow a business to the next level. The stock market is a resale market of speculation, which reflects the anticipated direction given signals in the market place.

The efficient market hypothesis is irrelevant and works only on paper or as a thought experiment. Most investors do not read the annual reports, do not understand the financial statements, and do not share the same knowledge concerning the market or the condition of a firm. As a result, the efficient market hypothesis does not apply to pricing stocks and bonds, especially when there has been excessive government intervention in the market.

Keynesian economics is the handmaiden of the central banking business model that encourages unsustainable sovereign debt through fiscal stimulus programs. Keynesian economic theory and central banking practices interfere with the free market and distort price levels. If left alone, the free market is capable of determining fair value for products, services, and labor. Inflation is not a result of the viscous wage-price spiral. Inflation is the result of a central bank's monetary policy that devalues the currency, interest rates, and underwriting guidelines, which together cause price levels to rise and fall.

The worst thing that can happen is another generation of students that parrot back answers for a grade. Students should challenge everything that is presented in the text books and taught in the classrooms and deconstruct every theoretical model that too many have mistakenly assumed to be facts. Educators need to take the lead and encourage vigorous inquiry since knowledge comes by dissecting and understanding comes by reassembling.

American citizens and voters respond. Fear and anger gripped many Americans as a result of the $700 billion Wall Street bailout. Some viewed the election of Barack Obama as the nation's first black president with liberal and progressive leanings as the lightning rod that absorbed the American people's fiery concerns. The dissenting public's emotions were channeled through patriotic language and over the top rhetoric of the Tea Party movement under the Gadson flag with the "don't tread on me" theme.

That over the top rhetoric made sense and was widespread and supported by the findings of Rasmussen Reports national telephone survey findings published March 22, 2010 that indicated only 11 percent of Americans believed Congress was doing a good or an excellent job. That same study indicated that 76 percent of Americans thought most members of Congress were more interested in their own careers rather than serving the American people.[254]

The loss of the American people's trust in many members of Congress is perhaps best illustrated in Countrywide's VIP program for "friends of Angelo" and Senator Christopher Dodd (D-Connecticut). The mainstream media narrowly focused on favorable loan terms that Countrywide Home Loans offered for Dodd's two properties. That, however, was not the real story. Dodd's mortgage applications had every appearance of mortgage fraud. Dodd reported different incomes for the different applications tied to his primary residence and his second home. Lenders typically extend higher interest rates on second homes. Dodd's likely motive was to obtain the lower owner occupied interest rates for both properties. The mortgage applications also revealed dramatically different debt-to-income ratios when quality control checking the reported incomes for misrepresentation.[255] That type of run of the mill mortgage fraud in stated income loans across the industry was guided and enabled by Countywide Home Loans. After the Select Committee on Ethics investigation spent one year to consider alleged wrongdoing, Dodd was cleared—though the facts indicated otherwise.[256] That in turn called into question the credibility of the ability of the Senate to self regulate.

What those affiliated with the Tea Party share in common with the Association of Community Organizations for Reform Now, ACORN for short, and Service Employees International Union, or the SEIU, is opposition to the financial sector's abuse of customers and clients, that sector's widespread fiscal mismanagement, and the government intervention that permitted the outrageous bonuses to be paid to employees at Goldman Sachs and American International Group, Inc., or AIG. These areas, however, may be where the common shared concerns end. The Coffee Party USA took a poll that echoed similar mainstream concerns.[257] In its April 14, 2010 poll, 92 percent believed that Coffee Party USA "should address the role of money in politics. Moreover, 89 percent believed that Coffee Party USA "should prioritize making Wall Street accountable to Main Street."[258] While these groups may appear to be poles apart given how the mainstream media has controlled the narrative and manufactured villains for the sport of public spectacle, these very different organizations in fact share fairly similar views concerning the financial sector.

The Tea Party is an organic social movement with two components. First, it is a top down driven movement to breath life into a failed Republican Party through the Tea Party Express. It is funded by oil and health care interests, which explains the "drill, baby drill" messages, the corporate driven opposition to healthcare reform, and the anger in the Town Hall meetings. It is also a media driven phenomenon as a result of Glenn Beck of *FOX News*. Second, it is a bottom up driven populist movement that rejects the Republican and Democratic parties as well as the mainstream media.[259] As such, the Tea Party is not a subculture or a counterculture. It represents the American mainstream that is largely made up of middle aged Americans. Adherents are mostly white, and politically and fiscally right of center. Many are cynical and feel disillusioned by the two party system and the role the mainstream media has played in dividing the American people against each other.

Many other subculture or counterculture groups, however, support the Tea Party's key ideas and have rode on the coat tails of the movement's growth and populist appeal. Political libertarians and liberals are among the ranks. Racial minorities are active in the many subgroups as well. The politically wounded Republican Party has rode on the coat tails of the movement in the form of the Tea Party Express, which many grassroots organizers have claimed they oppose since the two party system of equally unappealing choices that cater to either big unbridled government or big unbridled corporations have consistently produced legislative and fiscal disasters for the American people.

Tea Party adherents ascribe to four key ideas: opposition to government bailouts, opposition to excessive taxation, demand to respect the Constitution, and demand to respect individual freedom. Like the Boston and San Francisco Tea Party groups that had rejected the *9/11 Commission Report* on December 16, 2006 when the phrase Tea Party was first used in modern history to express political dissent, Tea Party adherents in the aftermath of the Wall Street bailout and the Panic of 2008 that followed also in large numbers question the need for the "Documents of Tyranny"—Patriot Acts, Military Commission Acts, Presidential Directive 51, as well as any other presidential directive or Congressional Act that curbs liberty, usurps individual rights, or has any appearance of heavy handed federal government, or manufactured consent as a result of an orchestrated crisis. Many subgroups like We Are Change question the official account of the terror attacks of September 11, 2001 and want a new investigation to takes into account the views of architects and engineers. Many fear that the global war on terror that followed those terror attacks was a pretext to create a police state in America and to build a New World Order.[260]

That over the top rhetoric among some who attend Tea Party rallies sent a chill through many who suspected and feared a resurgence of racism and bigotry in America. The Tea Party slogan "We want our country back" was interpreted by the Southern Poverty Law Center and those with a skin deep understanding of politics to make the repeated assertion that Tea Party activists were radical right wing extremists and racists and the breeding ground for hate groups.[261] Some from the southern states carried Confederate flags in the protest rallies, and that controversial flag reverberated with double meanings. On one hand that flag symbolized secession from the union, which supported one Tea Party theme that the federal government had become tyrannical. On the other hand, that flag symbolized white supremacy, the belief in the inferiority of blacks, and the economic exploitation of enslaved Africans that hade defined the Confederate southern states. The media did not question the allegations of the Southern Poverty Law Center, did not investigate on their own, but reported the defamations, which based on the actions of a few served to smear the majority within the Tea Party that were engaged in lawful political dissent.

According to a *USA Today*/Gallup Poll conducted March 26 - 28, 2010 and published April 5th, 28 percent of Americans called themselves supporters of the Tea Party.[262] Only 49 percent of Republicans supported the Tea Party while 51 percent of Independents and Democrats supported the Tea Party. According to the same poll, those who embraced the values put forward by the Tea Party based on age, education, employment status, and race reflected the general public. In other words, the Tea Party was quite reflective of America, not the fringes.

What makes Tea Party different from the rest of the population is that 87 percent opposed passage of healthcare legislation whereas only 50 percent of all Americans were opposed to its passage. The findings stated that 65 percent considered themselves pro-life on the abortion issue. Only 26 percent were pro-choice. Nationally, 46 percent of Americans were pro-choice. These findings suggest that many Tea Party supporters embrace traditional values while those within who differ on other core issues may be Democrats, Independents, and Libertarians. The political dissent and engagement concerning abortion and healthcare reflected another chapter in America's ongoing culture war.

The findings of the *USA Today*/Gallup Poll also suggested that much of the mainstream media was out of touch with both the nation's true pulse beat and had violated sound journalistic practices. The widespread failure in investigative news reporting was due to embedded journalism, inbuilt media bias, misguided producers that had confused news with entertainment and advocacy journalism where television personalities become the story rather than report the story, and what many media critics have labeled as propaganda on behalf of the government and the corporate sector.

Some, however, indeed took their over the topic rhetoric and engaged in senseless acts of vandalism as was the case when the health reform bill passed. Others, not associated with the Tea Party, snapped when the economy collapsed and in a last desperate act committed suicide as was the case of Andrew Joseph Stack, who flew a plane into a building that housed the Internal Revenue Service. These types of unfortunate and tragic events served as opportunities for critics of the Tea Party to spread more disinformation and misinformation.

The "We want our country back" slogan popular with the Tea Party, however, spoke to the widespread recognition and demand that government:

Abide by the U.S. Constitution and Bill of Rights;

Rid the nation of the inordinate influence of the Council on Foreign Relations on the nation's domestic and foreign policies;

Stay focused on America as an economically viable sovereign nation rather than bent on building a global empire with political puppets that produce populist rage abroad directed back at America;

Permit corporate bankruptcies rather than provide government bailouts of the private sector;

Remind elected officials that they represent voters not think tanks and corporations;

Not cater to the corporate or financial sector at the expense of citizens, who have been made victims by both corporations and the federal government;

Cease and desist from resorting to Keynesian economic theories that increase the federal deficit to the delight of the Federal Reserve and the member banks that are shareholders; and

Audit and abolish the Federal Reserve and have the U.S. Treasury resume its originally intended role with an asset-backed currency in order to protect Americans from the ravages of inflation.[263]

The mainstream media, it would seem, vilified the Tea Party, because of its policy threats posed by the core populist messages directed against the military-financial-industrial-media complex. Beneath that "We want our country back" message, moreover, was the desperate cries of the Republican Party that had forfeited the right to control the White House and the Congress.

Political dissent is healthy and revitalizing for America. These require reliable information. The change that is needed most in America is widespread citizen-driven journalism that investigates, documents, and delivers real news independent of the establishment utilizing social networking media, alternative media, and independent media. This is important to ensure a truly informed rather than propagandized citizenry so that this Republic with democratic values and freedoms can have a more enlightened discussion on key topics without the misinformation, disinformation, and demonization that characterizes news coverage and over the top commentary in the mainstream media.

The financial sector's war on the American household and investor continues. After the $700 billion Wall Street bailout, the financial sector did not declare a cease fire on the mortgaged American household and real estate investor. The Wall Street Reform and Consumer Protection Act may deliver about 90 percent of the needed reform. But, the most important 10 percent is missing. Through the reform bill, the financial sector preempted the Financial Crisis Inquiry Commission by pressuring law makers to sign this bill into law prior to the commission's report to Congress, the White House, and the American people. Congress praised the bill and the White House blamed lobbyists for pushing for a one sided bill. There is no audit of the Federal Reserve. The central bank is held harmless. The Bureau of Consumer Financial Protection is embedded inside of the Federal Reserve. This is the regulatory equivalent of embedded reporting in journalism. In journalism, the end result is propaganda. In regulation, it means that Congress will be told that victims of predatory lending and unilateral credit terms that devastate households will have enjoyed the freedoms that come with abundant consumer choice. The Federal Reserve does not have primary obligations to the American people, but to its shareholders, which are the member banks that helped ruin the American economy. The central bank has secondary obligations as a federal agency to Congress and is less than completely transparent. The Bureau of Consumer Financial

Protection should be an independent agency, and it should have a healthy adversarial relationship with the Federal Reserve and the financial sector. There is still no legal definition of predatory lending. The battle lines remain drawn between Wall Street and K Street that hold the strategic high ground on Capitol Hill against the America people.

End Notes

Preface

[1] Bob Tedeschi, "Mortgages; The Widening Web of Fraud," *The New York Times*, April 6, 2008.

[2] Ryan J. Donmoyer and Dawn Kopecki, "Fannie, Freddie May Pay Lower Taxes After Rule Change (Update2)," *Bloomberg*, April 23, 2008.

[3] The higher estimate of 8 million foreclosures came from Fannie Mae's former chief risk officer Edward Pinto in testimony before the Committee on Oversight and Reform titled "The Role of Fannie Mae and Freddie Mac in the Financial Crisis" on December 9, 2008.

[4] Matt Taibi of *Rolling Stone* magazine deserves credit with the *coup d'état* assessment and analogy.

[5] Neil Irwin, "Don't Confuse Wall Street With Princeton," *The Washington Post*; January 18, 2008; Page A10.

Chapter 1 – Financing the American Dream

[6] Over the course of the author's career, he has worked with every manner of loan officer and type of manager. The most insensitive viewed customers as those, who once stripped of equity, no longer had any value for the firm. The phrase management applied was that the customer was "used up." That manager was one of the most valued managers with this unnamed national mortgage lender.

[7] Alvin Toffler and Heidi Toffler, *Revolutionary Wealth,* Alfred A. Knopf, 2006; Page 14.

[8] "Mortgage," Oxford English Dictionary, 1981.

[9] Walter W. Skeat, "Mortgage," Concise Etymological Dictionary of the English Language, 1951.

[10] Freddie Mac, "Notes and Note Addenda," 2008.

[11] Mortgage Lists, Wall Street List, Inc., 2007.

[12] In 1914, President Woodrow Wilson signed the FTC Act into law, and the Federal Trade Commission (FTC) has since served as the nation's primary federal level consumer protection agency.

[13] Lew Sichelman, "NAR Fears 'Trigger Lists,'" Realty Times®, November 14, 2006.

[14] Veneris in Lew Sichelman, "NAR Fears 'Trigger Lists,'" Realty Times®, November 14, 2006.

[15] Veneris in Lew Sichelman, "NAR Fears 'Trigger Lists,'" Realty Times®, November 14, 2006.

[16] Kenneth R. Harney, "Home Mortgage Applications 'Trigger' Sales of Private Financial Information," Realty Times®, September 11, 2006.

[17] DeLoach in Kenneth R. Harney, "Home Mortgage Applications 'Trigger' Sales of Private Financial Information," Realty Times®, September 11, 2006.

[18] DeLoach in Kenneth R. Harney, "Home Mortgage Applications 'Trigger' Sales of Private Financial Information," Realty Times®, September 11, 2006.

[19] Byron Acohido and Jon Swartz, "FTC under fire as credit bureaus sell consumers' data," USA Today, December 16, 2007.

[20] Kuttner inside Byron Acohido and Jon Swartz, "FTC under fire as credit bureaus sell consumers' data," USA Today, December 16, 2007.

[21] Byron Acohido and Jon Swartz, "FTC under fire as credit bureaus sell consumers' data," USA Today, December 16, 2007.

[22] Byron Acohido and Jon Swartz, "FTC under fire as credit bureaus sell consumers' data," USA Today, December 16, 2007.

[23] Byron Acohido and Jon Swartz, "FTC under fire as credit bureaus sell consumers' data," USA Today, December 16, 2007.

[24] Pratt inside Byron Acohido and Jon Swartz, "FTC under fire as credit bureaus sell consumers' data," USA Today, December 16, 2007.

[25] The book's website www.MortgagedAndArmed.com has a collection of consumer-oriented warnings issued by the government.

[26] Long & Foster Real Estate, Inc., Today's Mortgage Rates, 2008. See www.longandfoster.com.

[27] This is a word-for-word quote made to me by a real estate sales manager when I worked for a nationwide mortgage company.

[28] At a private event in May 2008, the author briefly discussed several tactics that real estate agents could do to increase their business. A Coldwell Banker agent said, "I wish I could tape record you." The author replied, "Better yet, how about having me as a guest speaker in your office?" She said, "That's not going to happen. Coldwell Banker has its own in-house lender."

[29] Weichert Realtors®, About Us, 2008. See www.weichert.com.

[30] Rachel Sams, "Wells Fargo faces another Baltimore housing lawsuit," Baltimore Business Journal, January 11, 2008.

[31] Rachel Sams, "Wells Fargo faces another Baltimore housing lawsuit," Baltimore Business Journal, January 11, 2008.

[32] Howard A. Lax, "Class Action Filed Against Bank and Real Estate Broker Alleging Sham," The Mortgage News, A Mortgage Banking Newsletter, Lipson, Neilson, Cole, Seltzer & Garin, P.C., December 2007 Edition.

[33] Kendra Marr, "Grand New Headquarter for Long & Foster," The Washington Post, May 19, 2008.

[34] This is an account of a friend of the author's that had worked for a major new homebuilder in the Washington, D.C. area. She left the builder's employment after she realized that the builder's business strategies and mortgage lending practices were not competitive.

[35] Consumers can take greater control in how the Consumer Credit Reporting Companies manage their data by submitting an Opt-In or Opt-Out request by calling the toll free number 1(888) 567-8688. Hearing impaired consumers can access the TDD service at 1(877) 730-4105. Information is also online at www.optoutprescreen.com.

[36] Sarah Max, "8 credit score myths," CNNMoney.com, March 16, 2005.

[37] FICO inside Sarah Max, "8 credit score myths," CNNMoney.com, March 16, 2005.

[38] This was an unpublished study the author conducted in the MBA program at Mount St. Mary's University.

[39] That was proven when the author arranged mortgage financing for a high school home economics teacher, who candidly told him that she was ill equipped to navigate the mortgage lending process.

[40] Mark Kutner, Elizabeth Greenberg, Ying Jin, Bridget Boyle, Yung-chen Hsu, Eric Dunleavy, "2003 National Assessment of Adult Literacy Public-Use Data File User's Guide," National Center for Education Statistics, April 4, 2007; Online at http://nces.ed.gov/NAAL/kf_demographics.asp. In his 2009 film *Capitalism: A Love Story*, Michael Moore reported that 40 percent of Americans are functionally illiterate. He was close, but it is actually worse than what he reported.

[41] The two anecdotal accounts are real life examples.

[42] Suze Orman online at www.suzeorman.com.

[43] Dave Ramsey, "Should you borrow money to invest in real estate?" Dave Ramsey.com, August 19, 2008.

[44] Jim Cramer online at www.cnbc.com.

[45] Similarly, if Cramer described the economic theory or insights described in George Soros' book *The New Paradigm for Financial Markets*, ratings would drop as well since Soros is too philosophical for the layperson looking for the quick tip for the day.

[46] Jon Stewart, "Interview with Jim Cramer," The Daily Show, Comedy Central, March 12, 2008. See www.thedailyshow.com.

[47] To learn more about Over Draft Protection, consumers should speak with the people where they have a checking account, and also visit the Federal Reserve online at www.federalreserve.gov.

[48] The author turned down a management position at one of the nation's leading mortgage banking firms during the boom in part due to the fact that upper management had absolutely no problem hiring and keeping loan officers who were smoking marijuana on the job and those with criminal backgrounds – so long as they made the company money.

[49] The Annual Credit Report Request Service can be reached at (877) 322-8228 and also online at www.annualcreditreport.com.

[50] Information is also online at www.annualcreditreport.com.

[51] Edward M. Gramlich, Statement of Edward M. Gramlich Member Board of Governors of the Federal Reserve System before the Committee on Banking, Housing, and Urban Affairs, United States Senate, May 17, 2005.

[52] Edward Gramlich testimony inside James D. Scurlock, "Maxed Out," 2006.

[53] During the boom, the author saved those direct mailers and it resulted in a three inch folder of mortgage refinance offers. The majority looked like they came from con artists and amateur brokers posing as government agencies. The ones that came from the top four banks made the author also laugh since they were in small type and came from a "senior vice president." The big banks were quite happy to outsource production to the brokers, who they would later blame.

[54] Primary Mortgage Market Survey®. See www.freddiemac.com.

[55] "A Summary of Your Rights Under the Fair Credit Reporting Act," Federal Trade Commission, not dated.

[56] "Credit & Loans," Federal Trade Commission, October 23, 2008. See www.ftc.gov/credit.

[57] The Annual Credit Report Request Service can be reached at (877) 322-8228 and also online at www.annualcreditreport.com. This is the official website, and the service is free. There are imposter websites that seek to charge consumers for this free service.

[58] "Fair And Accurate Credit Transactions Act of 2003," U.S. Senate and House of Representatives of the United States, December 4, 2003; See http://frwebgate.access.gpo.gov/cgi-bin/getdoc.cgi?dbname=108_cong_public_laws&docid=f:publ159.108.pdf.

[59] "Title VII - Equal Credit Opportunity Act," Housing Section Documents, Civil Rights Division, United States Department of Justice, not dated. See http://www.usdoj.gov/crt/housing/documents/ecoafulltext_5-1-06.php

[60] "Equal Credit Opportunity," Facts for Consumers, Federal Trade Commission, March 1998. See http://www.ftc.gov/bcp/edu/pubs/consumer/credit/cre15.shtm.

[61] "A Consumer's Guide to Mortgage Settlement Costs," The Federal Reserve Board, October 7, 2008. See www.federalreserve.gov/pubs/settlement/default.htm.

[62] "RESPA - Real Estate Settlement Procedures Act," U.S. Department of Housing and Urban Development, November 21, 2008. See www.hud.gov/offices/hsg/sfh/res/respa_hm.cfm; "More Information About RESPA," U.S. Department of Housing and Urban Development. See www.hud.gov/offices/hsg/sfh/res/respamor.cfm.

[63] "FDIC Law, Regulations, Related Acts," Federal Deposit Insurance Corporation. See www.fdic.gov/regulations/laws/rules/6500-1400.html; and "Truth in Lending, Comptroller's Handbook," Comptroller of the Currency Administrator of National Banks. October 2008. See www.occ.treas.gov/handbook/til.pdf.

[64] "Joint Report to the Congress Concerning Reform to the Truth in Lending Act and the Real Estate Settlement Procedures Act," Board of Governors of the Federal Reserve System Department of Housing and Urban Development, July 1998, page 7.

[65] Carole Gould, "Changes Loom for Home Equity Loans," The New York Times, February 26, 1989.

[66] "Facts for Consumers: High-Rate, High-Fee Loans (HOEPA/Section 32 Mortgages)," Federal Trade Commission, February 2008. See www.ftc.gov/bcp/edu/pubs/consumer/homes/rea19.shtm.

[67] "Facts for Consumers: High-Rate, High-Fee Loans (HOEPA/Section 32 Mortgages)," Federal Trade Commission, February 2008. See www.ftc.gov/bcp/edu/pubs/consumer/homes/rea19.shtm.

[68] "Facts for Consumers: High-Rate, High-Fee Loans (HOEPA/Section 32 Mortgages)," Federal Trade Commission, February 2008. See www.ftc.gov/bcp/edu/pubs/consumer/homes/rea19.shtm.

Chapter 2 – Loan Officers Originate for Underwriting

[69] Peter Hébert, "Underwriting on the Front Line," Scotsman Guide, January 2008, Cover Story.

[70] "The 3 Cs of Underwriting Factors Used in Loan Prospector's Assessment," Freddie Mac, 2008.

[71] Minimum credit score requirements are not a cut and dry topic. A mortgage banker may have a higher score requirement than a agency, government, or a private labeled securitizer. That higher standard may be due to a need to mitigate an array of risks that come with lending.

[72] "FHA TOTAL Scorecard," U.S. Housing and Urban Development, 2008.

[73] Fitch Ratings is a one of the three rating agencies that provides among other things opinions on fixed income investments, such as the credit grade of mortgage issuances.

[74] James Grant, "Paying the Price for the Fed's Success," The New York Times, January 27, 2008; Op-Ed Page WK 16.

[75] Louis Leibowitz, a certified public accountant, Personal Communications, 2008.

[76] Claude Romano, a certified financial planner with Prudential Financial, Personal Communications, 2008.

[77] The Patriot Act Reauthorization Tackles Terrorism Financing. This bill enhances penalties for terrorism financing and closes a loophole concerning terrorist financing through "hawalas" (informal money transfer networks) rather than traditional financial institutions (White House, USA PATRIOT Act, 2008).

Chapter 3 – The Product

[78] "About Ginnie Mae," Ginnie Mae, 2008.

[79] "About Ginnie Mae," Ginnie Mae, 2008.

[80] Zvi Bodie, Alex Kane, and Alan J. Marcus, Investments, 7th Edition. McGraw-Hill Irwin, 2008.

[81] "About Ginnie Mae," Ginnie Mae, 2008.

[82] "About Ginnie Mae," Ginnie Mae, 2008.

[83] "For Issuers," Ginnie Mae, 2008.

[84] "About Ginnie Mae," Ginnie Mae, 2008.

[85] "Your Path to Homeownership," Ginnie Mae, 2008.

[86] "For Issuers," Ginnie Mae, 2008.

[87] "For Issuers," Ginnie Mae, 2008.

[88] "203(b) Mortgage Insurance," U.S. Housing and Urban Development, May 10, 2006.

[89] Henry Savage, "Is an FHA Refi 'Mini-Boom' on the Horizon?" Realty Times®, March 21, 2006.

[90] Kenneth R. Harney, "Martinez's 'Appraiser Watch' Proposal Adds New Worries for Appraisers," Realty Times®, February 25, 2002.

[91] Kenneth R. Harney, "Martinez's 'Appraiser Watch' Proposal Adds New Worries for Appraisers," Realty Times®, February 25, 2002.

[92] "Rehab a Home w/HUD's 203(k) Rehab Program," U.S. Housing and Urban Development, November 3, 2005.

[93] "Streamline Your FHA Mortgage," U.S. Housing and Urban Development, not dated.

[94] Ruthie Ackerman, "Thornburg's Jumbo Loss," Forbes, June 12, 2008.

[95] This is a tongue-in-cheek reference from the author's real estate work experience from the 1980s.

[96] Richard Bitner was the former co-owner of the subprime wholesaler Kellner Mortgage that operated during part of the refinance boom.

[97] Richard Bitner, *Greed, Fraud & Ignorance: A Subprime Insider's Look at the Mortgage Collapse*, LTV Media LLC, 2008.

[98] Mortgage Bankers Association of America inside "Lender Loses Round," Bloomberg, October 4, 2007.

[99] UBS AG and Credit Suisse Group inside "Lender Loses Round," Bloomberg, October 4, 2007.

[100] Ben S. Bernanke, "The Housing Market and Subprime Lending," International Monetary Conference, June 5, 2007.

[101] *Inside Mortgage Finance* inside Senator Charles E. Schumer and Representative Carolyn B. Maloney, "The Subprime Lending Crisis: The Economic Impact of Wealth, Property Values and Tax Revenues, and How We Got Here," Report and Recommendations by the Majority Staff of the Joint Economic Committee, U.S. Senate, October 2007. Author's note: There is an apparent discrepancy between the data from Wholesale Access and Inside Mortgage Finance. Schumer and Maloney appear to have relied on the latter's figures. The issue is that the subprime lending peak was the result of investment banks and big banks using brokers as storefronts.

[102] Senator Charles E. Schumer and Representative Carolyn B. Maloney, "The Subprime Lending Crisis: The Economic Impact of Wealth, Property Values and Tax Revenues, and How We Got Here," Report and Recommendations by the Majority Staff of the Joint Economic Committee, U.S. Senate, October 2007.

[103] Olson, Personal Communications, 2007 through 2010.

[104] Senator Charles E. Schumer and Representative Carolyn B. Maloney, "The Subprime Lending Crisis: The Economic Impact of Wealth, Property Values and Tax Revenues, and How We Got Here," Report and Recommendations by the Majority Staff of the Joint Economic Committee, U.S. Senate, October 2007.

[105] Standard language in a promise note for a fully amortized loan.

[106] Calyx® Point® loan origination software suggests that by amortizing the loan over 256 months instead of 360 months, the reduced interest payment is more significant: $38,325.75.

[107] Unnamed economists inside Tomoeh Murakami Tse, "Growth Slows in Housing Market Appreciation Rate Lowest Since 1999," The Washington Post; Page D1, September 6, 2006.

[108] June Fletcher, *House Poor: Pumped Up Prices, Rising Rates, and Mortgages on Steroids, How to Survive the Coming Housing Crisis*, Harper Collins, 2005.

[109] LoanPerformance inside David Leonhardt and Motoko Rich, "The Trillion-Dollar Bet." The New York Times, June 16, 2005.

[110] Anya Sostek, "The Intrigue of Interest-Only: Loans Cut Monthly Payments, but Carry Risks," The Washington Post; Page F01 (Originally MortgagePro News); June 19, 2004.

[111] "Multistate Fixed Rate Balloon Note," Freddie Mac, January 2001.

[112] "Multistate Adjustable Rate Note," Freddie Mac, January 2001.

[113] Valerie Bauerlein, "Golden West Didn't Sink Thompson, Sandler Says," The Wall Street; Journal. Page B1, June 7, 2008.

[114] Golden West Financial Corp. was the parent company of World Savings Bank.

[115] Liu inside David Leonhardt and Motoko Rich, "The Trillion-Dollar Bet." The New York Times, June 16, 2005.

[116] James R. Hagerty and Ruth Simon, "Option ARMs Emerge: As Home-Loan Worry," The Wall Street Journal, April 19, 2007.

[117] John N. Dunlevy, James M. Manzi, Jeremy I. Garfield, Edward Santevecchi, Diana Berezina, "RMBS: New Wrinkle in Option ARM Lending," Nomura Fixed Income Strategy, May 10, 2006.

[118] John N. Dunlevy, James M. Manzi, Jeremy I. Garfield, Edward Santevecchi, Diana Berezina, "RMBS: New Wrinkle in Option ARM Lending," Nomura Fixed Income Strategy, May 10, 2006.

[119] Valerie Bauerlein and Ruth Simon, "Wachovia to Discontinue Option-ARMs," The Wall Street Journal, July 1, 2008.

[120] Marshall Eckblad, "Wachovia Posts $8.66 Billion Loss, Slashes Dividend, Will Sell Assets," The Wall Street Journal, July 22, 2008.

[121] Barclays Capital inside Valerie Bauerlein and Ruth Simon, "Wachovia to Discontinue Option-ARMs," The Wall Street Journal, July 1, 2008.

[122] Jack Guttentag, "Simple Interest," www.mtgprofessor.com, 2006.

[123] Jack Guttentag, "Simple Interest," www.mtgprofessor.com, 2006.

[124] Jack Guttentag, "Simple Interest," www.mtgprofessor.com, 2006.

[125] "Reverse Mortgages: Get the Facts Before Cashing in on Your Home's Equity." Federal Trade Commission, June 2005.

[126] "Reverse Mortgages: Get the Facts Before Cashing in on Your Home's Equity." Federal Trade Commission, June 2005.

[127] "Top Ten Things to Know if You're Interested in a Reverse Mortgage." U.S. Department of Housing and Urban Development, August 10, 2006.

[128] Henry Hebeler in Christopher Farrell, "Choosing Where to Grow Old," Business Week, July 14 & 21, 2008; Page 47.

[129] Christopher Farrell, "Choosing Where to Grow Old," Business Week, July 14 & 21, 2008; Page 47.

[130] "Reverse Mortgages: Get the Facts Before Cashing in on Your Home's Equity." Federal Trade Commission, June 2005.

[131] The author has taught these concepts as part of continuing education credit courses to licensed real estate agents and loan officers, and was stunned to uncover that many in the classes reacted as if they had been psychologically programmed. They also reacted as if they had been snapped out of a trance during the author's presentations. The author noted little to no intact critical and independent thinking and analysis on the topics in the many of the audiences. The author's assumption is that if this is the case within the industry, it is probably similar in the general public but on a broader scale.

Chapter 4 – The Price

[132] "Federal Open Market Committee." Board of Governors of the Federal Reserve System, April 8, 2008.

[133] George Clack, Executive Editor, "Glossary of Economic Terms," An Outline of the U.S. Economy, U.S. Department of State's Bureau of International Information Programs, 2001.

[134] "Adjustable Rate Mortgage Index," Wachovia, 2009. See http://www.wachovia.com/misc/0,,1412,00.html.

[135] "11th District Cost of Funds Indices," Federal Home Loan Bank of San Francisco, 2000 - 2009. See www.fhlbsf.com/cofi/default.asp.

[136] "Adjustable Rate Mortgage Index," Wachovia, 2009. See www.wachovia.com/misc/0,,1412,00.html.

[137] M. Anthony Carr, "Is The Two Percent Mortgage Too Good To Be True?" Realty Times®, July 25, 2003.

[138] "Adjustable Rate Mortgage Index," Wachovia, 2009. See www.wachovia.com/misc/0,,1412,00.html.

[139] Over the course of the author's career, he has had countless customers literally cry on the phone due to emotional distress and complain that they were told by other loan officers that it was okay to not make a scheduled payment to later find that closing was delayed and that their credit was damaged as a result.

[140] Mortgage-X is online at http://mortgage-x.com.

[141] "High-Rate, High-Fee Loans (HOEPA/Section 32 Mortgages)," Federal Trade Commission. Online at www.ftc.gov/bcp/edu/pubs/consumer/homes/rea19.shtm

Chapter 5 - The Promotion

[142] "FTC Consumer Alert: Shopping For a Mortgage? Your Application May Trigger Competing Offers." Federal Trade Commission, February 2007.

[143] The Federal Trade Commission has two vehicles by which consumers can opt-out from prescreened offers and to be on a do not call list. The site www.optoutprescreen.com permits consumers to be removed from the sale of data initiated by the credit bureaus. The National Do No Call Registry at www.donotcall.gov permits consumers to put commercial vendors on notice to not call. Though the author has his home number on the National Do No Call Registry, the author periodically receives phone calls from mortgage lenders soliciting business. To illustrate, on April 15, 2008, a woman called the author's home and asked for the author by mispronouncing his last name. She then asked if the author was familiar with the phrase "improved cash flow," and that her manager had asked her to call. Apparently, she dialed against her will. She had the hook baited with an interest only or Option ARM product. The author then asked that she communicate the Federal Trade Commission's position to her manager. Lenders violating a consumer's wish to not be contacted can be subjected to a fine as high as $10,000 per instance.

[144] While Ditech is a lender, Lending Tree acts as both a lead provider to other lenders as well as a mortgage broker.

[145] See Countrywide advertisement online at www.countrywidehomeloans.com/no_cost_refi.php.

[146] Stuart Elliott, "Ameriquest Mortgage Spots Are Winners in Super Bowl Competition," The New York Times, February 9, 2005.

[147] Lenox Financial Mortgage, LLC. Online at www.lenoxfinancial.com.

[148] Lenox Financial Mortgage, LLC. Online at www.lenoxfinancial.com.

[149] The author saved a several inch folder of direct mail pieces from every mortgage company that took the time to send an offer in the mail.

[150] Bloomberg news accounts inside "E*Trade Wholesale Lending - Wholesale & Retail," The Mortgage Lender Implode-O-Meter, April 22, 2008. See http://ml-implode.com/imploded/lender_E*TradeWholesaleLending_2008-04-22.html.

[151] Rob Snow, Personal Communications, August 2007 through June 2008.

[152] Metatags are just a series of words, no different than ingredients in a cooking mix. Though they cannot be copyrighted because of this, they have significant competitive value for a company serious about an Internet presence and search engine optimization.

Chapter 6 – The Placement

[153] Martin Mayer, *Whatever Happened to Madison Avenue?* Little Brown & Co., May 1991.

[154] This important discussion resulted from personal communications with Guy Cecala of *Inside Mortgage Finance* and David Olson of Wholesale Access.

[155] David Olson, Personal Communications, August 2008.

[156] David Olson, Personal Communications, August 2008; and "Mission." National Association of Mortgage Brokers, 2008.

[157] David Olson, Personal Communications, Fall 2005.

[158] Inside Mortgage Finance in Senator Charles E. Schumer and Representative Carolyn B. Maloney, "The Subprime Lending Crisis: The Economic Impact of Wealth, Property Values and Tax Revenues, and How We Got Here," Report and Recommendations by the Majority Staff of the Joint Economic Committee. U.S. Senate, October 2007.

[159] David Olson, "Retail Vs. Wholesale," Scotsman Guide, 2008.

[160] David Olson, Personal Communications, 2008.

[161] Jack M. Guttentag is Professor of Finance Emeritus at the Wharton School of the University of Pennsylvania, and founder of GHR Systems, Inc., a mortgage technology company. He runs a website called the Mortgage Professor at www.mtgprofessor.com.

[162] Jack Guttentag, "What is a Correspondent?," www.mtgprofessor.com, September 4, 2006.

[163] John Wilson, Personal Communications, April 2008.

[164] Jack Guttentag, "What is a Correspondent?," www.mtgprofessor.com, September 4, 2006.

[165] David Olson, Personal Communications, 2008.

[166] Morgan Brown, "Dead Man Walking - Wholesale Lending is Marching Towards Extinction," Mortgage Musings. (Also published by the Arizona Association of Mortgage Brokers), October 15, 2007.

[167] Morgan Brown, "Dead Man Walking - Wholesale Lending is Marching Towards Extinction," Mortgage Musings. (Also published by the Arizona Association of Mortgage Brokers), October 15, 2007.

[168] Morgan Brown, "Dead Man Walking - Wholesale Lending is Marching Towards Extinction," Mortgage Musings. (Also published by the Arizona Association of Mortgage Brokers), October 15, 2007.

[169] David Olson, Personal Communications, 2008.

[170] A Google search takes any site visitor to HUD's Neighborhood Watch website. This is a remarkable database that private-labeled lenders would do well to emulate as part of their best practices and risk management measures.

[171] HUD has pulled back the cloak of mystery with its Neighborhood Watch. In its own words: "Neighborhood Watch is intended to aid HUD/FHA staff in monitoring lenders and our programs, and to aid lenders and the public in self-policing the industry. The system is designed to highlight exceptions, so that potential problems are readily identifiable." See "Neighborhood Watch." Housing and Urban Development, 2008.

[172] Michellle Singletary, "Prosecute the Mortgage Sharks," The Washington Post; Page F1, April 27, 2008.

[173] Author's note: The use of Salary.com further supports the argument of the lack of due diligence and faulty thinking in the industry.

Chapter 7 – Key Market Players

[174] Guy Cecala, Personal Communications, May 2008.

[175] David Olson, Personal Communications, 2008.

[176] "Allied Home Mortgage (AHMCC) and PushMX Agree to Offer Workflow Management, Productivity and Management Reporting Solutions to Allied Branches Nationwide Who Use Calyx Point Software," Market Wire, September 2005.

[177] Brad Finkelstein, "Large Net Branch Firms Agree to Combine Units," Origination News, September 2005; Vol. 14, No. 12.

[178] Georgia Steele, "2006's Top Brokers," Broker, Volume 9, Number 6, June 2007.

[179] "Carteret Mortgage Corporation - Retail, Net Branch," The Mortgage Lender Implode-O-Meter, August 26, 2008. Online at http://ml-implode.com/imploded/lender_CarteretMortgageCorporation_2008-08-26.html. This site functions as a link to the legal complaints.

[180] Inside Mortgage Finance inside Randall Dodd, "Subprime: Tentacles of a Crisis," Finance & Development, December 2007; Page 16.

[181] Inside Mortgage Finance inside Randall Dodd, "Subprime: Tentacles of a Crisis," Finance & Development, December 2007; Page 17.

[182] James R. Hagerty and Damian Paletta, "Oversight Compromise Reached on Fannie, Freddie," The Wall Street Journal, May 21, 2008.

[183] Senator Charles E. Schumer and Representative Carolyn B. Maloney, "The Subprime Lending Crisis: The Economic Impact of Wealth, Property Values

and Tax Revenues, and How We Got Here," Report and Recommendations by the Majority Staff of the Joint Economic Committee. U.S. Senate, October 2007.

[184] Giovanni Dell'Ariccia, Deniz Igan, and Luc Laeven, "Credit Booms and Lending Standards: Evidence from the Subprime Mortgage Market," IMF Working Paper Research Department, International Monetary Fund, April 2008; Page 37.

[185] Brian Hargrave, Marianna Fassinotti, and Steve Bergantino, "An Introduction to the Non-Agency CMO Market," Lehman Brothers Fixed Income Research, June 27, 2002; page 1.

[186] Shane M. Sherlund, "The Jumbo-Conforming Spread: A Semiparametric Approach," Board of Governors of the Federal Reserve System, January 31, 2008.

[187] James Grundy, Sharif Mahdavian, and Monica Perelmuter, "RMBS Trends: U.S. RMBS Subprime Securitization Volume Declines Amid More-Stringent Guidelines," Standard & Poor's, August 31, 2007.

[188] Deutsche Bank inside David Leonhardt and Motoko Rich, "The Trillion-Dollar Bet." The New York Times, June 16, 2005.

[189] Cutts inside David Leonhardt and Motoko Rich, "The Trillion-Dollar Bet." The New York Times, June 16, 2005.

[190] Alan Greenspan, "Understanding household debt obligations," Remarks at the Credit Union National Association 2004 Governmental Affairs Conference, Washington, D.C., February 23, 2004; and Greg Ip, "His Legacy Tarnished, Greenspan Goes on Defensive: Future of U.S. Financial Reform is at Stake; 'I am right,'" The Wall Street Journal; Page A1, April 8, 2008.

[191] "Cash-Out Refinance Report," Office of the Chief Economist, Freddie Mac, 4th Quarter 2008.

[192] Brian Sullivan, "FHA Suspends Taylor, Bean & Whitaker Mortgage Corp. and Proposes to Sanction Two Top Officials, Ginnie Mae Issues Default Notice and Transfers Portfolio," U.S. Department of Housing and Urban Development, August 4, 2009.

[193] "J.D. Power and Associates Reports: Wachovia Ranks Highest in Customer Satisfaction with Home Equity Loan Servicers," J.D. Power and Associates, December 16, 2008.

[194] As reported to the author from a would-be Citi hire who declined the job offer as he came to better understand the financial health of the company.

[195] "J.D. Power and Associates Reports: Wachovia Ranks Highest in Customer Satisfaction with Home Equity Loan Servicers," J.D. Power and Associates, December 16, 2008.

196 Zachary A. Goldfarb and Tomoeh Murakami Tse, "Judge Delays Bank of America's Settlement," The Washington Post, August 11, 2009; Ann Woolner, "Slamming Bank of America With Fine Slams Victims," Business Week, February 23, 2010; and Larry Neumeister, "Judge OK's revised Bank of America settlement in Merrill deal," Associated Press, February 23, 2010.

197 Center for Public Integrity inside Nomi Prins, "The Real Size of the Bailout," Mother Jones and the Foundation for National Progress, January/February 2010.

Chapter 8 – Real Estate Niches

198 Daniel McGinn, *House Lust: America's Obsession With Our Homes*. Doubleday Publishing, 2008.

199 Compiled from August 2008 data from the National Association of REALTORS® and the National Association of Home Builders. These numbers are estimates only.

200 Walter Maloney, Personal Communications, National Association of REALTORS®, August 2008.

201 These are generic guidelines, while the historic norm may change.

202 Margaret Winfrey, "Luxury Consumer Research---affluent Market For Vacation Homes Looks Gloomy For Full Ownership," The American Affluence Research Center, April 21, 2009.

203 See William Grim, "The Ugly American Expatriate -- Deconstructing Today's Expatriate American Haters," Free Republic, November 27, 2003. A scathing take on expatriation, online at http://209.157.64.200/focus/f-news/1029999/ posts. See also JustLanded.com for global perspective.

204 Kathleen Madigan, "After the Housing Boom, What the coming slow down means for the economy and you," Business Week, April 11, 2005; Page 86.

205 Leslie Peterson, "Rule Changes Made Easy: Fannie Mae and Freddie Mac have new investment property guidelines," Broker; Page 18, June 2008.

206 The author became familiar with Andy Kane in the early 1980s as a result of a television interview that focused on his book *Care and Feeding of Tenants*.

207 "Income Stable, Poverty Rate Increases, Percentage of Americans Without Health Insurance Unchanged," U.S. Census Bureau, August 30, 2005.

208 Bruce H. Webster Jr. and Alemayehu Bishaw, "Income, Earning, and Poverty Data From the 2006 American Community Survey," U.S. Census Bureau, August 2007.

209 IRS' Income Statistics Division inside Jesse Drucker, "Richest See Income Share Rise," The Wall Street Journal, July 23, 2008; Page A3.

[210] The author checked out this book from a Maryland public library as part of the research for this book, and it came from a library in Georgia two months later.

[211] Andy Kane, *Care and Feeding Tenants.* Paladin Press, 1981; page 45.

[212] Andy Kane, *Care and Feeding Tenants.* Paladin Press, 1981; page 47.

[213] Guadalupe (Lupe) Barrera is the author's wife's personal nail technician, who makes house calls as a value add that gives her a competitive advantage.

[214] Guadalupe Barrera, Personal Communication, 2008.

[215] "Buyers are liars" is an adage that applies to what buyers *think* they want in the way of a home since they oftentimes buy something quite different. This phenomenon is typically driven by deep-seated emotional and psychological needs tied to associating a certain quality in a home with a memory that could be as simple as the smell of fresh cooked bread or even a tree house in the back yard associated with growing up in a parent's home.

[216] David Goldman, "New home sales hit 13-year low," CNNMoney.com, March 26, 2008.

[217] Ethan Butterfield, "Builder 100 Over The Years," Builder, May 1, 2008.

[218] Haas in Hovanesian, Bonfire of the Builders, Business Week, 2007.

[219] Haas in Hovanesian, Bonfire of the Builders, Business Week, 2007.

[220] John Burns, "Housing Market Outlook: Fighting Through the Banking Crisis," Real Estate Consulting, Inc., November 7, 2008.

[221] Hector Vega is the dean of the College of Engineering in Bogotá, Colombia. He is also the author's brother-in-law.

[222] Hector Vega, Personal Communications, July 2008.

[223] Kendra Marr, "Luxury Foreclosures," The Washington Post, May 15, 2008.

[224] Duane Marsteller and Jennifer Rich, "Tales from inside: Borrowers discuss housing crunch," Bradenton Herald, May 25, 2008.

[225] Quote is taken from www.fear.org; Henry Hyde, *Forfeiting Our Property Rights: Is Your Property Safe From Seizure?* CATO Institute, 1995.

[226] Terrance G. Reed, "American Forfeiture Law: Property Owners Meet the Prosecutor," Policy Analysis no. 179, CATO Institute, September 29, 1992; and Leon Felkins, "Federal Asset Forfeiture Laws Need To Be Amended To Restore Due Process And Protect Property Rights In The Forfeiture Process," Forfeiture Endangers American Rights Foundation, March 27, 2002.

Chapter 9 – Needed Change

[227] Joseph Chatham, "Home Prices: This slide is but a taste of things to come," Gerson Lehrman Group and CNN.com, June 4, 2009.

228 RealtyTrac Staff, "RealtyTrac® Year-End Report Shows Record 2.8 Million U.S. Properties with Foreclosure Filings in 2009," January 14, 2010.

229 Scott Pelley, "The Mortgage Meltdown: New Wave Of Mortgage Rate Adjustments Could Force More Homeowners To Default," 60 Minutes, December 14, 2008.

230 Many loan closings are delayed due to the customer not providing the lender with the required supporting documents. That, however, is not the reason many loans do not close as promised. Many lenders deliberately mislead their customers, and as a result, they should be held accountable or forced out of the business.

231 See the apostle Paul's letter to Timothy. 1 Timothy, chapter 6, verse 10 in the New Testament.

232 See *Genesis*, chapter 25, verse 34, Hebrew Bible (any translation will suffice).

233 Author's note: "Borrowing while black" is a phrase adapted from the phrase "driving while black," which was used as an indictment against the Los Angeles Police Department. The author's usage of the phrase is an indictment against the financial sector and mortgage lenders for engaging in target marketing and reverse red lining.

234 Roy De Young, "Bank of America Walkout," YouTube, April 21, 2009. Online at www.youtube.com/watch?v=u6hy4PBo4tE&NR=1.

235 Personal communications with Roy De Young, branding strategist, September 21 and 22, 2009.

236 Carroll Quigley, *Tragedy and Hope: A History of the World in Our Time*, The Macmillan Company, 1966; page 43.

237 The author's observation is based on his first hand experience teaching continuing education credit courses to licensed loan officers and real estate agents. Based on a show of hands, one third of the lenders and real estate agents in many of the classes he taught did not read a daily newspaper or periodic magazine. Most did not understand the historical basis for an array of lending and real estate related laws and regulations designed to protect consumers. Moreover, the author's observation was that there was a significant gap in many of the training environments where loan officers demonstrated a failure to connect ethics as the foundational basis for protective legislation designed to curb predatory business behavior.

238 John Mechem, spokesman for the Mortgage Bankers Association inside Donna Leinwand, "Cities sue home lenders," USA Today, May 15, 2008.

[239] David Lereah, *Are You Missing the Real Estate Boom? : Why Home Values and Other Real Estate Investments Will Climb Through the End Of The Decade - And How You Can Profit from It,* Broadway Business, February 22, 2005.

[240] Personal communications with Chris Sorenson, September 15, 2009.

[241] James Tyson, Craig Torres and Alison Vekshin, "Fed Says It Could Have Acted Sooner on Subprime Rout" (Update3), Bloomberg, March 22, 2007.

[242] Scott M. Albinson, "Interagency Guidance on Nontraditional Mortgage Product Risks," Office of Thrift Supervision, October 10, 2006.

[243] "Federal Financial Regulatory Agencies Issue Final Statement on Subprime Mortgage Lending," Office of the Comptroller of the Currency, Board of Governors of the Federal Reserve System, Federal Deposit Insurance Corporation, Office of Thrift Supervision, and National Credit Union Administration; June 29, 2007.

[244] Dawn Kopecki and Catherine Dodge, "U.S. Rescue May Reach $23.7 Trillion, Barofsky Says (Update3)," Bloomberg, July 20, 2009; And the author's first hand knowledge given that Citi had doubled the author's credit line and tripled the interest rate. The bank's justification was "changes in market conditions." The federal government money was cheap, and the changes in the marketplace were due to the banks, not households. The author terminated the banking relationship.

[245] Dawn Kopecki and Catherine Dodge, "U.S. Rescue May Reach $23.7 Trillion, Barofsky Says (Update3)," Bloomberg, July 20, 2009; and Emily Kaiser, "The real cost of the bailout," The New York Times, October 15, 2008.

[246] Nomi Prins, "The Real Size of the Bailout," Mother Jones and the Foundation for National Progress, January/February 2010 Issue.

[247] Neil Barofsky, "Testimony of Neil Barofsky," United States Committee on the Judiciary, February 11, 2009; Dawn Kopecki and Catherine Dodge, "U.S. Rescue May Reach $23.7 Trillion, Barofsky Says (Update3)," Bloomberg, July 20, 2009; Jennifer Liberto, "Bailout cop busy on the beat: Neil Barofsky, who is overseeing the $700 billion TARP, says he has 20 criminal probes and calls for changes to prevent fraud," CNNMoney.com, April 21 2009; and Kate Pickert, "TARP Oversight Report," Time, February 6, 2009; and Frances Romero, "TARP Watchdog Neil Barofsky," Time, July 21, 2009.

[248] "Employment Situation Summary," U.S. Bureau of Labor Statistics, June 5, 2009.

[249] "The Employment Situation-March 2010," Bureau of Labor Statistics, U.S. Department of Labor, April 2, 2010; page 26; Online at www.bls.gov/news.re-

lease/pdf/empsit.pdf; and personal communications with Eleni Theodossiou, economist with the Bureau of Labor Statistics.

[250] David Lazarus, "Suicide hotlines see rise in calls as economy tanks," Los Angeles Times, December 24, 2008.

[251] Dr. Robert Simon, a psychiatrist at Suburban Hospital in Bethesda, Maryland, and professor at Georgetown University School of Medicine in Washington, D.C., inside Jill U. Adams, "Is the economic crisis leading to more suicides?" Los Angeles Times, October 27, 2008.

[252] Harvard University psychologist Matthew Nock inside Jill U. Adams, "Is the economic crisis leading to more suicides?" Los Angeles Times, October 27, 2008.

[253] Archives of General Psychiatry study of 96,000 psychiatric patients in Denmark inside Jill U. Adams, "Is the economic crisis leading to more suicides?" Los Angeles Times, October 27, 2008.

[254] "Congressional Performance: 64% Say Congress Is Doing A Poor Job," Rasmussen Reports, March 22, 2010; and "Most Say Tea Party Has Better Understanding of Issues than Congress," Rasmussen Reports, March 28, 2010.

[255] The mainstream media chose to make a story out of favorable treatment. The fact is, almost all loan officers have pricing control and can extend favorable treatment. Dodd, given this scenario, should have had the good judgment to refuse special treatment given that he was the Senate Committee Chairman on Banking, Housing, and Urban Affairs. The author did the due diligence on the mortgage loan applications that Dodd had made with Countrywide Home Loans (that he had withheld from media scrutiny for close to one year). The author concluded lender directed mortgage fraud for the benefit of the borrower with the borrower participating in that fraud. That was a very common occurrence during the refinance boom. The only difference here was Dodd's high-profile position and position.

[256] Michael M. Forester, Todd Krell, and James A. Jorgensen, "Review of the Terms and Conditions of Certain Residential Mortgage Loans," CrossCheck Compliance LLC, July 22, 2008.

[257] The Coffee Party USA poll was not based on a random sampling of the American population. It was based on those who aligned with the cause and had participated on Facebook.

[258] "Poll Results," Coffee Party USA, April 14, 2010.

[259] These comments rest on surveying alternative and independent media as well as social networking websites like Facebook. Gary Franchi of Restore the Republic magazine and the Reality Report (an Internet based news cast) and Alex

Jones of Infowars.com may be the best examples of those who promote a view that Americans need to bypass, or transcend, the two party system and the mainstream media since both serve to divide Americans against each other.

260 This is a synthesis based on statements (analysis and commentary) from Alex Jones, Steve Quayle, and Gary Franchi who ascribe to a conspiratorial view of history and current events. Their assessments are based on the statements of political and business leaders. See Gary Franchi,, "Reality Report #31 – Tea Parties Co-opted, Mass Resignations, New Enemy of the State, Assassinating Americans, Super Bowl Conditioning,' Restore the Republic, February 10, 2010; Doug McIntosh, "Playing the Patriots," SteveQuayle.com, February 8, 2010; and Kurt Nimmo, "Republicans and Democrats Determined to Turn Tea Parties into Circus Sideshow," Infowars.com, April 14, 2009.

261 Mark Potok, "Rage on the Right, The Year in Hate and Extremism," Southern Poverty Law Center, Intelligence Report, Issue Number 137, Spring 2010; and Sonia Scherr, "The Unlikeliest Conspiracy-Monger: Colorado Public TV," Southern Poverty Law Center, March 11, 2010. Author's note: the author's assertion that Southern Poverty Law Center is a smear campaign center rests on the observations of appearances of its representatives in the mainstream media and how the Tea Party has been portrayed. The clearest example was seen in Dylan Ratigan, "Anger in America," Dylan Ratigan Show, MSNBC, March 2, 2010. Ratigan made himself look like a complete fool when he discredited the journalistic integrity of MSNBC. His rant followed an interview with Mark Potok of Southern Poverty Law Center. See Dylan Ratigan, "Anger in America," Dylan Ratigan Show, MSNBC, March 2, 2010; Online at www.youtube.com/watch?v=nObPplOGUdI.

262 Lydia Saad, "Tea Partiers Are Fairly Mainstream in Their Demographics, Skew right politically, but have typical profile by age, education, and employment," Gallup, Inc., April 5, 2010.

263 This is the author's synthesis given what is published in alternative and independent media as well as organizations that advance the many causes of the Tea Party. The mainstream media either promoted the Tea Party on behalf of the Republican Party as was the case of *FOX News* or vilified the Tea Party as was the case with *MSNBC*. Regarding *CNN*, it is abundantly clear that many Tea Party adherents do not care for *CNN*.

References

Alternative Media

Franchi, Gary. "Reality Report #31 – Tea Parties Co-opted, Mass Resignations, New Enemy of the State, Assassinating Americans, Super Bowl Conditioning.' Restore the Republic, February 10, 2010.

McIntosh, Doug. "Playing the Patriots." SteveQuayle.com, February 8, 2010.

Nimmo, Kurt. "Republicans and Democrats Determined to Turn Tea Parties into Circus Sideshow." Infowars.com, April 14, 2009.

Articles from Academic Studies and Journals

Kutner, Mark, Elizabeth Greenberg, Ying Jin, Bridget Boyle, Yung-chen Hsu, and Eric Dunleavy. "2003 National Assessment of Adult Literacy Public-Use Data File User's Guide." National Center for Education Statistics, April 4, 2007.

Blogs and Social-Political Groups

———· "Poll Results." Coffee Party USA. April 14, 2010.

Grim, William. "The Ugly American Expatriate -- Deconstructing Today's Expatriate American Haters." Free Republic, November 27, 2003.

Krowne, Aaron. "E*Trade Wholesale Lending - Wholesale & Retail." The Mortgage Lender Implode-O-Meter, April 22, 2008.

Books

Bitner, Richard. *Greed, Fraud & Ignorance: A Subprime Insider's Look at the Mortgage Collapse.* LTV Media LLC, 2008.

Bodie, Zvi, Alex Kane, and Alan J. Marcus. *Investments.* 7th Edition. McGraw-Hill Irwin, 2008.

Fletcher, June. *House Poor: Pumped Up Prices, Rising Rates, and Mortgages on Steroids, How to Survive the Coming Housing Crisis.* Harper Collins, 2005.

Hyde, Henry. *Forfeiting Our Property Rights: Is Your Propoerty Safe From Seizure?* CATO Institute, 1995.

Kane, Andy. *Care and Feeding Tenants.* Paladin Press, 1981.

Lereah, David. *Are You Missing the Real Estate Boom? : Why Home Values and Other Real Estate Investments Will Climb Through the End Of The Decade - And How You Can Profit from It.* Broadway Business, February 22, 2005.

Mayer, Martin. *Whatever Happened to Madison Avenue?* Little Brown & Co., May 1991.

McGinn, Daniel. *House Lust: America's Obsession With Our Homes.* Doubleday Publishing, 2008.

Quigley, Carroll. *Tragedy and Hope: A History of the World in Our Time.* The Macmillan Company, 1966.

Toffler, Alvin and Heidi Toffler. *Revolutionary Wealth.* Alfred A. Knopf, 2006.

Congressional Websites, Studies, or Hearings
Barofsky, Neil. "Testimony of Neil Barofsky." United States Committee on the Judiciary, February 11, 2009.

Schumer, Senator Charles E. and Representative Carolyn B. Maloney. "The Subprime Lending Crisis: The Economic Impact of Wealth, Property Values and Tax Revenues, and How We Got Here." Report and Recommendations by the Majority Staff of the Joint Economic Committee. U.S. Senate, October 2007.

Conferences
——· "Congressional Performance: 64% Say Congress Is Doing A Poor Job." Rasmussen Reports, March 22, 2010.

Bernanke, Ben S. "The Housing Market and Subprime Lending." International Monetary Conference, June 5, 2007.

·Felkins, Leon. "Federal Asset Forfeiture Laws Need To Be Amended To Restore Due Process And Protect Property Rights In The Forfeiture Process." Forfeiture Endangers American Rights Foundation, March 27, 2002.

Potok, Mark. "Rage on the Right, The Year in Hate and Extremism." Intelligence Report, Issue Number: 137, Spring 2010.

Reed, Terrance G. "American Forfeiture Law: Property Owners Meet the Prosecutor." Policy Analysis no. 179, CATO Institute, September 29, 1992.

Saad, Lydia. "Tea Partiers Are Fairly Mainstream in Their Demographics, Skew right politically, but have typical profile by age, education, and employment." Gallup, Inc., April 5, 2010.

Scherr, Sonia. "The Unlikeliest Conspiracy-Monger: Colorado Public TV." Southern Poverty Law Center, March 11, 2010.

Credit Related Organizations

Annual Credit Report Request Service

Opt Out Services LLC

Editorials or Opinions

Grant, James. "Paying the Price for the Fed's Success." The New York Times. Op-Ed. Page WK.16, January 27, 2008.

Governmental Branches, Agencies, or Presidential Libraries

·——· "203(b) Mortgage Insurance." U.S. Housing and Urban Development, May 10, 2006.

·——· "A Consumer's Guide to Mortgage Settlement Costs." The Federal Reserve Board. October 7, 2008.

·——· "A Summary of Your Rights Under the Fair Credit Reporting Act." Federal Trade Commission, not dated.

·———· "About Ginnie Mae." Ginnie Mae, 2008.

·———· "Credit & Loans." Federal Trade Commission, October 23, 2008.

·———· "Employment Situation Summary." U.S. Bureau of Labor Statistics, June 5, 2009.

·———· "Equal Credit Opportunity." Facts for Consumers. Federal Trade Commission, March 1998.

·———· "Facts for Consumers: High-Rate, High-Fee Loans (HOEPA/Section 32 Mortgages)." Federal Trade Commission, February 2008.

·———· "Fair and Accurate Credit Transactions Act of 2003." U.S. Senate and House of Representatives of the United States. December 4, 2003.

·———· "FDIC Law, Regulations, Related Acts." Federal Deposit Insurance Corporation, not dated.

·———· "Federal Financial Regulatory Agencies Issue Final Statement on Subprime Mortgage Lending." Office of the Comptroller of the Currency, Board of Governors of the Federal Reserve System, Federal Deposit Insurance Corporation, Office of Thrift Supervision, and National Credit Union Administration, June 29, 2007.

·———· "Federal Open Market Committee." Board of Governors of the Federal Reserve System, April 8, 2008.

·———· "FHA TOTAL Scorecard." U.S. Housing and Urban Development, 2008.

·———· "For Issuers." Ginnie Mae, 2008.

·———· "FTC Consumer Alert: Shopping For a Mortgage? Your Application May Trigger Competing Offers." Federal Trade Commission, February 2007.

———· "Joint Report to the Congress Concerning Reform to the Truth in Lending Act and the Real Estate Settlement Procedures Act." Board of Governors of the Federal Reserve System, U.S. Department of Housing and Urban Development. July 1998

———· "Rehab a Home w/HUD's 203(k) Rehab Program." U.S. Housing and Urban Development, November 3, 2005.

———· "RESPA - Real Estate Settlement Procedures Act," U.S. Department of Housing and Urban Development, November 21, 2008.

———· "Reverse Mortgages: Get the Facts Before Cashing in on Your Home's Equity." Federal Trade Commission, June 2005.

———· "Streamline Your FHA Mortgage." U.S. Housing and Urban Development, not dated.

———· "The Employment Situation-March 2010." Bureau of Labor Statistics, U.S. Department of Labor, April 2, 2010.

———· "Title VII - Equal Credit Opportunity Act." Housing Section Documents, Civil Rights Division, U.S. Department of Justice, not dated.

———· "Top Ten Things to Know if You're Interested in a Reverse Mortgage." U.S. Department of Housing and Urban Development, August 10, 2006.

———· "Truth in Lending, Comptroller's Handbook," Comptroller of the Currency Administrator of National Banks. October 2008.

———· "Your Path to Homeownership." Ginnie Mae, 2008.

Albinson, Scott M. "Interagency Guidance on Nontraditional Mortgage Product Risks." Office of Thrift Supervision, October 10, 2006.

Clack, George, Executive Editor. "Glossary of Economic Terms." An Outline of the U.S. Economy. U.S. Department of State's Bureau of International Information Programs, 2001.

Greenspan, Alan. "Understanding household debt obligations." Remarks at the Credit Union National Association 2004 Governmental Affairs Conference, Washington, D.C., February 23, 2004.

Sullivan, Brian. "FHA Suspends Taylor, Bean & Whitaker Mortgage Corp. and Proposes to Sanction Two Top Officials, Ginnie Mae Issues Default Notice and Transfers Portfolio." U.S. Department of Housing and Urban Development, August 4, 2009.

Webster Jr., Bruce H. and Alemayehu Bishaw. "Income, Earning, and Poverty Data From the 2006 American Community Survey." U.S. Census Bureau, August 2007.

Government Sponsored Enterprise Publications
——— "11th District Cost of Funds Indices," Federal Home Loan Bank of San Francisco, 2000 - 2009.

——— "Cash-Out Refinance Report." Office of the Chief Economist, Freddie Mac, 4th Quarter 2008.

——— "COFI: Frequently Asked Questions." Federal Home Loan Bank of San Francisco, 2008.

——— "Income Stable, Poverty Rate Increases, Percentage of Americans Without Health Insurance Unchanged." U.S. Census Bureau, August 30, 2005.

——— "Multistate Adjustable Rate Note." Freddie Mac, January 2001.

——— "Multistate Fixed Rate Balloon Note." Freddie Mac, January 2001.

——— "Multistate Note." Freddie Mac, January 2001.

——— "Neighborhood Watch." Housing and Urban Development, 2008.

——— "Notes and Note Addenda." Freddie Mac, 2008.

——— "Primary Mortgage Market Survey®." Freddie Mac, 2008.

———· "The 3 Cs of Underwriting Factors Used in Loan Prospector's Assessment." Freddie Mac, 2008.

Sherlund, Shane M. "The Jumbo-Conforming Spread: A Semiparametric Approach." Board of Governors of the Federal Reserve System, January 31, 2008.

Holy Bible
Moses. "Genesis." Tanach: The Torah / Prophets / Writings. Mesorah Publications, Ltd., May 2000.

Paul. "The First Epistle of Paul the Apostle to Timothy." The New Testament. The Holy Bible, King James Version. Oxford University Press, 1945.

Industry Reports or Trade Publications
———· "Allied Home Mortgage (AHMCC) and PushMX Agree to Offer Workflow Management, Productivity and Management Reporting Solutions to Allied Branches Nationwide Who Use Calyx Point Software." Market Wire, September 2005.

———· "Carteret Mortgage Corporation - Retail, Net Branch." The Mortgage Lender Implode-O-Meter, August 26, 2008.

———· "J.D. Power and Associates Reports: Wachovia Ranks Highest in Customer Satisfaction with Home Equity Loan Servicers." J.D. Power and Associates, December 16, 2008.

Brown, Morgan. "Dead Man Walking - Wholesale Lending is Marching Towards Extinction." Mortgage Musings. (Also published by the Arizona Association of Mortgage Brokers), October 15, 2007.

Butterfield, Ethan. "Builder 100 Over The Years." Builder, May 1, 2008.

Carr, M. Anthony. "Is The Two Percent Mortgage Too Good To Be True?" Realty Times®, July 25, 2003.

Dodd, Randall. "Subprime: Tentacles of a Crisis." Finance & Development, December 2007.

Dunlevy, John N., James M. Manzi, Jeremy I. Garfield, Edward Sante-vecchi, Diana Berezina. "RMBS: New Wrinkle in Option ARM Lending." Nomura Fixed Income Strategy, May 10, 2006.

Finkelstein, Brad. "Large Net Branch Firms Agree to Combine Units." Origination News, Vol. 14, No. 12, September 2005.

Forester, Michael M., Todd Krell, and James A. Jorgensen. "Review of the Terms and Conditions of Certain Residential Mortgage Loans." CrossCheck Compliance LLC, July 22, 2008.

Grundy, James, Sharif Mahdavian, and Monica Perelmuter. "RMBS Trends: U.S. RMBS Subprime Securitization Volume Declines Amid More-Stringent Guidelines." Standard & Poor's, August 31, 2007.

Hargrave, Brian, Marianna Fassinotti, and Steve Bergantino. "An Introduction to the Non-Agency CMO Market." Lehman Brothers Fixed Income Research, June 27, 2002.

Harney, Kenneth R. "Martinez's 'Appraiser Watch' Proposal Adds New Worries for Appraisers." Realty Times®, February 25, 2002.

Harney, Kenneth R. "Home Mortgage Applications 'Trigger' Sales of Private Financial Information." Realty Times®, September 11, 2006.

Hébert, Peter. "Underwriting on the Front Line: As loan officers battle a new market, they have control over their client's funding." Scotsman Guide Residential Edition; Cover Story, January 2008.

Lax, Howard A. "Class Action Filed Against Bank and Real Estate Broker Alleging Sham." The Mortgage News, A Mortgage Banking Newsletter. Lipson, Neilson, Cole, Seltzer & Garin, P.C., December 2007 Edition.

Olson, David. "Retail Vs. Wholesale: Which Costs Less? In a tightening environment, it helps to know if the broker channel really is cheaper for lenders." Scotsman Guide Residential Edition, February 2008.

Peterson, Leslie. "Rule Changes Made Easy: Fannie Mae and Freddie Mac have new investment property guidelines." Broker, June 2008.

RealtyTrac Staff. "RealtyTrac® Year-End Report Shows Record 2.8 Million U.S. Properties with Foreclosure Filings in 2009." January 14, 2010.

Sams, Rachel. "Wells Fargo faces another Baltimore housing lawsuit." Baltimore Business Journal, January 11, 2008.

Savage, Henry. "Is an FHA Refi 'Mini-Boom' on the Horizon? " Realty Times®, March 21, 2006.

Sichelman, Lew. "NAR Fears 'Trigger Lists.'" Realty Times®, November 14, 2006.

Steele, Georgia. "2006's Top Brokers," *Broker*, Volume 9, Number 6, June 2007.

Winfrey, Margaret. "Luxury Consumer Research---affluent Market For Vacation Homes Looks Gloomy For Full Ownership." The American Affluence Research Center, April 21, 2009.

Magazines

Farrell, Christopher. "Choosing Where to Grow Old." Business Week, July 14 & 21, 2008.

Hovanesian, Mara Der. "Bonfire of the Builders." Business Week, August 13, 2007.

Madigan, Kathleen. "After the Housing Boom, What the coming slow down means for the economy and you." Business Week, April 11, 2005.

Pickert, Kate. "TARP Oversight Report." Time, February 6, 2009.

Marketing Companies

·———· "Mortgage Lists." Wall Street List, Inc., 2007.

Movies, Documentaries, Plays, and Songs
Jones, Alex. *Fall of the Republic: The Presidency of Barack H. Obama.* Free Speech Systems, LLC, October 21, 2009.

Moore, Michael. *Capitalism: A Love Story.* Starz / Anchor Bay, March 9, 2010.

Scurlock, James D. *Maxed Out.* Magnolia, June 5, 2007.

Mortgage Lender Web Sites*
·———· "Adjustable Rate Mortgage Index." Wachovia, 2008.

Lenox Financial Mortgage, LLC. Online at www.lenoxfinancial.com.

Wachovia Corporation. Online at www.wachovia.com.

Washington Mutual. No longer on the Internet.

Wells Fargo Bank, N.A. Online at www.wellsfargo.com.

*(Retrieved between 2007 and 2008)

Newspaper Articles
Acohido, Byron and Jon Swartz. "FTC under fire as credit bureaus sell consumers' data." USA Today, December 16, 2007.

Adams, Jill U. "Is the economic crisis leading to more suicides?" Los Angeles Times, October 27, 2008.

Bauerlein, Valerie. "Golden West Didn't Sink Thompson, Sandler Says." The Wall Street; Journal; June 7, 2008.

Bauerlein, Valerie and Ruth Simon. "Wachovia to Discontinue Option-ARMs." The Wall Street Journal, July 1, 2008.

Drucker, Jesse. "Richest See Income Share Rise." The Wall Street Journal, July 23, 2008.

Eckblad, Marshall. "Wachovia Posts $8.66 Billion Loss, Slashes Dividend, Will Sell Assets." The Wall Street Journal, July 22, 2008.

Elliott, Stuart. "Ameriquest Mortgage Spots Are Winners in Super Bowl Competition," The New York Times, February 9, 2005.

Goldfarb, Zachary A. and Tomoeh Murakami Tse. "Judge Delays Bank of America's Settlement." The Washington Post, August 11, 2009.

Gould, Carole. "Changes Loom for Home Equity Loans." The New York Times, February 26, 1989.

Hagerty, James R. and Damian Paletta. "Oversight Compromise Reached on Fannie, Freddie." The Wall Street Journal, May 21, 2008.

Hagerty, James R. and Ruth Simon. "Option ARMs Emerge: As Home-Loan Worry." The Wall Street Journal, April 19, 2007.

Ip, Greg. "His Legacy Tarnished, Greenspan Goes on Defensive: Future of U.S. Financial Reform is at Stake; 'I am right.'" The Wall Street Journal, April 8, 2008.

Irwin, Neil. "Don't Confuse Wall Street with Princeton." The Washington Post, January 18, 2008.

Lazarus, David. "Suicide hotlines see rise in calls as economy tanks." Los Angeles Times, December 24, 2008.

Leinwand, Donna. "Cities sue home lenders." USA Today, May 15, 2008.

Leonhardt, David and Motoko Rich. "The Trillion-Dollar Bet." The New York Times, June 16, 2005.

Kendra Marr. "Grand New Headquarter for Long & Foster." The Washington Post, May 19, 2008.

Marr, Kendra. "Luxury Foreclosures." The Washington Post, May 15, 2008.

Marsteller, Duane and Jennifer Rich. "Tales from inside: Borrowers discuss housing crunch." Bradenton Herald, May 25, 2008.

Singletary, Michellle. "Prosecute the Mortgage Sharks." The Washington Post, April 27, 2008.

Sostek, Anya. "The Intrigue of Interest-Only: Loans Cut Monthly Payments, but Carry Risks." The Washington Post; Page F01 (Originally MortgagePro News); June 19, 2004.

Tedeschi, Bob. "Mortgages; The Widening Web of Fraud." The New York Times, April 6, 2008.

Tse, Tomoeh Murakami. "Growth Slows in Housing Market Appreciation Rate Lowest Since 1999." The Washington Post; Page D1, September 6, 2006.

Online Publications
——· "Lender Loses Round." Bloomberg, October 4, 2007.

Ackerman, Ruthie. "Thornburg's Jumbo Loss." Forbes, June 12, 2008.

Chatham, Joseph. "Home Prices: This slide is but a taste of things to come." Gerson Lehrman Group and CNN.com, June 4, 2009.

Donmoyer, Ryan J. and Dawn Kopecki, "Fannie, Freddie May Pay Lower Taxes After Rule Change (Update2)," Bloomberg, April 23, 2008.

Goldman, David. "New home sales hit 13-year low." CNNMoney.com, March 26, 2008.

Guttentag, Jack. "What is a Correspondent Lender?" The Mortgage Professor, September 4, 2006.

Guttentag, Jack. "Simple Interest Mortgages: A Trap For the Unwary." The Mortgage Professor, October 16, 2006.

Kopecki, Dawn and Catherine Dodge. "U.S. Rescue May Reach $23.7 Trillion, Barofsky Says (Update3)." Bloomberg, July 20, 2009.

Liberto, Jennifer. "Bailout cop busy on the beat: Neil Barofsky, who is overseeing the $700 billion TARP, says he has 20 criminal probes and calls for changes to prevent fraud." CNNMoney.com, April 21 2009.

Max, Sarah. "8 credit score myths." CNNMoney.com, March 16, 2005.

Prins, Nomi. "The Real Size of the Bailout," Mother Jones and the Foundation for National Progress, January/February 2010 Issue.

Tyson, James, Craig Torres and Alison Vekshin. "Fed Says It Could Have Acted Sooner on Subprime Rout" (Update3). Bloomberg, March 22, 2007.

Personal Communications

Barrera, Guadalupe. Self-Employed Real Estate Speculator and Investor. June 2008.

Cecala, Guy. President of *Inside Mortgage Finance, Inc.* May 2008.

Clifford, Christine. Vice President, Wholesale Access Mortgage Research & Consulting, Inc., August 2007 through April 28, 2008.

De Young, Roy. Branding strategist with an undisclosed company, September 21 and 22, 2009.

Leibowitz, Louis. Certified Public Accountant and Tax Preparer. February 1, 2008 and February 8, 2008.

Maloney, Walter. National Association of REALTORS®. August 2008.

Olson, David. Founder and President of Wholesale Access Mortgage Research & Consulting, Inc. August 2007 through March 2010.

Person, Carl E. New York City attorney. September 2009.

Romano, Claude. Insurance Agent and Investment Planner. Prudential, February 4, 2008.

Snow, Rob. President of Snow Portfolio Management, LLC. August 2007 through June 2008.

Sorenson, Chris. Founder of Homeownership Education Learning Program (USA HELP), September 15, 2009.

Theodossiou, Eleni. Economist with the Bureau of Labor Statistics. April 9, 2010.

Wilson, John. Washington Mutual (subprime operations until 2008), April through May 2008.

Vega, Hector. Foreign Real Estate Investor and Speculator (author's brother-in-law), July 2008.

Popular Financial Advisors

Cramer, Jim. Online at www.thestreet.com, www.madmoney.com, www.madmoneylightninground.com, and www.cnbc.com.

Orman, Suze. Online at www.suzeorman.com.

Ramsey, Dave. Online at www.daveramsey.com.

Real Estate Companies

———· "About Us." Weichert, Realtors®, 2008.

———· "Today's Mortgage Rates are brought to you by Prosperity Mortgage." Long & Foster Real Estate, Inc., 2008.

Reference Books

Skeat, Walter W. "Mortgage." A Concise Etymological Dictionary of the English Language; Page 336, 1951.

The Compact Edition of the Oxford English Dictionary. Volume I, A-O. "Mortgage." Page 1854 of Volume I, 1981.

The Compact Edition of the Oxford English Dictionary. Volume II, P-Z. "Usury." Page 3577 of Volume II, 1981.

Research Studies

Burns, John. "Housing Market Outlook: Fighting Through the Banking Crisis." Real Estate Consulting, Inc., November 7, 2008.

Dell'Ariccia, Giovanni, Deniz Igan, and Luc Laeven. "Credit Booms and Lending Standards: Evidence from the Subprime Mortgage Market." IMF Working Paper Research Department, International Monetary Fund, April 2008.

Television or News Shows

Pelley, Scott. "The Mortgage Meltdown: New Wave Of Mortgage Rate Adjustments Could Force More Homeowners To Default." 60 Minutes, December 14, 2008.

Ratigan, Dylan. "Anger in America." Dylan Ratigan Show, MSNBC, March 2, 2010.

Stewart, Jon. "Interview with Jim Cramer." The Daily Show, Comedy Central, March 12, 2008.

Trade Associations

·——· "Mission." National Association of Mortgage Brokers, 2008.

You Tube Video Clips

De Young, Roy. "Bank of America Walkout." You Tube, April 21, 2009.

1003: The Ten-O-Three is the standard loan application issued by Fannie Mae and Freddie Mac for loan originators to collect borrower information in connection with a mortgage application.

1099: IRS Form 1099 used to report self-employed or independent contractor income.

203(b): FHA program which provides mortgage insurance to protect lenders from default; used to finance the purchase of new or existing one- to four-family housing; characterized by low down payment, flexible qualifying guidelines, limited fees, and a limit on maximum loan amount.

203(k): This FHA mortgage insurance program enables homebuyers to finance both the purchase of a house and the cost of its rehabilitation through a single mortgage loan.

4506-T: The form in a complete loan application authorizing the lender and assigns to pull a borrower's federal tax returns in order to conduct spot check quality control and determine if there was mortgage fraud in the event of default.

A

A-minus: A Fannie Mae and Freddie Mac underwriting designation that places the borrower's application between A-paper and B-C-D paper rates.

A-Paper: A Fannie Mae, Freddie Mac, or Government loan product. Also referred to as a prime loan. (Has nothing to do with the prime rate.)

Accounting: Recording, summarizing, and classifying financial information related to income, cash flow, and assets with the assurance that is essential for sound business decision making.

Adjustable Rate Mortgage (ARM) Disclosure: This document describes the features of the adjustable-rate mortgage (ARM) program. It includes information about how interest rates and payments are determined, how the interest rate can change, and how the monthly payment can change. The lender is required to provide this document to you when you hand in your application or before you pay a nonrefundable fee (whichever is earlier).

Adverse Selection: Compensation incentives that may contribute to a mortgage banker or broker to originate a loan that may be less advantageous to the borrower. To illustrate, a 1 percent yield spread premium at the same mortgage loan note rate may have a lower margin associated with an ARM. A 2 percent yield spread premium, however, not only increases compensation but also increases the ARM's margin, which means higher borrower payments after the rate adjusts. Or, a marginal borrower is placed into a subprime 2/28 adjustable rate mortgage rather than a 30-year fixed-rate government loan for the reason of adding to a portfolio of potential future refinances.

Affiliated Business Arrangement: A business partnership established between entities, that may include a mortgage lender, real estate broker, or homebuilder, that results in sharing customer information and fees.

Agent: An appointed person or entity acting on behalf of and with the authority of another.

Agency: The law governing the conduct of an agent. A department within the government.

Agency Loan: A loan that goes to Fannie Mae or Freddie Mac. Sometimes referred to as a prime loan. (Not to be confused with the prime rate.)

Alt-A: Limited documentation loans offered to relatively high credit score borrowers perceived to be low risk.

Amenity: A feature of the home or property that serves as a benefit to the buyer but that is not necessary to its use; may be natural (like location, woods, water) or man-made (like a swimming pool or garden).

Amortization: Repayment of a mortgage loan through monthly install-ments of principal and interest; the monthly payment amount is based on a schedule that will allow you to own your home at the end of a specific time period (for example, 15 or 30 years).

Amortization Schedule: A table showing the repayment schedule of inter-est and principal necessary to pay off a loan by maturity.

Annual Percentage Rate (APR): Calculated by using a standard formula, the APR shows the cost of a loan; expressed as a yearly interest rate, it includes the interest, points, mortgage insurance, and other fees associ-ated with the loan. The APR provides the true cost of a loan expressed as one number that enables you to compare all types of loans. The APR is higher than the Note Rate, and the two should not be confused since the borrower pays the Note Rate. The APR is the ideal means of comparing costs.

Annuity: An amount paid yearly or at other regular intervals, often at a guaranteed minimum amount. Also, a type of insurance policy in which the policy holder makes payments for a fixed period or until a stated age, and then receives annuity payments from the insurance company.

Antitrust Law: A policy or action that seeks to curtail monopolistic pow-ers within a market.

Application: The first step in the official loan approval process; this form is used to record important information about the potential borrower necessary to the underwriting process.

Application Fee: The fee that a mortgage lender or broker charges to ap-ply for a mortgage to cover preliminary costs like a credit report and an appraisal.

Appraisal: A document that gives an estimate of a property's fair market value; an appraisal is generally required by a lender before loan approval to ensure that the mortgage loan amount is not more than the value of the property.

Appraiser: A qualified and licensed individual who uses his or her experience and knowledge to prepare the appraisal estimate.

Appreciation: An increase in the market value of a home due to changing market conditions and/or home improvements that add value.

Arbitration: A process during which disputes are settled by referring them to a fair and neutral third party (arbitrator). The disputing parties agree in advance to agree with the decision of the arbitrator. There is a hearing where both parties have an opportunity to be heard, after which the arbitrator makes a decision.

ARM: Adjustable Rate Mortgage; a mortgage loan subject to changes in interest rates; when rates change, ARM monthly payments increase or decrease at intervals determined by the lender; the change in monthly payment amount, however, is usually subject to a cap.

Asbestos: A toxic material that once was used in housing insulation and fireproofing. Because some forms of asbestos have been linked to certain lung diseases, it is no longer used in new homes. However, some older homes may still have asbestos in these materials.

Assessor: A government official who is responsible for determining an assessed value of a property for the purpose of taxation.

Assessment: The assessed value is not a property's fair market value or appraised value. Instead, it is a value based on a formula that varies from jurisdiction to jurisdiction for the purpose of levying real estate property taxes.

Asset: A possession of value, usually measured in terms of money, which can take the form of on of the three asset classes: real estate, a debt claim against an asset in the form of a note or bond that produces income, or an equity stake as in an ownership claim on a company.

Asset Backed Security (ABS): A debt security made up of student loans, home equity lines of credit, auto loans, and/or leases that monetizes the underlying assets into predictable income streams.

Assignment of Mortgage: A document evidencing the transfer of owner-ship of a mortgage from one person to another.

Assumable Mortgage: A mortgage loan that can be taken over (assumed) by the buyer when a home is sold. An assumption of a mortgage is a transaction in which the buyer of real property takes over the seller's ex-isting mortgage; the seller remains liable unless released by the lender from the obligation. If the mortgage contains a due-on-sale clause, the loan may not be assumed without the lender's consent.

Assumption: A homebuyer's agreement to take on the primary responsi-bility for paying an existing mortgage from a home seller.

Assumption Fee: A fee a lender charges a buyer who will assume the sell-er's existing mortgage.

Attorney General: The primary legal counsel for federal and state govern-ments, and in some jurisdictions may have law enforcement responsibilities for public prosecutions involving consumer-related and class action cases.

Audit: A review of a system or process in accounting or after loan closing in order for the quality controller or certified third party to assure that the process was in compliance with regulations.

Award Letter: Verification of fixed income from the source, like the Social Security Administration, or a pension manager.

Auditor: The person conducting an audit. In accounting, a certified public accountant. In lending, it may be a person from HUD.

Automated Underwriting: An automated process performed by a technol-ogy application that streamlines the processing of loan applications and provides a recommendation to the lender to approve the loan or refer it for manual underwriting.

Automated Valuation Model (AVM): An alternative to the traditional full appraisal that relies on a database of public records to determine current market value of real estate.

B

B – C – D Lending: Subprime credit extend to borrowers with less than perfect credit or borrowers who do not meet agency or government underwriting guidelines.

Bait and Switch: A predatory lending practice that entices prospective borrowers to apply for product "A" and then offered product "B," oftentimes without adequate prior disclosure or borrower consent.

Balance Sheet: One of the three main financial statements that shows assets, liabilities, and net worth as of a specific date. (See also Income Statement and Statement of Cash Flows).

Balloon Mortgage: A mortgage that typically offers low rates for an initial period of time (usually five, seven, or ten) years; after that time period elapses, the balance is due or is refinanced by the borrower.

Balloon Payment: A final lump sum payment that is due, often at the maturity date of a balloon mortgage.

Bankruptcy: A federal law whereby a person's assets are turned over to a trustee and used to pay off outstanding debts; this usually occurs when someone owes more than they have the ability to repay. Chapter 7 is a complete discharge of obligations for businesses and individuals. Chapter 11 is a corporate reorganization plan whereby debtor in possession financing permits a large distressed company to still run its business. Chapter 13 is a debt restructuring and repayment plan for individuals and small businesses.

Bear Market: A market in which, in a time of falling prices, shareholders may rush to sell their stock shares, adding to the downward momentum. A bear market is the flip side of a bull market.

Before-Tax Income: Income before taxes are deducted. Also known as "gross income."

Biweekly Payment Mortgage: A mortgage with payments due every two weeks (instead of monthly).

Bona Fide: In good faith, without fraud.

Bond: A certificate reflecting a firm's promise to pay the holder a periodic interest payment until the date of maturity and a fixed sum of money on the designated maturing date.

Bond Market: The financial market where investors buy and sell debt securities related to government, agency, municipal, corporate, and mortgage issuances.

Borrower: A person who has been approved to receive a loan and then is obligated to repay it and any additional fees according to the loan terms.

Bridge Loan: A short-term loan secured by the borrower's current home (which is usually for sale) that allows the proceeds to be used for building or closing on a new house before the current home is sold. Also known as a "swing loan."

Broker: An individual or firm that acts as an agent between providers and users of products or services, such as a mortgage broker or real estate broker. See also "Mortgage Broker." Not all mortgage brokers, however, are agents. Some act as independent contractors.

Broker Price Opinion (BPO): A paid opinion rendered by a real estate professional usually delivered to a loan servicer or a loss mitigation department.

Building Code: Based on agreed upon safety standards within a specific area, a building code is a regulation that determines the design, construction, and materials used in building. In addition, the codes address maintenance and occupancy of buildings. The codes are designed to provide for the safety, health and welfare of the public.

Budget: A detailed record of all income earned and spent during a specific period of time.

Budget Deficit: The amount each year by which spending is greater than income.

Budget Surplus: The amount each year by which income exceeds spending. This is the opposite of a budget deficit.

Bull Market: A market in which there is a continuous rise in stock prices. Bull markets could indicate strong performance within a sector, an economic cycle, or a bubble.

Bump to the Rate: Cost adjustments reflected in a higher interest rate or additional points due to objective criteria that include a higher than normally accepted debt-to-income ratio, higher loan-to-value ratio, a lower credit score, or limited documentation.

Business Ethics: Not taught in most business schools. Not about right and wrong, or what is legal or illegal. A systematic and objective approach that takes into account different methods to determine an appropriate course of action in complex business scenarios. It does not presume a right or wrong answer to a chosen course of action.

Buydown: An arrangement whereby the property developer or another third party provides an interest subsidy to reduce the borrower's monthly payments typically in the early years of the loan.

Buydown Account: An account in which funds are held so that they can be applied as part of the monthly mortgage payment as each payment comes due during the period that an interest rate buydown plan is in effect.

C

Cap: A limit, such as that placed on an adjustable rate mortgage, on how much a monthly payment or interest rate can increase or decrease. See also "Lifetime Payment Cap," "Lifetime Rate Cap," "Periodic Payment Cap," and "Periodic Rate Cap."

Capacity: The ability to make mortgage payments on time. This depends on income and income stability (job history and security), assets and savings, and the amount of income each month that is left over after paying housing costs, debts, and other obligations.

Capital: The physical equipment (buildings, equipment, human skills) used in the production of goods and services. Also used to refer to corporate equity, debt securities, and cash.

Capital Asset Pricing Model (CAPM): A model for pricing securities that describes the relationship between risk and expected return for the time value of money.

Capital Market: The market in which corporate equity and longer-term debt securities (those maturing in more than one year) are issued and traded.

Capitalism: An economic system in which the means of production are privately owned and controlled and which is characterized by competition and the profit motive.

Cash-Out Refinance: A refinance transaction in which the borrower receives additional funds over and above the amount needed to repay the existing mortgage, closing costs, points, and any subordinate liens.

Cash Reserves: A cash amount sometimes required to be held in reserve in addition to the down payment and closing costs; the amount is determined by the lender.

Central Bank: A country's principal monetary authority, responsible for such key functions as issuing currency and regulating the supply of credit in the economy.

Certificate of Deposit (CD): A document issued by a bank or other financial institution that is evidence of a deposit, with the issuer's promise to return the deposit plus earnings at a specified interest rate within a specified time period.

Certificate of Eligibility: A document issued by the U.S. Department of Veterans Affairs (VA) certifying a veteran's eligibility for a VA-guaranteed mortgage loan.

Certificate of Title: A document provided by a qualified source (such as a title company) that shows the property legally belongs to the current owner; before the title is transferred at closing, it should be clear and free of all liens or other claims.

Chain of Title: The history of all of the documents that have transferred title to a parcel of real property, starting with the earliest existing document and ending with the most recent.

Change Orders: A change in the original construction plans ordered by the property owner or general contractor.

Civil Lawsuit: A private action in law between two parties.

Class Action: A criminal action leveled by the federal government or the state where numerous claims are consolidated for the purpose of expediting the judicial process.

Clear Title: Ownership that is free of liens, defects, or other legal encumbrances.

Closing: The process of completing a financial transaction. For mortgage loans, the process of signing mortgage documents, disbursing funds, and, if applicable, transferring ownership of the property. In some jurisdictions, closing is referred to as "escrow," a process by which a buyer and seller deliver legal documents to a third party, who completes the transaction in accordance with their instructions. See also "Settlement."

Closing Agent: The person or entity that coordinates the various closing activities, including the preparation and recordation of closing documents and the disbursement of funds. (May be referred to as an escrow agent or settlement agent in some jurisdictions.) Typically, the closing is conducted by title companies, escrow companies or attorneys.

Closing Costs: Customary costs above and beyond the sale price of the property that must be paid to cover the transfer of ownership at closing; these costs generally vary by geographic location and are typically detailed to the borrower in the Good Faith Estimate after submission of a loan application and confirmed at closing in the HUD1/Settlement Statement, which details the accounting of the transaction. The costs are broken down into four sections: origination, discount, and broker fees; hard costs for lender charges appraisal, processing, and underwriting; and title charges for closing, document preparation, and title insurance; escrows that include taxes and insurance; and daily interest due from the day of closing and calculated to last day of that month. In the case of a purchase, the closing costs will also itemize the real estate broker fees, transfer taxes, and closing help also known as a seller or lender concession.

Closing Date: The date on which the sale of a property is to be finalized and a loan transaction completed. Often, a real estate sales professional coordinates the setting of this date with the buyer, the seller, the closing agent, and the lender.

Closing Statement: See "HUD-1 Settlement Statement."

Coborrower: Any borrower other than the first borrower whose name appears on the application and mortgage note, even when that person owns the property jointly with the first borrower and shares liability for the note.

Combined Loan-to-Value (CLTV): The ratio that results from adding the loan-to-value on the first mortgage with the loan-to-value of the second mortgage and others, and then dividing that into the property value.

Collateral: An asset that is pledged as security for a loan. The borrower risks losing the asset if the loan is not repaid according to the terms of the loan agreement. In the case of a mortgage, the collateral would be the house and real property.

Collateral Risk: The lender's risk tied to the collateral, or the property. A higher loan-to-value, for example, increases a lender's collateral risk.

Collateralized Debt Obligation: A security that does not specialize in any one single type of debt, but rather pools many types together to include bonds, car loans, student loans, and so forth. The levels of credit risk are transferred to investors, who in turn take different levels of return depending on the rated class.

Collateralized Mortgage Obligation (CMO): A Special Purpose Entity, or Trust, that owns pools of mortgages. The mortgages are the collateral containing several bonds sliced into differently rated classes, or tranches, modeled to generate an expected income stream.

Commercial Bank: A bank that offers a broad range of deposit accounts, including checking, savings, and time deposits, and extends loans to individuals and businesses, in contrast to investment banking firms such as brokerage firms, which generally are involved in arranging for the sale of corporate or municipal securities.

Commission: An amount, usually a percentage of the property sales price that is collected by a real estate professional as a fee for negotiating the transaction along with other rendered services.

Commitment Letter: A binding offer from a lender that includes the amount of the mortgage, the interest rate, and repayment terms.

Competitive Market Analysis: An opinion of a real estate agent rendered to either a homeowner or home buyer that estimates the current fair market value given current market conditions where similar properties within a tight radius to the subject property are compared. Typically, adjustments are made for time on the market, property features that either enhance or detract from value, and closing help that may have impacted a comparable property's sale price.

Common Areas: Those portions of a building, land, or improvements and amenities owned by a planned unit development (PUD,) a condominium project, a homeowners' association, or a cooperative project's cooperative corporation that are used by all of the unit owners, who share in the common expenses of their operation and maintenance. Common areas typically include swimming pools, tennis courts, play grounds, walking trails, roof tops, and other recreational facilities, as well as common corridors of buildings, parking areas, means of ingress and egress, etc.

Comparables: An abbreviation for "comparable properties," which are used as a comparison in determining the current value of a property that is being appraised. Also referred to as a comp.

Compliance: The conduct of a person or business in meeting licensing or regulatory requirements.

Concession: Something given up or agreed to in negotiating the sale of a house. For example, the sellers may agree to help pay for closing costs.

Condominium: A form of ownership in which individuals purchase and own a unit of housing in a multiunit complex; the owner also shares financial responsibility for common areas.

Conduit: A channel into the private-labeled mortgage market that excludes Fannie Mae, Freddie Mac, or HUD.

Conforming Loan: A loan that conforms to Fannie Mae and Freddie Mac underwriting guidelines.

Construction Loan: A loan for financing the cost of construction or improvements to a property; the lender disburses payments to the builder at periodic intervals during construction.

Consumer Price Index: A measure of the U.S. cost of living as tabulated by the U.S. Bureau of Labor Statistics based on the actual retail prices of a variety of consumer goods and services at a given time and compared to a base period that is changed from time to time.

Contingency: A condition that must be met before a contract is legally binding. For example, home purchasers often include a home inspection contingency; the sales contract is not binding unless and until the purchaser has the home inspected.

Controlled Business Arrangement: An arrangement by several businesses to share customer information, fees, and profits.

Conventional Loan: A private sector loan, one that is not guaranteed or insured by the U.S. government. Also called a fixed-rate mortgage or a traditional mortgage, the interest rate remains the same for the life of the loan. The loan term is typically 15 or 30 years. In the strictest sense of this phrase, it is a loan that is sold to Fannie Mae or Freddie Mac.

Conversion Option: A provision of some adjustable-rate mortgage (ARM) loans that allows the borrower to change the ARM to a fixed-rate mortgage at specified times after loan origination.

Convertible ARM: An adjustable-rate mortgage (ARM) that allows the borrower to convert the loan to a fixed-rate mortgage under specified conditions.

Cooperative (Co-op): Residents purchase stock in a cooperative corporation that owns a structure; each stockholder is then entitled to live in a specific unit of the structure and is responsible for paying a portion of the loan. As surprising as it may sound, a co-op is not real estate, and fair housing laws do not apply.

Correspondent Lender: A lending institution that uses a line of credit to fund loans.

Cost of Deposit Index (CODI): An index calculated by averaging the previous 12 interest rates paid on the 3 month certificate of deposit.

Cost of Funds Index (COFI): An index that is used to determine interest rate changes for certain adjustable-rate mortgage (ARM) loans. The COFI index is based on the weighted monthly average cost of deposits, advances, and other borrowings of members of the Federal Home Loan Bank of San Francisco.

Cost of Savings Index (COSI): The weighted average of interest rates paid on deposits held by World Savings.

Counter-Offer: An offer made in response to a previous offer. For example, after the buyer presents their first offer, the seller may make a counter-offer with a slightly higher sale price.

CPA Letter: A letter from a certified public accountant that typically states that he has reviewed a borrower's tax returns and financial statements thus attesting to the validity of the business.

Cram Down: An action that can result in loss of value to shareholders and bond holders. If a financial sector firm was nationalized and received an infusion of capital from the U.S. Treasury, stockholders were wiped out since technically the firm was financially insolvent. In a judicial modification, a bankruptcy judge restructures a promise note for a distressed borrower to relieve him with perhaps a lower balance and a lower interest. That judicial action would invariably result in a cram down on the bond holder, who would see the value of his asset decline accordingly.

Credit: The ability of a person to borrow money, or buy goods by paying over time. Credit is extended based on a lender's opinion of the person's financial situation and reliability, among other factors.

Credit Bureau: A company that gathers information on consumers who use credit. These companies sell that information to lenders and other businesses in the form of a credit report.

Credit Default Swap: Credit enhancements, or insurance, to protect an asset's value by covering possible default. The purchaser of the swap secures credit protection, while the seller of the swap insures the credit worthiness of the credit-related asset. In this transaction, the default risk is transferred from the holder of the security to the seller of the swap, also known as the counter party.

Credit History: History of an individual's debt payment; lenders use this information to gauge a potential borrower's ability and willingness to repay a loan.

Credit Life Insurance: A type of insurance that pays off a specific amount of debt or a specified credit account if the borrower dies while the policy is in force.

Credit Report: A record that lists all past and present debts and the timeliness of their repayment; it documents an individual's credit history. The report includes identifying information and details about your credit accounts, loans, bankruptcies, late payments, and recent credit inquiries. Prospective lenders will obtain these reports, with your permission, to evaluate your creditworthiness. Every year, you should order a free copy of your credit report and review it for accuracy.

Credit Score: A number representing the possibility a borrower may default; it is based upon credit history, and is used to determine ability to qualify for a mortgage loan. It is calculated using a standardized formula. There are many factors that could damage a credit score, including late payments and poor credit card use. Lenders may use your credit score to determine whether to give you a loan and what rate to charge. The better your credit score, the better the rate you can get on a loan.

Creditor: A person who extends credit to whom you owe money.

Creditworthy: The ability to qualify for credit and repay debts.

Criminal Lawsuit: An action by either the state or the federal government against an individual or entity.

Curtailment: The reduction of the loan balance.

D

DD-214: Defense Department Form 214 is a veteran's discharge papers that evidences VA loan eligibility.

Debt: Money owed from one person or institution to another person or institution.

Debt-to-Income Ratio (DTI): A comparison of gross income to housing and nonhousing expenses expressed as a percentage. With the FHA, the monthly mortgage payment should be no more than 29 percent of monthly gross income (before taxes) and the mortgage payment combined with nonhousing debts should not exceed 41 percent of income. This would be presented as 29/41 ratios. The lender uses these ratios to help determine how much it will lend. For conventional conforming loans, if the percentage is greater than 33/36, these ratios could negatively impact the credit score because the lender considers that as too much debt. Jumbo loans permit 33/38 ratios. Private-labeled lenders permit a higher single percent ratio at 50 percent to 55 percent.

Deed: The document that transfers ownership of a property.

Deed-in-Lieu: To avoid foreclosure ("in lieu" of foreclosure), a deed is given to the lender to fulfill the obligation to repay the debt; this process doesn't allow the borrower to remain in the house but helps avoid the costs, time, and effort associated with foreclosure.

Deed of Trust: A legal document in which the borrower transfers the title to a third party (trustee) to hold as security for the lender. When the loan is paid in full, the trustee transfers title back to the borrower. If the borrower defaults on the loan the trustee will sell the property and pay the lender the mortgage debt.

Default: The inability to pay monthly mortgage payments in a timely manner or to otherwise meet the mortgage terms.

Deficit Judgment: In some short sales or claims made by lenders against borrowers, the lender's loss that is held against a borrower and duly noted on a credit report. In such cases, consumers are barred further extensions of mortgage credit until such time that a deficit judgment is cleared.

Delinquency: Failure of a borrower to make timely mortgage payments under a loan agreement.

Delegated Underwriting: The lender's authority to approve loans that is passed onto a correspondent lender.

Demand: The total quantity of goods and services consumers are willing and able to buy at all possible prices during some time period.

Deposit Insurance: U.S. government backing of bank deposits up to a certain amount; currently, $100,000 (as of 2007).

Depreciation: A decline in the value of a house due to changing market conditions or lack of upkeep on a home.

Depression: A severe decline in general economic activity in terms of magnitude and/or length.

Deregulation: Lifting of government controls over an industry.

Discount Point: Normally paid at closing and generally calculated to be equivalent to 1 percent of the total loan amount, discount points are paid to reduce the interest rate on a loan.

Disintermediation: The removal of intermediaries in the chain that connect the supplier with the consumer. In lending and securitization, it is the passing of the borrower's credit risk from the lending bank to the investor.

Discount Rate: The interest rate paid by commercial banks to borrow funds from Federal Reserve Banks.

Discounted Rate: A below-market interest rate that is secured by financing discount points, which typically are a percentage of the loan amount.

Do Not Call List: A federally mandated list of names and numbers that prohibit commercial communications from parties with no existing relationship.

Down Payment: The portion of a home's purchase price that is paid in cash and is not part of the mortgage loan.

Due Care: In law, the degree of care that a person of ordinary prudence and reason would exercise under given circumstances. Failure to exercise due care is negligence.

Due Diligence: Refers to the care a reasonable person takes prior to entering into an agreement with others, which is done by confirming the material facts associated with a sale, purchase, or making of a loan. This "homework" serves to prevent unnecessary harm to parties to the transaction.

Due-on-Sale Clause: A provision in a mortgage that allows the lender to demand repayment in full of the outstanding balance if the property securing the mortgage is sold.

E

Earnest Money: Money put down by a potential buyer to show that he or she is serious about purchasing the home; it becomes part of the down payment if the offer is accepted, is returned if the offer is rejected, or is forfeited if the buyer pulls out of the deal.

Easement: A right to the use of, or access to, land owned by another.

Economic Growth: An increase in a nation's capacity to produce goods and services.

Employer-Assisted Housing: A program in which companies assist their employees in purchasing homes by providing assistance with the down payment, closing costs, or monthly payments.

Encroachment: The intrusion onto another's property without right or per-mission.

Encumbrance: Any claim on a property, such as a lien, mortgage or easement.

Energy Efficient Mortgage: An FHA program that helps homebuyers save money on utility bills by enabling them to finance the cost of adding energy efficiency features to a new or existing home as part of the home purchase

Equal Credit Opportunity Act (ECOA): A federal law that requires lenders to make credit equally available without regard to the applicant's race, color, religion, national origin, age, sex, or marital status; the fact that all or part of the applicant's income is derived from a public assistance program; or the fact that the applicant has in good faith exercised any right under the Consumer Credit Protection Act. It also requires various notices to consumers.

Equity: This is the owner's financial interest in a property that is calculated by subtracting the difference between the current fair market value of the property and the outstanding balances on the mortgage(s) and home equity lines of credit.

Equity-Based Lending: The extension of credit irrespective of a borrower's documented ability or willingness to repay whereby the loan-to-value is low enough to minimize the collateral risk in the event of default and the rate is high enough to justify the interest rate risk so that a loan can be made.

Escrow: An item of value, money, or documents deposited with a third party to be delivered upon the fulfillment of a condition. For example, the deposit by a borrower with the lender of funds to pay taxes and insurance premiums when they become due, or the deposit of funds or documents with an attorney or escrow agent to be disbursed upon the closing of a sale of real estate.

Escrow Account: A separate account into which the lender puts a portion of each monthly mortgage payment; an escrow account provides the funds needed for such expenses as property taxes, homeowners insurance, mortgage insurance, etc.

Escrow Analysis: The accounting that a mortgage servicer performs to deter-mine the appropriate balances for the escrow account, compute the borrower's monthly escrow payments, and deter-mine whether any shortages, surpluses or deficiencies exist in the account.

Eviction: The legal act of removing someone from real property.

Exclusive Right-to-Sell Listing: The traditional kind of listing agreement under which the property owner appoints a real estate broker (known as the listing broker) as exclusive agent to sell the property on the owner's stated terms, and agrees to pay the listing broker a commission when the property is sold, regardless of whether the buyer is found by the broker, the owner or another broker. This is the kind of listing agreement that is commonly used by a listing broker to provide the traditional full range of real estate brokerage services. If a second real estate broker (known as a selling broker) finds the buyer for the property, then some commission will be paid to the selling broker.

Exclusive Agency Listing: A listing agreement under which a real estate broker (known as the listing broker) acts as an exclusive agent to sell the property for the property owner, but may be paid a reduced or no commission when the property is sold if, for example, the property owner rather than the listing broker finds the buyer. This kind of listing agreement can be used to provide the owner a limited range of real estate brokerage services rather than the traditional full range. As with other kinds of listing agreements, if a second real estate broker (known as a selling broker) finds the buyer for the property, then some commission will be paid to the selling broker.

Executor: A person named in a will and approved by a probate court to administer the deposition of an estate in accordance with the instructions of the will.

F

Fair Credit Reporting Act (FCRA): A consumer protection law that imposes obligations on credit bureaus (and similar agencies) that maintain consumer credit histories, lenders and other businesses that buy reports from credit bureaus, and parties who furnish consumer information to credit bureaus. Among other provisions, the FCRA limits the sale of credit reports by credit bureaus by requiring the purchaser to have a legitimate business need for the data, allows consumers to learn the information on them in credit bureau files (including one annual free credit report), and specifies procedure for challenging errors in that data.

Fair Housing Act: A law that prohibits discrimination in all facets of the home buying process on the basis of race, color, national origin, religion, sex, familial status, or disability.

Fair Market Value: The hypothetical price that a willing buyer and seller will agree upon when they are acting freely, carefully, and with complete knowledge of the situation.

Fair Value Accounting: A transparent based measurement of assets and liabilities. Also known as mark-to-market.

Fannie Mae: Federal National Mortgage Association (FNMA); a federally-chartered enterprise owned by private stockholders that purchases residential mortgages and converts them into securities for sale to investors; by purchasing mortgages, Fannie Mae supplies funds that lenders may loan to potential homebuyers.

Fannie Mae-Seller/Servicer: A lender that Fannie Mae has approved to sell loans to it and to service loans on Fannie Mae's behalf.

Fannie Mae/Freddie Mac Loan Limit: The 2006 Fannie Mae/Freddie Mac loan limit for a single-family home is $417,000 and is higher in Alaska, Guam, Hawaii, and the U.S. Virgin Islands. The Fannie Mae loan limit is $533,850 for a two-unit home; $645,300 for a three-unit home; and $801,950 for a four-unit home. Also referred to as the "conventional loan limit." For updates, visit www.fanniemae.com and www.freddiemac.com.

Feasibility Study: A detailed report assembled by a real estate agent, developer, or builder to determine the marketability and potential profitability of rezoning land, as well as assessing the appropriate features and benefits for a new home community.

Federal Accounting Standards Board (FASB): A non-profit organization authorized by the SEC to develop generally accepted accounting principles.

Federal Deposit Insurance Corporation (FDIC): Created in 1933 in response to bank failures, and extended to protect consumer deposits up to $100,000 after the S&L crisis of the 1980s.

Federal Home Loan Bank Board (FHLBB): A government sponsored entity established in 1932 that serves as a stable source of mortgage capital across the U.S. through its member banks.

Federal Housing Authority: Federal Housing Administration (FHA); established in 1934 to advance homeownership opportunities for all Americans; assists homebuyers by providing mortgage insurance to lenders to cover most losses that may occur when a borrower defaults; this encourages lenders to make loans to borrowers who might not qualify for conventional mortgages.

Federal Housing Finance Agency (FHFA): The Federal Housing Finance Agency was created on July 30, 2008 by the Housing and Economic Recovery Act of 2008 to launch "a world-class, empowered regulator" for Fannie Mae, Freddie Mac, and the Federal Home Loan Banks.

Federal Reserve Bank: One of the twelve operating arms of the Federal Reserve System, located throughout the United States, that together with their 25 branches carry out various functions of the U.S. central bank system.

Federal Reserve System: The principal monetary authority (central bank) of the United States, which issues currency and regulates the supply of credit in the economy. It is made of a seven-member Board of Governors in Washington, D.C., twelve regional Federal Reserve Banks, and their 25 branches. Often referred to as "the Fed," but has nothing to do with the federal government.

Federal Trade Commission (FTC): A federal agency tasked by Congress to protect the public from unfair and deceptive trade practices.

Fiduciary: In law, a requirement of loyalty, trust, utmost good faith, and confidence from an agent toward others in specific obligations.

First Mortgage: A mortgage that is the primary lien against a property.

First-Time Homebuyer: A person with no ownership interest in a principal residence during the three-year period preceding the purchase of the security property.

Fiscal Policy: The federal government's decisions about the amount of money it spends and collects in taxes to achieve full employment and noninflationary economy.

Fixed-Rate Mortgage: A mortgage with payments that remain the same throughout the life of the loan because the interest rate and other terms are fixed and do not change.

Fixed-Period Adjustable-Rate Mortgage: An adjustable-rate mortgage (ARM) that offers a fixed rate for an initial period, typically three to ten years, and then adjusts every six months, annually, or at another specified period, for the remainder of the term. Also known as a "hybrid loan."

Flood Certification Fee: A fee charged by independent mapping firms to identify properties located in areas designated as flood zones.

Flood Insurance: Insurance that protects homeowners against losses from a flood; if a home is located in a flood plain, the lender will require flood insurance before approving a loan. Homeowners can go to the FEMA website at www.FEMA.gov to see the designation of their property.

Force majeure: A French phrase that means a major or superior force, or implies an act of God. The phrase may be used in contracts to address the impact of unforeseen events on obligations.

Foreclosure: A legal process in which mortgaged property is sold to pay the loan of the defaulting borrower.

Forensic Loan Auditing: A technique used to deconstruct a loan application for the purpose of identifying inadequate disclosure or violations of the law with the end result being legal recourse against the mortgage lender.

Forfeiture: The loss of an earnest money deposit, money, property, rights, or privileges due to a breach of a legal obligation.

Freddie Mac: Federal Home Loan Mortgage Corporation (FHLMC); a federally-chartered corporation that purchases residential mortgages, securitizes them, and sells them to investors; this provides lenders with funds for new mortgage borrowers.

Free Enterprise System: An economic system characterized by private ownership of property and productive resources, the profit motive to stimulate production, competition to ensure efficiency, and the forces of supply and demand to direct the production and distribution of goods and services.

Fully Amortized Mortgage: A mortgage in which the monthly payments are designed to retire the obligation at the end of the mortgage term.

Fundamental Analysis: An analysis based on financials or income streams out of which ratios can be established.

G

General Contractor: A person who oversees a home improvement or construction project and handles various aspects such as scheduling workers and ordering supplies.

Generally Accepted Accounting Practices (GAAP): The set of principles, standards and procedures governing accounting. The SEC requires publicly traded companies to comply with GAAP.

Gift Letter: A letter that a family member writes verifying that s/he has provided a certain amount of money as a gift and that does not have to be repaid. This money can be used toward a portion of the down payment with some mortgages.

Ginnie Mae: Government National Mortgage Association (GNMA); a government-owned corporation overseen by the U.S. Department of Housing and Urban Development, Ginnie Mae pools FHA-insured, VA-guaranteed loans, Rural Housing Service loans, and Public and Indian Housing loans to back securities for private investment. As with Fannie Mae and Freddie Mac, the investment income provides funding that may then be lent to eligible borrowers by lenders.

GNMA I: Government securities that are comprised of fixed-rate mortgages.

GNMA II: Government securities that are comprised of both ARMs and fixed-rate mortgages.

Good Faith Estimate: An estimate of all closing fees including prepaid and escrow items as well as lender charges; must be given to the borrower within three days after submission of a loan application.

Government Mortgage: A mortgage loan that is insured or guaranteed by a federal government entity such as the Federal Housing Administration (FHA), the U.S. Department of Veterans Affairs (VA), the Rural Housing Service (RHS), or Public and Indian Housing (PIH).

Government Sponsored Enterprise (GSE): Corporations with a public mission like Fannie Mae, Freddie Mac, and the Federal Home Loan Bank Board System.

Great Depression: Period of time tied to the stock market crash on October 29, 1929, or Black Tuesday, and ended about 1939 on the eve of World War II. One of out four Americans were out of work, foreclosures were at record numbers, and bank runs led to many banks failing – all in the wake of a stock market bubble driven by irrational exuberance and no standardized accounting rules.

Gross Domestic Product: The total value of a nation's output, income, or expenditure produced within its physical boundaries.

Gross Monthly Income: Income earned in a month before taxes and other deductions. It also may include rental income, self-employed income, income from alimony, child support, public assistance payments, and retirement benefits.

Ground Rent: Payment for the use of land when title to a property is held as a leasehold estate (that is, the borrower does not actually own the property, but has a long-term lease on it).

Gross Up: To add a percentage to an income figure. For example, grossing up nontaxable income adds back what otherwise would have taken out for taxes. This technique permits a retired borrower on social security income to qualify with the same footing as a borrower whose income is taxed.

Growing-Equity Mortgage (GEM): A fixed-rate mortgage in which the monthly payments increase according to an agreed-upon schedule, with the extra funds applied to reduce the loan balance and loan term.

H

Hard Money: See Equity Based Lending.

Hazard Insurance: Insurance coverage that compensates for physical damage to a property from fire, wind, vandalism, or other covered hazards or natural disasters.

HELP: Homebuyer Education Learning Program; an educational program from the FHA that counsels people about the home buying process; HELP covers topics like budgeting, finding a home, getting a loan, and home maintenance; in most cases, completion of the program may entitle the homebuyer to a reduced initial FHA mortgage insurance premium-from 2.25 percent to 1.75 percent of the home purchase price.

High Cost Test: Section 32 of regulation Z that processors and underwriters follow to stay in compliance with regulations that limit interest rates and fees charged to borrowers.

Home Equity Conversion Mortgage (HECM): A special type of mortgage developed and insured by the Federal Housing Administration (FHA) that enables home owners 62 and older to convert the equity they have in their homes into cash, or monthly income with a variety of payment options to address their specific financial needs. More popularly called a "reverse mortgage."

Home Equity Line of Credit (HELOC): A type of revolving loan that enables a home owner to obtain multiple advances of the loan proceeds at his or her own discretion, up to an amount that represents a specified percentage of the borrower's equity in the property.

Home Inspection: A professional inspection of a home to determine the condition of the property. The inspection should include an evaluation of the plumbing, heating and cooling systems, roof, wiring, foundation, and evidence of wood-boring insects.

Home Ownership Equity Protection Act (HOEPA): A 1994 federal law that amends the Truth in Lending Act and sets a high cost test on lenders in order to protect consumers from unfair and deceptive practices.

Home Warranty: Offers protection for mechanical systems and attached appliances against unexpected repairs not covered by homeowner's insurance; overage extends over a specific time period and does not cover the home's structure.

Homeowners' Association: An organization of homeowners residing within a particular area whose principal purpose is to ensure the provision and maintenance of community facilities and services for the common benefit of the residents.

Homeowner's Insurance: An insurance policy that combines protection against damage to a dwelling and its contents with protection against claims of negligence or inappropriate action that result in someone's injury or property damage.

Homeowner's Warranty (HOW): Insurance offered by a seller that covers certain home repairs and fixtures for a specified period of time.

Housing Counseling Agency: Provides counseling and assistance to individuals on a variety of issues, including loan default, fair housing, and home buying.

Housing Expense Ratio: The percent-age of gross monthly income that goes toward paying for housing expenses.

HUD-1 Settlement Statement: A final listing of the closing costs of the mortgage transaction. It provides the sales price and down payment, as well as the total settlement costs required from the buyer and seller.

HUD: The U.S. Department of Housing and Urban Development; established in 1965, HUD works to create a decent home and suitable living environment for all Americans; it does this by addressing housing needs, improving and developing American communities, and enforcing fair housing laws.

HVAC: Heating, Ventilation and Air Conditioning; a home's heating and cooling system.

Hybrid ARM: These ARMs are a mix—or a hybrid—of a fixed-rate period and an adjustable-rate period. The interest rate is fixed for the first several years of the loan; after that, the rate could adjust annually. For example, hybrid ARMs can be advertised as 3/1 or 5/1—the first number tells you how long the fixed interest-rate period will be and the second number tells you how often the rate will adjust in either months or years after the initial period.

I

Income Property: Real estate developed or purchased to produce income, such as a rental unit.

Income Statement: One of the three main financial statements that summarizes firm's revenues and expenses over a specified period, and concludes with net income or loss for that period. (See also and Balance Sheet and Statement of Cash Flows).

Income Tax: An assessment levied by government on the net income of individuals and businesses.

Independent Contractor: An employment arrangement that has different IRS reporting and legal responsibilities than that of an employee.

Index: A number used to compute the interest rate for an adjustable-rate mortgage (ARM). The index is generally a published number or percentage, such as the average interest rate or yield on U.S. Treasury Bills. A margin is added to the index to determine the interest rate that will be charged on the ARM. This interest rate is subject to any caps on the maximum or minimum interest rate that may be charged on the mortgage, stated in the note.

Individual Retirement Account (IRA): A tax-deferred plan that can help build a retirement nest egg.

Inflation: A rate of increase in the general price level of all goods and services. (This should not be confused with increases in the prices of specific goods relative to the prices of other goods.) Also, the number of dollars in circulation that exceeds the amount of goods and services available for purchase. Inflation results in a decrease in the dollar's value, which can take place due to low interest rates or scarcity of goods.

Initial Interest Rate: The original interest rate for an adjustable-rate mortgage (ARM). Sometimes known as the "start rate."

Inquiry: A request for a copy of a credit report by a lender or other business, often at the time of credit application and/or request more credit. Too many inquiries on a credit report can hurt a credit score; however, most credit scores are not affected by multiple inquiries from auto or mortgage lenders within a short period of time.

Installment: The regular periodic payment that a borrower agrees to make to a lender.

Installment Debt: A loan that is repaid in accordance with a schedule of payments for a specified term (such as an automobile loan).

Interest: The cost paid to borrow money. It is the payment made to a lender for the money it has loaned. Interest is usually expressed as a percentage of the amount borrowed.

Interest Accrual Rate: The percentage rate at which interest accumulates or increases on a mortgage loan.

Interest Rate Cap: For an adjustable-rate mortgage (ARM), a limitation on the amount the interest rate can change per adjustment or over the lifetime of the loan, as stated in the note.

Interest Rate Ceiling: For an adjust-able-rate mortgage (ARM), the maximum interest rate, as specified in the mortgage note.

Interest Rate Floor: For an adjustable-rate mortgage (ARM), the minimum interest rate, as specified in the mortgage note.

Investment Property: A property purchased to generate rental income, tax benefits, or profitable resale rather than to serve as the borrower's primary residence. Contrast with "second home."

Interest-Only Mortgage: The borrower is required only to make interest payments for a specified number of years. When this initial period expires, the loan changes so the monthly payment includes principal and interest. At this point, the mortgage begins to fully amortize and monthly payments could increase significantly. The monthly principal payment could be greater than the conventional fixed-rate mortgage payment because there are fewer years to pay down the principal.

Interest-Only Payment ARM: An I/O Payment ARM plan allows the borrower to pay only the interest for a specified number of years. After that, the borrower must repay both the principal and the interest over the remaining term of the loan.

Interest Rate: The amount of interest charged on a monthly loan payment; usually expressed as a percentage.

Interest Rate Risk: This is a secondary market and depository institution concern. A retail banking example is when a depository institution has obligations to pay on certificates of deposit at one rate at say 4 percent but rates on deposits are declining given market conditions to 3 percent. That 1 percent spread is the risk and is measured as a loss, which can be substantial even for small banks. Another example is in the yield curve risk, which is the risk that comes about from the changes in short-term and long-term interest rates. Banks typically borrow on lower short-term rates and then lend out at higher long-term rates. If the yield curve inverts, which is a sign of an impending recession, then the interest rate risk rises as short-term rates rise and long-term rates drop. Finally, in the secondary market, pricing a security to model versus to market exemplifies the interest risk inherent in securities that may not normally trade in a stable market.

Insurance: Protection against a specific loss over a period of time that is secured by the payment of a regularly scheduled premium.

Investment: The purchase of a security, such as a stock or bond.

J

Judgment: A legal decision; when requiring debt repayment, a judgment may include a property lien that secures the creditor's claim by providing a collateral source.

Judicial Foreclosure: A legal action in a civil dispute over a mortgage contract that requires a court hearing and permission by a judge to grant a foreclosure and eviction.

Jumbo Loan: A loan that exceeds the mortgage amount eligible for purchase by Fannie Mae or Freddie Mac. Also called "nonconforming loan."

Junior Mortgage: A loan that is subordinate to the primary loan or first-lien mortgage loan, such as a second or third mortgage.

K

Keogh Funds: A tax-deferred retirement-savings plan for small business owners or self-employed individuals who have earned income from their trade or business. Contributions to the Keogh plan are tax-deductible.

L

Labor Force: As measured in the United States, the total number of people employed or looking for work.

Laissez-Faire: French phrase meaning "leave alone." In economics and politics, a doctrine that the economic system functions best when there is little to no interference in the market place by the government.

Late Charge: A penalty imposed by the lender when a borrower fails to make a scheduled payment on time.

Lease Purchase: Assists low- to moderate-income homebuyers in purchasing a home by allowing them to lease a home with an option to buy; the rent payment is made up of the monthly rental payment plus an additional amount that is credited to an account for use as a down payment.

Letter of Explanation (LOE): A letter from the borrower directed to the loan officer and underwriter that explains the reason for the application, consumer credit late payments, and other issues triggered by the contents of a credit report or public records.

Leverage: The ability to use income and assets to make other acquisitions. It is a ratio that in this example is expressed as 10:1, which indicates a ten to one ratio, or $1 in equity for every $10 borrowed and owed. This is a financial technique used by both individuals and corporations to maximize possible gains. But, it can cut both ways and multiple losses as well.

Liabilities: A person's debts and other financial obligations.

Liability Insurance: Insurance coverage that protects property owners against claims of negligence, personal injury or property damage to another party.

LIBOR Index: An index used to determine interest rate changes for certain adjustable rate mortgage (ARM) plans, based on the average interest rate at which international banks lend to or borrow funds from the London Inter-bank Market.

Lien: A legal claim against property that must be satisfied when the property is sold.

Lifetime Cap: For an adjustable-rate mortgage (ARM), a limit on the amount that the interest rate or monthly payment can increase or decrease over the life of the loan.

Liquid Asset: A cash asset or an asset that is easily converted into cash.

Loan: Money borrowed that is usually repaid with interest.

Loan Fraud: Purposely giving incorrect information on a loan application in order to qualify for a loan; may result in civil liability or criminal penalties.

Loan Origination: The process by which a loan is made, which may include taking a loan application, processing and underwriting the application, and closing the loan.

Loan Origination Fees: Fees paid to the mortgage lender or broker for processing the mortgage application. This fee is usually in the form of points. One point equals one percent of the mortgage amount.

Loan-to-Value (LTV): The relationship between the loan amount and the value of the property (the lower of appraised value or sales price), expressed as a percentage of the property's value. For example, a $100,000 home with an $80,000 mortgage has an LTV of 80 percent.

Lock-in: Since interest rates can change frequently, many lenders offer an interest rate lock-in that guarantees a specific interest rate if the loan is closed within a specific time.

Long Bond: The ten-year U.S. Treasury bond.

Loss Mitigation: A process to avoid foreclosure; the lender tries to help a borrower who has been unable to make loan payments and is in danger of defaulting on his or her loan. Typically, borrowers who have become delinquent in their obligations may be eligible to restructure their loan with refinance provided that their hardship was through no fault of their own.

Low-Down-Payment Feature: A feature of some mortgages, usually fixed-rate mortgages, that helps purchasers buy a home with only a low down payment.

M

Manual Underwriting: When an automated underwriting decision can not be secured due to a variety of borrower-related risk characteristics, the loan file must be carefully reviewed and underwritten the old fashioned way: by a human being.

Manufactured Housing: Homes that are built entirely in a factory in accordance with a federal building code ad-ministered by the U.S. Department of Housing and Urban Development (HUD). Manufactured homes may be single- or multisection and are transported from the factory to a site and installed. Homes that are permanently affixed to a foundation often may be classified as real property under applicable state law, and may be financed with a mortgage. Homes that are not permanently affixed to a foundation generally are classified as personal property, and are financed with a retail installment sales agreement.

Margin: A percentage added to the index for an adjustable rate mortgage (ARM) to establish the interest rate on each adjustment date.

Mark-to-Market: The valuation of an asset based on current values rather than historical cost.

Mark-to-Model: The valuation of an asset based on assumptions and variables that produce a theoretical forecast.

Market: A setting in which buyers and sellers establish prices for identical or very similar products, and exchange goods or services.

Market Risk: Market factors, anticipated and unforeseen, that may positively or negatively impact the value of an investment in one of the three asset classes: stocks, bonds, or real estate.

Market Economy: The national economy of a country that relies on market forces to determine levels of production, consumption, investment, and savings without government intervention.

Market Value: The current value of real estate based on what a purchaser would pay in an arm's length transaction. An appraisal is sometimes used to determine market value.

Maturity Date: The date on which a mortgage loan is scheduled to be paid in full, as stated in the note.

Merged Credit Report: A credit report issued by a credit reporting company that combines information from two or three major credit bureaus.

Modification: Any change to the terms of a mortgage loan, including changes to the interest rate, loan balance, or loan term.

Minimum Monthly Payment (MMP): This required payment typically covers only a portion of the interest and none of the principal.

Monetary Policy: Federal Reserve System actions to influence the availability and cost of money and credit as a means of helping to promote high employment, economic growth, price stability, and a sustainable pattern of international transactions.

Money Supply: The amount of money (coins, paper currency, and checking accounts) that is in circulation in the economy.

Monopoly: The sole seller of a good or service in a market.

Moral Hazard: A concept that addresses the risks to parties to a transaction associated with rewarding poor decision making or the business behavior of individuals and corporations that shield them from the consequences of their actions.

Mortgage: A lien on the property that secures the promise to repay a loan.

Mortgagee: The institution or individual to whom a mortgage is given.

Mortgage Backed Security (MBS): A securitized pool of mortgages that serve as an asset whose value is determined by the anticipated cash flows of principal and interest payments.

Mortgagee Clause: A clause in an insurance policy that names the mortgage lender as beneficiary in the event of a loss associated with a claim so that the building can be repaired or rebuilt in order to preserve the lender's vested interest in the collateral.

Mortgage Banker: A company that originates loans and resells them to secondary mortgage lenders like: Fannie Mae or Freddie Mac.

Mortgage Broker: An individual or firm that that brings borrowers and lenders together, and originates and processes loans for a number of lenders.

Mortgage Electronic Registration Systems, Inc.: It is a third party registry of mortgages created by the mortgage banking industry. The courts have ruled that it is a nominee, not a beneficial owner, of a promissory note.

Mortgage Insurance: A policy that protects lenders against some or most of the losses that can occur when a borrower defaults on a mortgage loan; mortgage insurance is required primarily for borrowers with a down payment of less than 20 percent of the home's purchase price.

Mortgage Insurance Premium (MIP): A monthly payment—usually part of the mortgage payment—paid by a borrower for mortgage insurance. And, an upfront premium added to the loan balance. MIP is always associated with FHA loans. These premiums serve to ensure timely payments even when borrowers are not on time, and also insure against loss in the case of foreclosure.

Mortgage Lender: The lender providing funds for a mortgage. Lenders also manage the credit and financial information review, the property and the loan application process through closing.

Mortgage Life Insurance: A type of insurance that will pay off a mortgage if the borrower dies while the loan is out-standing; a form of credit life insurance.

Mortgage Modification: A loss mitigation option that allows a borrower to refinance and/or extend the term of the mortgage loan and thus reduce the monthly payments.

Mortgage Rate: The interest rate you pay to borrow the money to buy your house.

Mortgagee: The institution or individual to whom a mortgage is given.

Mortgagor: The owner of real estate who pledges property as security for the repayment of a debt; the borrower.

Moving Treasury Average (MTA): A less widely used index based on the twelve-month average of U.S. Treasury securities.

Multifamily Mortgage: A mortgage loan on a building with five or more dwelling units.

Multifamily Properties: Typically, buildings with five or more dwelling units.

Multiple Listing Service (MLS): A clearinghouse through which member real estate brokerage firms regularly and systematically exchange information on listings of real estate properties and share commissions with members who locate purchasers. The MLS for an area is usually operated by the local, private real estate association as a joint venture among its members designed to foster real estate brokerage services.

N

Negative Amortization: Occurs when the monthly payments do not cover all the interest owed. The interest that is not paid in the monthly payment is added to the loan balance. This means that even after making many payments, you could owe more than you did at the beginning of the loan. Negative amortization can occur when an ARM has a payment cap that results in monthly payments that are not high enough to cover the interest due or when the minimum payments are set at an amount lower than the amount owed in interest. Deferring interest owed results in a higher loan balance.

Net Tangible Benefit: Normally determined by the free market when informed consumers and disclosing financers meet in an efficient market, but imposed as a consumer protection and compliance check by underwriters prior to loan funding.

Net Monthly Income: Take-home pay after taxes. It is the amount received in a paycheck.

Net Worth: The value of a company or individual's assets, including cash, less total liabilities.

NINA: A documentation type that means No Income, No Asset.

NINJA: A documentation type that means No Income, No Job, No Assets.

Nonconforming Loan: A mortgage loan that does not conform to Fannie Mae or Freddie Mac underwriting guidelines.

Non-Judicial Foreclosure: A foreclosure proceeding initiated by a trustee pursuant to the terms of a deed of trust.

Nonliquid Asset: An asset that cannot easily be converted into cash.

Nonprime: Synonymous with B-C-D and subprime. The term used in both industry trade publications and annual reports of lenders.

Nontraditional Mortgages: These products are more complex than traditional fixed-rate or adjustable-rate mortgages. They present greater risk of negative amortization and payment shock. Typically referred to as *alternative* or *exotic*, these products take many different forms. They include interest only mortgages, payment-option ARMS, low-doc. and no-doc. loans, piggybacks (simultaneous second lien loans—i.e., loans that cover the down payment) and 40- or 50-year mortgages. Although these products may provide flexibility for some, for others they may simply lead to increased future payment obligations and possibly financial disaster.

Note: See Promissory Note.

Note Rate: The interest rate listed on the application, Good Faith Estimate, and the Promise Note. Note to be confused with the Payment Rate, which is a phrase used in association with Option ARMs where the product may be presented as a loan with a 1 percent payment rate.

New Deal: Economic reform programs of the 1930s established to help lift the United States out of the Great Depression.

O

Offer: Indication by a potential buyer of his willingness to purchase a home at a specific price; generally put forth in writing. It is a formal bid from the homebuyer to the home seller to purchase a home, and starts the negotiating process.

Office of the Comptroller of the Currency (OCC): The Office of the Comptroller of the Currency charters, regulates, and supervises all national banks.

Office of Thrift Supervision (OTS): Established by Congress in 1989 as the primary banking regulator for federally charted savings associations.

Office of Federal Housing Enterprise Oversight: The regulator of Fannie Mae and Freddie Mac.

Open House: When the seller's real estate agent opens the seller's house to the general public for inspection for the purpose of attracting potential buyers.

Option ARM: This product typically offers the borrower three different monthly payment options: 1) payments of principal and interest, 2) interest only payments, or 3) minimum monthly payments ("teaser" payment options that are less than interest only payments). Choosing minimum monthly payments means the unpaid interest is added to the principal loan amount. To ensure that the loan is repaid within the agreed-upon time, these loans "recast" after a set number of years (usually three or five) or when negative amortization drives the loan amount to a certain level above the original loan amount. Monthly payments increase so that the loan fully amortizes.

Origination: The process of preparing, submitting, and evaluating a loan application; generally includes a credit check, verification of employment, and a property appraisal.

Original Principal Balance: The total amount of principal owed on a mortgage before any payments are made.

Origination Fee: A fee paid to a lender or broker to cover the administrative costs of processing a loan application. The origination fee typically is stated in the form of points. One point is one percent of the mortgage amount.

Owner Financing: A transaction in which the property seller provides all or part of the financing for the buyer's purchase of the property.

Owner-Occupied Property: A property that serves as the borrower's primary residence.

P

Panic: A series of unexpected cash withdrawals from a bank caused by a sudden decline in depositor confidence or fear that the bank will be closed by the chartering agency, i.e., many depositors withdraw cash almost simultaneously. Since the cash reserve a bank keeps on hand is only a small fraction of its deposits, a large number of withdrawals in a short period of time can deplete available cash and force the bank to close and possibly go out of business.

Par Rate: An interest rate costs either the lender or consumer zero points to acquire. A wholesaler's par rate will be slightly marked up when retailed to the consumer. The par rate a consumer may elect is a zero point loan.

Partial Claim: A loss mitigation option offered by the FHA that allows a borrower, with help from a lender, to get an interest-free loan from HUD to bring their mortgage payments up to date.

Partial Payment: A payment that is less than the scheduled monthly payment on a mortgage loan.

Payment Change Date: The date on which a new monthly payment amount takes effect, for example, on an adjust-able-rate mortgage (ARM) loan.

Payment Option ARM: An ARM that allows you to choose among several payment options each month. The options typically include (1) a traditional amortizing payment of principal and interest, (2) an interest only payment, or (3) a minimum (or limited) payment that may be less than the amount of interest due that month. With the minimum-payment option, the amount of any interest not paid is added to the principal of the loan (see negative amortization).

Payment Cap: For an adjustable-rate mortgage (ARM) or other variable rate loan, a limit on the amount that payments can increase or decrease during any one adjustment period.

Payment Rate: Note to be confused with the Note Rate. The payment rate is a phrase often used in association with Option ARMs where the product may be presented as a loan with a 1 percent payment rate.

Payment Shock: Payment shock is a large and sudden increase in monthly payments. It occurs primarily in interest only products and option-adjustable-rate mortgages (Option ARMs).

Personal Property: Any property that is not real property.

PITI Reserves: A cash amount that a borrower has available after making a down payment and paying closing costs for the purchase of a home. The principal, interest, taxes, and insurance (PITI) reserves must equal the amount that the borrower would have to pay for PITI for a predefined number of months.

PITI: An acronym for the four primary components of a monthly mortgage payment: Principal, Interest, Taxes, and Insurance—the four elements of a monthly mortgage payment; payments of principal and interest go directly toward repaying the loan while the portion that covers taxes and insurance (homeowner's and mortgage, if applicable) goes into an escrow account to cover the fees when they are due. Oftentimes, MIP/Condo/HOA are added to this formula to take into account the monthly cost of mortgage insurance premiums, condo fees, or homeowner association fees as applicable.

Planned Unit Development (PUD): A real estate project in which individuals hold title to a residential lot and home while the common facilities are owned and maintained by a homeowners' association for the benefit and use of the individual PUD unit owners.

Points (may be called discount points): One point is equal to 1 percent of the principal amount of your mortgage. For example, if the mortgage is for $200,000, one point equals $2,000. Lenders frequently charge points in both fixed-rate and adjustable-rate mortgages in order to cover loan origination costs or to provide additional compensation to the lender or broker. These points usually are collected at closing and may be paid by the borrower or the home seller, or may be split between them. Discount points (sometimes called discount fees) are points that you voluntarily choose to pay in return for a lower interest rate.

Power of Attorney: A legal document that authorizes another person to act on one's behalf. A power of attorney can grant complete authority or can be limited to certain acts and/or certain periods of time.

Preapproval: A process by which a lender provides a prospective borrower with an indication of how much money he or she will be eligible to borrow when applying for a mortgage loan. This process typically includes a review of the applicant's credit history and may involve the review and verification of in-come and assets to close.

Preapprove: Lender commits to lend to a potential borrower; commitment remains as long as the borrower still meets the qualification requirements at the time of purchase.

Preapproval Letter: A letter from a mortgage lender indicating qualification for a mortgage of a specific amount. It also shows a home seller that the buyer is serious.

Predatory Lending: Abusive lending practices that include making mortgage loans to people who do not have the income to repay them or repeatedly refinancing loans, charging high points and fees each time and "packing" credit insurance onto a loan. During the housing boom, the practice, while clearly unethical, was legal given that RESPA, TILA, ECOA, and HOEPA left gaping holes for unethical lenders to penetrate, exploit, and victimize their own customers. Moreover, the nation's leading banking regulators: the Federal Reserve, the Office of the Comptroller of the Currency, and the Office of Thrift Supervision either did not enforce existing laws or fought against consumers and states seeking to curb abusive lending behavior.

Preforeclosure Sale: Allows a defaulting borrower to sell the mortgaged property to satisfy the loan and avoid foreclosure.

Premium: An amount paid on a regular schedule by a policyholder that maintains insurance coverage.

Premium Rate: This is an above market rate; it is higher than the prevailing Fannie Mae and Freddie Mac rates published on their websites.

Prepayment: Payment of the mortgage loan before the scheduled due date; may be subject to a prepayment penalty.

Prepayment Penalty: A fee that a borrower may be required to pay to the lender, in the early years of a mortgage loan, for repaying the loan in full or prepaying a substantial amount to reduce the unpaid principal balance.

Prequalification: A preliminary assessment by a lender of the amount it will lend to a potential home buyer. The process of determining how much money a prospective homebuyer may be eligible to borrow before he or she applies for a loan.

Prequalification Letter: A letter from a mortgage lender that states that the borrower prequalified to buy a home, but does not commit the lender to a particular mortgage amount.

Prequalify: A lender informally determines the maximum amount an individual is eligible to borrow.

Price Engine: An online program used by lenders to determine an interest and program given a borrower's overall credit and income profile.

Prime Loan: An agency (Fannie Mae or Freddie Mac) or government loan.

Prime Rate: An interest rate that banks offered to preferred customers; and the index to the Home Equity Line of Credit (HELOC).

Private-Labeled Investor: A nongovernment or non-agency buyer of mortgages. This could be a major Wall Street firm, a small hedge fund, or a private equity group with an appetite for mortgages in their investment portfolio.

Private Mortgage Insurance (PMI): PMI is required by lenders when a loan is originated and closed without a 20 percent down payment. This insurance protects the lender from default losses in the event a loan becomes delinquent. If the buyer is approved for a mortgage that requires PMI, he still has to apply for PMI and may not qualify. A borrower can be approved for a mortgage and not qualify for PMI.

Promissory Note: A contract. A written promise to repay a specified amount over a specified period of time under specified conditions.

Property Appreciation: See "Appreciation."

Principal: The amount of money borrowed or the amount still owed on a loan.

Price Fixing: Actions, generally by a several large corporations that dominate in a single market, to escape market discipline by setting prices for goods or services at an agreed-on level.

Price Supports: Federal assistance provided to farmers to help them deal with such unfavorable factors as bad weather and overproduction.

Private Labeled Lender: This could be a no name lender that exists in the wholesale channel for the purpose of acting as a conduit between its strategic relationships and lenders and brokers in the retail arena. It can also be a Wall Street investment banker that has a mortgage lending concern.

Privatization: The act of turning previously government-provided services over to private sector enterprises.

Purchase and Sale Agreement: A document that details the price and conditions for a transaction. In connection with the sale of a residential property, the agreement typically would include: information about the property to be sold, sale price, down payment, earnest money deposit, financing, closing date, occupancy date, length of time the offer is valid, and any special contingencies.

Purchase Money Mortgage: A mortgage loan that enables a borrower to acquire a property.

Pyramiding: Repeated cash-out refinances, typically in an appreciating real estate market, which support a borrower's lifestyle and expenses that are beyond his income.

Q

Qualifying Guidelines: Criteria used to determine eligibility for a loan.

Qualifying Ratios: Calculations that are used in determining the loan amount that a borrower qualifies for, typically a comparison of the borrower's total monthly income to monthly debt payments and other recurring monthly obligations.

Quality Control: A system of safeguards to ensure that loans are originated, underwritten and serviced according to the lender's standards and, if applicable, the standards of the investor, governmental agency, or mortgage insurer.

Quantitative Easing: An economic concept for dropping interest rates to zero percent and deflating the currency by printing more money in currencies backed by "the full faith" of the government. In the United States, this is when the Federal Reserve purchases mortgage backed securities and U.S. Treasury bills and notes when there is no market for them in order to stimulate the economy.

R

Radon: A radioactive gas found in some homes that, if occurring in strong enough concentrations, can cause health problems.

Rate Cap: The limit on the amount an interest rate on an adjustable rate mortgage (ARM) can increase or decrease during an adjustment period.

Rate Lock: An agreement in which an interest rate is "locked in" or guaranteed for a specified period of time prior to closing. See also "Lock-in Rate."

Ratified Sales Contract: A contract that shows both the buyer and the seller of the house have agreed to the offer. This offer may include sales contingencies, such as obtaining a mortgage of a certain type and rate, getting an acceptable inspection, making repairs, closing by a certain date, etc.

Real Estate Agent: An individual who is licensed to negotiate and arrange real estate sales; works for a real estate broker.

Real Estate Owned: Referred to as REO. Real estate that banks own as a result of foreclosures, unsuccessful auctions, or an inability or unwillingness to sell foreclosed properties on the open market.

REALTOR®: A real estate agent or broker who is a member of the National Association of REALTORS®, and its local and state associations.

Real Estate Professional: An individual who provides services in buying and selling homes. The real estate professional is paid a percentage of the home sale price by the seller. Unless specifically contracted with a buyer's agent, the real estate professional represents the interest of the seller. Real estate professionals may be able to refer buyers to local lenders or mortgage brokers, but are generally not involved in the lending process.

Real Estate Settlement Procedures Act (RESPA): A federal law that requires lenders to provide home mortgage borrowers with information about transaction-related costs prior to settlement, as well as information during the life of the loan regarding servicing and escrow accounts. RESPA also prohibits kickbacks and unearned fees in the mortgage loan business. RESPA protects consumers from abuses during the residential real estate purchase and loan process by requiring lenders to disclose all settlement costs, practices, and relationships.

Real Property: Land and anything permanently affixed thereto, including buildings, fences, trees, and minerals.

Receivership: A form of bankruptcy that permits a firm to reorganize with the aid of a trustee rather than liquidate assets. Also, the power granted by Congress to regulatory agencies authorizing them to step in and act as a trustee of an otherwise bankrupt agency.

Recession: A significant decline in general economic activity extending over a period of time. A recession is generally understood to be two consecutive quarters of negative economic growth as measured by the gross domestic product.

Receivable: In book keeping and accounting, money that is owed from customers for goods or services sold on credit.

Receivership: A form of bankruptcy that involves a court-appointed trustee to guide reorganization.

Rescission: The cancellation or annulment of a transaction or contract by operation of law or by mutual consent. Borrowers have a right to cancel certain mortgage refinance and home equity transactions within three business days after closing, or for up to three years in certain instances.

Recorder: The public official who keeps records of transactions that affect real property in the area. Sometimes known as a "Registrar of Deeds" or "County Clerk."

Recording: The filing of a lien or other legal documents in the appropriate public record. Also referred to as "recordation."

Reduced Documentation Loan: Commonly referred to as a Low Doc, Lite Doc, or No Doc loan, this is a loan for which the lender sets reduced or minimal standards for documenting the borrower's income and assets. For example, the borrower may state that her income is a certain amount, and the lender will accept that statement with little or no documentation. Low Doc loans may charge a higher interest rate than traditional products.

Refer Up/Refer Down: An internal policy with mortgage bankers that offer the full array of lending products—agency (prime), government, and subprime,—that is either silent on this topic or clearly states that qualified borrowers should be referred up to government or agency products of they appear to be eligible. In wholesale lending, there are prime and subprime account representatives that service the needs of the broker partners of mortgage bankers. Adverse selection can stem from the broker if the right hand does not know what the left hand is doing within the mortgage banker's operation.

Refinancing: Paying off one loan by obtaining another; refinancing is generally done to secure better loan terms (like a lower interest rate).

Regulation: The formulation and issuance by authorized agencies of specific rules or regulations, under governing law, for the conduct and structure of a certain industry or activity.

Rehabilitation Mortgage: A mortgage that covers the costs of rehabilitating (repairing or Improving) a property; some rehabilitation mortgages—like the FHA's 203(k)—allow a borrower to roll the costs of rehabilitation and home purchase into one mortgage loan.

Remaining Term: The original number of payments due on the loan minus the number of payments that have been made.

Repayment Plan: An arrangement by which a borrower agrees to make additional payments to pay down past due amounts while still making regularly scheduled payments.

Replacement Cost: The cost to replace damaged personal property without a deduction for depreciation.

Resolution Trust Corporation (RTC): A U.S. government owned asset management company. RTC liquidated real estate and mortgage-related assets received from savings and loan associations that became insolvent in the S&L crisis of the 1980s.

Retail Lender: A financial institution or broker that extends mortgage credit directly to the consumer.

Revenue: Payments received by businesses from selling goods and services.

Reverse Mortgage: See Home Equity Conversion Mortgage (HECM).

Revolving Debt: Credit that is extended by a creditor under a plan in which (1) the creditor contemplates repeated transactions; (2) the creditor may impose a finance charge from time to time on an outstanding unpaid balance; and (3) the amount of credit that may be ex-tended to the consumer during the term of the plan is generally made available to the extent that any outstanding balance is repaid.

Right of First Refusal: A provision in an agreement that requires the owner of a property to give another party the first opportunity to purchase or lease the property before he or she offers it for sale or lease to others.

Rural Housing Service (RHS): An agency within the U.S. Department of Agriculture (USDA), which operates a range of programs to help rural communities and individuals by providing loan and grants for housing and community facilities. The agency also works with private lenders to guarantee loans for the purchase or construction of single-family housing.

S

Sarbanes-Oxley Act of 2002 (SOX): Legislation that addresses, among other issues, corporate governance, auditing and accounting, executive compensation, and enhanced and timely disclosure of corporate information.

Sale-Leaseback: A transaction in which the buyer leases the property back to the seller for a specified period of time.

Second Mortgage: A mortgage that has a lien position subordinate to the first mortgage.

Secondary Mortgage Market: The market in which mortgage loan and mortgage-backed securities are bought and sold.

Secured Loan: A loan that is backed by property such as a house, car, jewelry, etc.

Securities: Paper certificates (definitive securities) or electronic records (book-entry securities) evidencing ownership of equity (stocks) or debt obligations (bonds).

Securitization: At the heart of structured finance, and entails pooling assets like individual mortgages and repackaging them into new financial assets called securities that produce cash flows for investors.

Securities and Exchange Commission (SEC): An independent, nonpartisan, quasi-judicial regulatory agency with responsibility for administering the federal securities laws. The purpose of these laws is to protect investors and to ensure that they have access to disclosure of all material information concerning publicly traded securities. The commission also regulates firms engaged in the purchase or sale of securities, people who provide investment advice, and investment companies.

Security: The property that will be given or pledged as collateral for a loan.

Seller Take-Back: An agreement in which the seller of a property provides financing to the buyer for the home purchase. See also "Owner Financing."

Servicemembers Civil Relief Act: A federal law that restricts the enforcement of civilian debts against certain military personnel who may not be able to pay because of active military service. It also provides other protections to certain military personnel.

Servicer: The financial entity tasked with collecting mortgage payments from borrowers, and paying the taxes and insurance premiums when due. At the other end of loan servicing is corporate trust, which takes the payments received and then disburses principal and interest payments to trusts, which exist on behalf of investors in mortgages.

Services: Economic activities, such as transportation, banking, insurance, tourism, telecommunications, advertising, entertainment, data processing, and consulting, that normally are consumed as they are produced, as contrasted with economic goods, which are more tangible.

Servicing: The tasks a lender performs to protect the mortgage investment, including the collection of mortgage payments, escrow administration, and delinquency management.

Settlement: Another name for closing. In some parts of the United States, the procedure is called escrow, as in to go to escrow (used as a verb).

Settlement Statement: A document that lists all closing costs on a consumer mortgage transaction. This is the accounting of the transaction.

Short Sale: The sale of real estate where the value is less than the balance owed on the mortgage(s). This type of transaction is cumbersome and time consuming. This requires third-party approval, i.e., the seller's lender(s) must authorize the sale and accept the purchase offer.

Single-Family Properties: One- to four-unit properties including detached homes, townhouses, condominiums, and cooperatives, and manufactured homes attached to a permanent foundation and classified as real property under applicable state law.

Simultaneous Second Lien Loan: This product, also called a *piggyback loan* or *soft second*, provides an alternative to paying private mortgage insurance. (Lenders typically require PMI if your down payment is less than 20 percent of the purchase price.) The loan is originated simultaneously with the first-lien mortgage. There are many government programs offering these products to low- and moderate-income first-time homebuyers. It is important to compare the cost of this second mortgage with the cost of purchasing PMI. If the borrower takes a simultaneous second-lien loan in place of making a down payment, he reduces the equity in the home. Also, if the second lien loan is a home equity line of credit (HELOC), the borrower may be exposed to increasing interest rates and higher monthly payments.

SISA: A documentation type that means Stated Income, Stated Assets. Borrowers tell the lender how much they make and how much they have in assets without providing any supporting documentation.

SIVA: A documentation type that means Stated Income, Verified Assets. Borrowers tell the lender how much they make without providing any supporting documentation, but state how much they have in assets and support that claim with documentation.

Social Regulation: Government-imposed restrictions designed to discourage or prohibit harmful corporate behavior (such as polluting the environment or putting workers in dangerous work situations) or to encourage behavior deemed socially desirable.

Social Responsibility: A concept within business ethics that argues that since businesses are corporate citizens, they therefore, should shoulder some of the challenges of society rather than leaving it to government and private organizations tasked with making our world a better place.

Social Security: A U.S. government pension program that provides benefits to retirees based on their own and their employers' contributions to the program while they were working.

Soft Second Loan: A second mortgage whose payment is forgiven or is deferred until resale of the property.

Special Forbearance: A loss mitigation option where the lender arranges a revised repayment plan for the borrower that may include a temporary reduction or suspension of monthly loan payments.

Standard of Living: A minimum of necessities, comforts, or luxuries considered essential to maintaining a person or group in customary or proper status or circumstances.

Stagflation: An economic condition of both continuing inflation and stagnant business activity.

Statement of Cash Flows: One of the three main financial statements that reports cash generated and used during a specific reporting period. (See also Income Statement and Balance Sheet).

Stock Exchange: An organized market for the buying and selling of stocks and bonds.

Structured Finance: Generic for a financial arrangement designed to transfer risk that starts with securitization. Structured finance arrangements include, but are not limited to, asset backed securities (ABS), mortgage backed securities (MBS), collateralized mortgage obligations (CMOs), collateralized debt obligations (CDOs), collateralized bond obligations (CBOs), and collateralized loan obligations (CLOs).

Subordinate: As a verb, to place in a rank of lesser importance or to make one claim secondary to another.

Subordinate Financing: Any mortgage or other lien with lower priority than the first mortgage.

Subordination Agreement: A contract whereby a second or third mortgage holder agrees to stand in line behind other lien holders. In the event of a suit claiming full or partial payment as in the case of a foreclosure, subordinate lien holders have a greater risk of loss.

Subprime: A lending niche that extends credit to borrowers who have credit risk profiles that do not conform to Fannie Mae and Freddie Mac underwriting guidelines.

Suitability Standard: The premise that lenders should only originate mortgages suitable for their borrowers given a documented ability to repay.

Supply: A schedule of how much producers are willing and able to sell at all possible prices during some time period.

Survey: A precise measurement of a property by a licensed surveyor, showing legal boundaries of a property and the dimensions and location of improvements.

Sweat Equity: A borrower's contribution to the down payment for the purchase of a property in the form of labor or services rather than cash.

T

Taxes and Insurance: Funds collected as part of the borrower's monthly payment and held in escrow for the payment of the borrower's, or funds paid by the borrower for, state and local property taxes and insurance premiums.

Teaser Rates: These are low rates that lenders offer to make mortgage products more attractive. When the "teaser-rate" period expires, the lender raises the interest rate for the remainder of the loan period. This new rate may be fixed or change periodically, depending upon the terms of the loan.

Technical Analysis: A technique for analyzing a market that relies on trend lines on charts.

Termite Inspection: An inspection to determine whether a property has termite infestation or termite damage. In many parts of the country, a home must be inspected for termites before it can be sold.

Third-Party Origination: A process by which a lender uses another party to completely or partially originate, process, underwrite, close, fund, or package a mortgage loan. See also "Mortgage Broker."

Title 1: An FHA-insured loan that allows a borrower to make nonluxury improvements (like renovations or repairs) to their home; Title I loans less than $7,500 do not require a property lien.

Title Insurance: Insurance that protects the lender against any claims that arise from arguments about ownership of the property; also available for homebuyers.

Title Search: A check of public records to be sure that the seller is the recognized owner of the real estate and that there are no unsettled liens or other claims against the property.

Trade Equity: Real estate or assets given to the seller as part of the down payment for the property.

Tranche: From the French, a word that means slice or section that is applied to mean a claim on an income stream from a Class A through Class C security.

Transfer Tax: State or local tax payable when title to property passes from one owner to another.

Treasury Index: An index that is used to determine interest rate changes for certain adjustable-rate mortgage (ARM) plans. It is based on the results of auctions by the U.S. Treasury of Treasury bills and securities.

Truth-in-Lending Act (TILA): A federal law obligating a lender to give full written disclosure of all fees, terms, and conditions associated with the loan initial period and then adjusts to another rate that lasts for the term of the loan.

Truth-in-Lending Disclosure: A core document in the loan application that discloses the Annual Percentage Rate as well as the total financing costs over the loan's term.

Two- to Four- Family Property: A residential property that provides living space (dwelling units) for two to four families, although ownership of the structure is evidenced by a single deed; a loan secured by such a property is considered to be a single-family mortgage.

U

Underwriting: The process of analyzing a loan application to determine the amount of risk involved in making the loan; it includes a review of the potential borrower's credit history and a judgment of the property value.

Uniform Residential Loan Application: A standard mortgage application that requests information about income, assets, liabilities, and a description of the property, among other things. See also "1003."

Unsecured Loan: A loan that is not backed by collateral.

V

VA: Department of Veterans Affairs: a federal agency that guarantees loans made to veterans; similar to mortgage insurance, a loan guarantee protects lenders against loss that may result from a borrower default.

VA Guaranteed Loan: A mortgage loan that is guaranteed by the U.S. Department of Veterans Affairs (VA).

Venture Capital: Investment in a new, generally possibly risky, enterprise.

Veterans Affairs (U.S. Department of Veterans Affairs): A federal government agency that provides benefits to veterans and their dependents, including health care, educational assistance, financial assistance, and guaranteed home loans.

W

W-2: IRS form used to report salaried employee or wage earner income.

Walk-Through: A common clause in a sales contract that allows the buyer to examine the property being purchased at a specified time immediately before the closing, for example, within the 24 hours before closing.

Warranties: Written guarantees of the quality of a product and the promise to repair or replace defective parts free of charge.

Well & Septic Certification: A certification by a specialist that attests to the potability of the drinking water and the soundness of the septic system.

Wholesale Lender: A lender that has no contact with consumers, but instead provides access to mortgage capital on a wholesale basis for retailers to lend to consumers.

Work Out Candidate: A delinquent borrower who qualifies to have arrearages and other fees capitalized due to a hardship that was through no fault of their own.

Sources: This select glossary of economic, financial, and real estate terms was developed from several sources.[1]

---

1   The glossary was developed from glossaries from the U.S. Department of Housing and Urban Development, Federal Reserve Bank of Boston, Federal Reserve Bank of San Francisco, Federal Reserve Bank of Minneapolis, the Virtual Trade Mission, the Wisconsin Economic Education Council, and the author's collection of business textbooks.

M

5764989R0

Made in the USA
Charleston, SC
30 July 2010